Heath
Mathematics

Walter E. Rucker

Clyde A. Dilley

D. C. Heath and Company
Lexington, Massachusetts   Toronto

About the authors

Walter E. Rucker Former Specialist in Education with the Curriculum Laboratory of the University of Illinois, has taught mathematics in public schools and is a coauthor of successful mathematics programs for elementary and junior high schools.

Clyde A. Dilley Professor, University of Toledo, Toledo, Ohio, is teaching methods courses in elementary and secondary mathematics. He has taught mathematics in public schools and is a coauthor of successful mathematics programs for elementary and junior high schools.

Illustrations Chris Czernota/True Kelley/Sally Mavor/Penny Carter

Photography Jonathan Barkan: 59, 66, 67, 71, 80, 81, 188, 189, 206, 216/ Fredrik D. Bodin: 87, 136, 138, 142, 146, 147, 154, 180, 181, 191, 207, 250, 268, 299, 317/Bohdan Hrynewych: 360, 361/Lou Jones: 14, 15, 168, 170, 171/ Michael Malyszko: 29, 46, 47, 140, 163/Julie O'Neil: 98, 99, 124 top, 157, 182, 205, 254, 312, 313/Frank Siteman, Stock Boston: 354, 355/Deidra Delano Stead: Cover, 1, 26, 55, 77, 133, 166, 213, 239, 243, 277, 286, 291, 306, 307, 344, 348, 349, 356, 357, 362, 363, 366, 367/John Urban: 24, 27, 52, 53, 54, 115, 122, 123, 124 bottom, 125, 126, 128, 130, 200, 246, 265, 278, 332/Photo Researchers, Inc., National Audubon Society Collection, Russ Kinne: 33

Published simultaneously in Canada.

Printed in the United States of America.

International Standard Book Number: 0-669-03413-4

Contents

1
Addition and Subtraction Facts

Addition facts

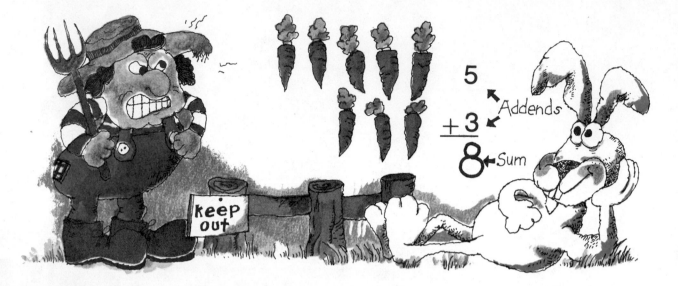

5
+3   ← Addends
8   ← Sum

EXERCISES
Add.

1. 3
    +2
    5

2. 0
    +4

3. 3
    +4

4. 3
    +6

5. 1
    +4

6. 2
    +6

7. 1
    +5

8. 5
    +4

9. 3
    +3

10. 3
    +7

11. 4
    +2

12. 2
    +5

13. 4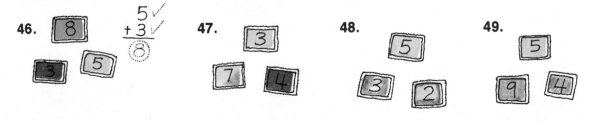
    +4

14. 6
    +4

15. 4
    +5

Give each sum.

16. 0
    +2

17. 4
    +3

18. 0
    +0

19. 3
    +1

20. 6
    +1

21. 1
    +2

22. 2
    +7

23. 1
    +4

24. 3
    +5

25. 1
    +1

26. 5
    +4

27. 0
    +7

28. 4
    +6

29. 8
    +2

30. 2
    +4

31. 0
    +5

32. 5
    +5

33. 5
    +2

34. 6
    +4

35. 6
    +2

36. 5
    +1

37. 0
    +1

38. 2
    +3

39. 1
    +8

40. 2
    +2

41. 6
    +3

42. 1
    +6

43. 7
    +3

44. 1
    +7

45. 1
    +9

Use the numbers in an addition fact. Check each addend. Circle the sum.

46. 8
    5 ✓
    + 3 ✓
    8
    3   5

47. 3
    7   4

48. 5
    3   2

49. 5
    9   4

Properties of addition

The Order Property of Addition

I can change the order of the addends without changing the sum.

$$4 + 5 = 9$$

$$5 + 4 = 9$$

The Adding 0 Property

If I add any number and 0, I get the number.

$$8 + 0 = 8$$

EXERCISES

Give each sum.

1. $\begin{array}{r} 3 \\ +2 \\ \hline \end{array}$

2. $\begin{array}{r} 2 \\ +3 \\ \hline \end{array}$

3. $\begin{array}{r} 6 \\ +4 \\ \hline \end{array}$

4. $\begin{array}{r} 4 \\ +6 \\ \hline \end{array}$

5. $\begin{array}{r} 7 \\ +1 \\ \hline \end{array}$

6. $\begin{array}{r} 1 \\ +7 \\ \hline \end{array}$

7. $\begin{array}{r} 5 \\ +3 \\ \hline \end{array}$

8. $\begin{array}{r} 3 \\ +5 \\ \hline \end{array}$

9. $\begin{array}{r} 6 \\ +2 \\ \hline \end{array}$

10. $\begin{array}{r} 2 \\ +6 \\ \hline \end{array}$

11. $\begin{array}{r} 7 \\ +3 \\ \hline \end{array}$

12. $\begin{array}{r} 3 \\ +7 \\ \hline \end{array}$

13. $\begin{array}{r} 2 \\ +0 \\ \hline \end{array}$

14. $\begin{array}{r} 0 \\ +2 \\ \hline \end{array}$

15. $\begin{array}{r} 8 \\ +2 \\ \hline \end{array}$

16. $\begin{array}{r} 2 \\ +8 \\ \hline \end{array}$

17. $\begin{array}{r} 9 \\ +1 \\ \hline \end{array}$

18. $\begin{array}{r} 1 \\ +9 \\ \hline \end{array}$

19. $\begin{array}{r} 7 \\ +0 \\ \hline \end{array}$

20. $\begin{array}{r} 0 \\ +7 \\ \hline \end{array}$

21. $\begin{array}{r} 5 \\ +1 \\ \hline \end{array}$

22. $\begin{array}{r} 1 \\ +5 \\ \hline \end{array}$

23. $\begin{array}{r} 9 \\ +0 \\ \hline \end{array}$

24. $\begin{array}{r} 0 \\ +9 \\ \hline \end{array}$

25. $\begin{array}{r} 6 \\ +3 \\ \hline \end{array}$

26. $\begin{array}{r} 3 \\ +6 \\ \hline \end{array}$

Add.

27. 3
    +0

28. 4
    +1

29. 1
    +2

30. 8
    +0

31. 0
    +0

32. 8
    +1

33. 0
    +8

34. 3
    +7

35. 2
    +2

36. 1
    +1

37. 2
    +5

38. 2
    +1

39. 0
    +5

40. 2
    +4

41. 6
    +0

42. 3
    +1

43. 0
    +6

44. 5
    +4

45. 5
    +5

46. 3
    +4

47. 6
    +1

48. 1
    +8

49. 4
    +2

50. 0
    +3

51. 1
    +6

52. 4
    +4

53. 3
    +3

54. 7
    +2

55. 4
    +3

56. 4
    +5

57. 2
    +7

58. 1
    +6

59. 5
    +5

60. 5
    +4

61. 9
    +0

62. 3
    +6

Who am I?

63. If you add me to 3, you get 8.

64. If you add me to 6, you get 10.

65. If you add me to 9, you get 9.

66. If you add me to myself, you get 6.

Sums to 18

The sum is **13**.

$$\begin{array}{r} 7 \\ +6 \\ \hline 13 \end{array}$$

7 and **6** makes **1** ten and **3**

EXERCISES
Give each sum.

1. $\begin{array}{r} 6 \\ +5 \\ \hline \end{array}$

2. $\begin{array}{r} 8 \\ +4 \\ \hline \end{array}$

3. $\begin{array}{r} 8 \\ +3 \\ \hline \end{array}$

4. $\begin{array}{r} 9 \\ +9 \\ \hline \end{array}$

5. $\begin{array}{r} 7 \\ +6 \\ \hline \end{array}$

6. $\begin{array}{r} 8 \\ +8 \\ \hline \end{array}$

7. $\begin{array}{r} 8 \\ +7 \\ \hline \end{array}$

8. $\begin{array}{r} 7 \\ +8 \\ \hline \end{array}$

9. $\begin{array}{r} 7 \\ +4 \\ \hline \end{array}$

10. $\begin{array}{r} 4 \\ +7 \\ \hline \end{array}$

11. $\begin{array}{r} 8 \\ +5 \\ \hline \end{array}$

12. $\begin{array}{r} 5 \\ +8 \\ \hline \end{array}$

13. $\begin{array}{r} 8 \\ +6 \\ \hline \end{array}$

14. $\begin{array}{r} 6 \\ +8 \\ \hline \end{array}$

15. $\begin{array}{r} 9 \\ +8 \\ \hline \end{array}$

16. $\begin{array}{r} 8 \\ +9 \\ \hline \end{array}$

17. $\begin{array}{r} 9 \\ +6 \\ \hline \end{array}$

18. $\begin{array}{r} 6 \\ +9 \\ \hline \end{array}$

19. $\begin{array}{r} 9 \\ +5 \\ \hline \end{array}$

20. $\begin{array}{r} 5 \\ +9 \\ \hline \end{array}$

21. $\begin{array}{r} 9 \\ +7 \\ \hline \end{array}$

22. $\begin{array}{r} 7 \\ +9 \\ \hline \end{array}$

23. $\begin{array}{r} 7 \\ +5 \\ \hline \end{array}$

24. $\begin{array}{r} 5 \\ +7 \\ \hline \end{array}$

Add.

25. 8
    +7

26. 9
    +4

27. 8
    +3

28. 6
    +9

29. 5
    +6

30. 9
    +5

31. 7
    +6

32. 6
    +8

33. 9
    +6

34. 9
    +3

35. 6
    +6

36. 4
    +9

37. 7
    +8

38. 9
    +7

39. 5
    +7

40. 7
    +7

41. 8
    +6

42. 8
    +8

43. 6
    +7

44. 4
    +7

45. 5
    +8

46. 9
    +9

47. 4
    +8

48. 3
    +8

49. 5
    +6

50. 9
    +4

51. 8
    +3

52. 6
    +4

53. 9
    +5

54. 2
    +8

55. 7
    +9

56. 2
    +9

57. 8
    +9

58. 3
    +9

59. 5
    +9

60. 9
    +8

Use the shortcut to find each sum.

Sometimes I use a double to find another sum. This sum is 1 more than 12.

61. 6
    +7
    ——
    13

    6
    +6
    ——
    12

62. 8
    +9

    8
    +8
    ——
    16

63. 7
    +8

    7
    +7
    ——
    14

64. 4
    +5

65. 8
    +7

66. 5
    +6

(seven) **7**

Addition equations

You can write addition in equation form, too.

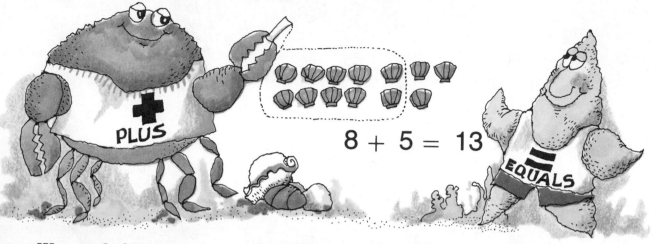

$$8 + 5 = 13$$

We read the equation as "8 plus 5 equals 13."

EXERCISES
Give each sum.

1. $9 + 5 = \underline{14}$

2. $6 + 7 = \underline{?}$

3. $8 + 3 = \underline{?}$

4. $9 + 6 = \underline{?}$

5. $6 + 9 = \underline{?}$

6. $8 + 8 = \underline{?}$

7. $5 + 6 = \underline{?}$

8. $8 + 4 = \underline{?}$

9. $5 + 8 = \underline{?}$

10. $7 + 9 = \underline{?}$

11. $6 + 6 = \underline{?}$

12. $8 + 9 = \underline{?}$

13. $7 + 8 = \underline{?}$

14. $4 + 8 = \underline{?}$

15. $9 + 4 = \underline{?}$

16. $7 + 7 = \underline{?}$

17. $9 + 8 = \underline{?}$

18. $8 + 7 = \underline{?}$

19. $9 + 7 = \underline{?}$

20. $8 + 6 = \underline{?}$

21. $5 + 9 = \underline{?}$

22. $9 + 3 = \underline{?}$

23. $6 + 9 = \underline{?}$

24. $9 + 9 = \underline{?}$

Give each sum.

25. $4 + 7 = \underline{?}$

26. $8 + 4 = \underline{?}$

27. $7 + 7 = \underline{?}$

28. $6 + 9 = \underline{?}$

29. $9 + 2 = \underline{?}$

30. $8 + 7 = \underline{?}$

31. $6 + 6 = \underline{?}$

32. $8 + 5 = \underline{?}$

33. $9 + 3 = \underline{?}$

34. $5 + 9 = \underline{?}$

35. $7 + 8 = \underline{?}$

36. $5 + 8 = \underline{?}$

37. $9 + 4 = \underline{?}$

38. $2 + 9 = \underline{?}$

39. $8 + 6 = \underline{?}$

40. $8 + 9 = \underline{?}$

41. $9 + 6 = \underline{?}$

42. $8 + 3 = \underline{?}$

43. $7 + 4 = \underline{?}$

44. $4 + 8 = \underline{?}$

45. $9 + 7 = \underline{?}$

46. $9 + 5 = \underline{?}$

47. $3 + 8 = \underline{?}$

48. $6 + 7 = \underline{?}$

49. $9 + 8 = \underline{?}$

50. $6 + 8 = \underline{?}$

51. $3 + 9 = \underline{?}$

52. $7 + 6 = \underline{?}$

53. $5 + 7 = \underline{?}$

54. $4 + 9 = \underline{?}$

55. $9 + 9 = \underline{?}$

56. $8 + 8 = \underline{?}$

57. $7 + 9 = \underline{?}$

Add across. Add down.

58.
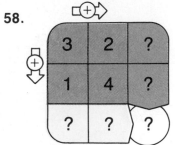

3	2	?
1	4	?
?	?	?

59.
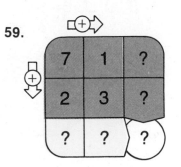

7	1	?
2	3	?
?	?	?

60.
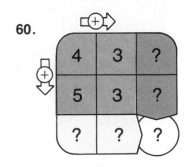

4	3	?
5	3	?
?	?	?

Missing addends

$3 + \underline{} = 5$
in all

$3 + \underline{2} = 5$
in all

EXERCISES
How many cars are in the box?

1. $3 + \underline{1} = 4$
in all

2. $5 + \underline{?} = 7$
in all

3. $4 + \underline{?} = 11$
in all

4. $2 + \underline{?} = 8$
in all

5. $3 + \underline{?} = 9$
in all

6. $8 + \underline{?} = 12$
in all

7. $5 + \underline{?} = 10$
in all

8. $2 + \underline{?} = 6$
in all

9. $3 + \underline{?} = 11$
in all

Give each missing addend.

10. 5 + _6_ = 11

11. 6 + _?_ = 12

12. 8 + _?_ = 11

13. 3 + _?_ = 11

14. 9 + _?_ = 16

15. 7 + _?_ = 16

16. 8 + _?_ = 16

17. 6 + _?_ = 11

18. 9 + _?_ = 14

19. 7 + _?_ = 15

20. 7 + _?_ = 14

21. 9 + _?_ = 17

22. 8 + _?_ = 14

23. 8 + _?_ = 17

24. 8 + _?_ = 15

25. 9 + _?_ = 18

26. 6 + _?_ = 15

27. 7 + _?_ = 16

28. _?_ + 4 = 11

29. _?_ + 5 = 13

30. _?_ + 9 = 12

31. _?_ + 9 = 13

32. _?_ + 6 = 11

33. _?_ + 8 = 16

34. _?_ + 5 = 14

35. _?_ + 8 = 12

36. _?_ + 7 = 15

37. _?_ + 8 = 11

38. _?_ + 7 = 16

39. _?_ + 7 = 11

40. _?_ + 7 = 12

41. _?_ + 9 = 11

42. _?_ + 9 = 18

Complete.

43.

+ →		
3	?	5
6	?	7
?	?	?

44.

+ →		
?	4	8
3	?	5
?	?	?

45.

+ →		
5	?	9
?	?	?
?	6	14

(eleven) **11**

Three addends

You can add numbers in any order and get the same sum.

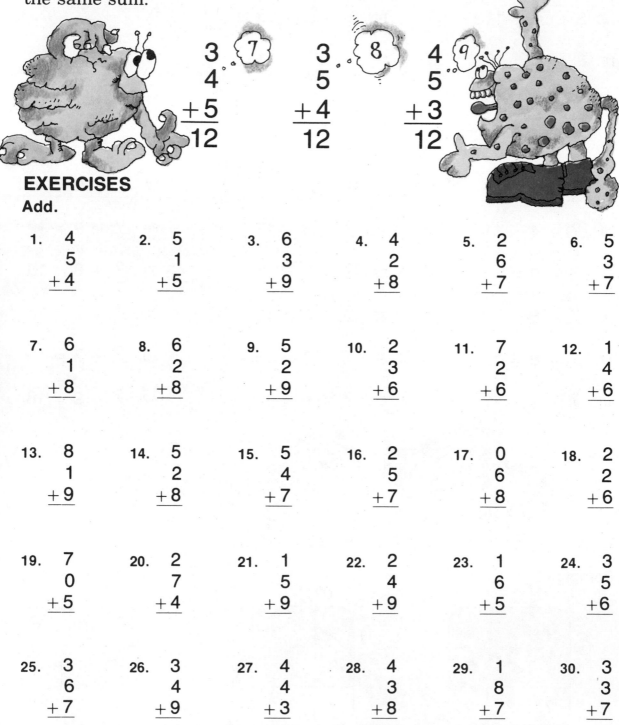

$$\begin{array}{r} 3 \\ 4 \\ +5 \\ \hline 12 \end{array} \quad \begin{array}{r} 3 \\ 5 \\ +4 \\ \hline 12 \end{array} \quad \begin{array}{r} 4 \\ 5 \\ +3 \\ \hline 12 \end{array}$$

EXERCISES
Add.

1. $\begin{array}{r} 4 \\ 5 \\ +4 \\ \hline \end{array}$
2. $\begin{array}{r} 5 \\ 1 \\ +5 \\ \hline \end{array}$
3. $\begin{array}{r} 6 \\ 3 \\ +9 \\ \hline \end{array}$
4. $\begin{array}{r} 4 \\ 2 \\ +8 \\ \hline \end{array}$
5. $\begin{array}{r} 2 \\ 6 \\ +7 \\ \hline \end{array}$
6. $\begin{array}{r} 5 \\ 3 \\ +7 \\ \hline \end{array}$

7. $\begin{array}{r} 6 \\ 1 \\ +8 \\ \hline \end{array}$
8. $\begin{array}{r} 6 \\ 2 \\ +8 \\ \hline \end{array}$
9. $\begin{array}{r} 5 \\ 2 \\ +9 \\ \hline \end{array}$
10. $\begin{array}{r} 2 \\ 3 \\ +6 \\ \hline \end{array}$
11. $\begin{array}{r} 7 \\ 2 \\ +6 \\ \hline \end{array}$
12. $\begin{array}{r} 1 \\ 4 \\ +6 \\ \hline \end{array}$

13. $\begin{array}{r} 8 \\ 1 \\ +9 \\ \hline \end{array}$
14. $\begin{array}{r} 5 \\ 2 \\ +8 \\ \hline \end{array}$
15. $\begin{array}{r} 5 \\ 4 \\ +7 \\ \hline \end{array}$
16. $\begin{array}{r} 2 \\ 5 \\ +7 \\ \hline \end{array}$
17. $\begin{array}{r} 0 \\ 6 \\ +8 \\ \hline \end{array}$
18. $\begin{array}{r} 2 \\ 2 \\ +6 \\ \hline \end{array}$

19. $\begin{array}{r} 7 \\ 0 \\ +5 \\ \hline \end{array}$
20. $\begin{array}{r} 2 \\ 7 \\ +4 \\ \hline \end{array}$
21. $\begin{array}{r} 1 \\ 5 \\ +9 \\ \hline \end{array}$
22. $\begin{array}{r} 2 \\ 4 \\ +9 \\ \hline \end{array}$
23. $\begin{array}{r} 1 \\ 6 \\ +5 \\ \hline \end{array}$
24. $\begin{array}{r} 3 \\ 5 \\ +6 \\ \hline \end{array}$

25. $\begin{array}{r} 3 \\ 6 \\ +7 \\ \hline \end{array}$
26. $\begin{array}{r} 3 \\ 4 \\ +9 \\ \hline \end{array}$
27. $\begin{array}{r} 4 \\ 4 \\ +3 \\ \hline \end{array}$
28. $\begin{array}{r} 4 \\ 3 \\ +8 \\ \hline \end{array}$
29. $\begin{array}{r} 1 \\ 8 \\ +7 \\ \hline \end{array}$
30. $\begin{array}{r} 3 \\ 3 \\ +7 \\ \hline \end{array}$

Use the shortcut to find each sum.

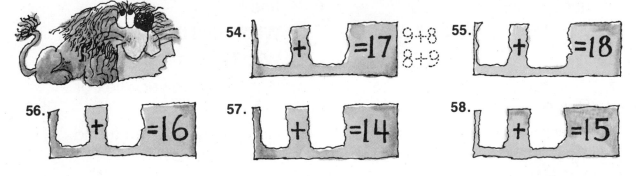

I first look for 10.

SHORTCUT

31. 5
     3
   +5
   13

10
+3

32. 6
     3
   +7

33. 2
     7
   +8

34. 4
     6
   +5

35. 3
     6
   +7

36. 5
     4
   +5

37. 4
     6
   +7

38. 6
     3
   +4

Add. Hint: First look for 10.

39. 5
     2
   +8

40. 6
     3
   +7

41. 1
     7
   +5

42. 4
     6
   +3

43. 5
     3
   +4

44. 3
     4
   +7

45. 7
     2
   +3

46. 1
     6
   +3

47. 3
     7
   +6

48. 3
     5
   +6

49. 2
     8
   +5

50. 3
     6
   +9

51. 3
     5
   +7

52. 8
     1
   +9

53. 7
     5
   +3

What could have been on each addition fact card?

54. ☐ + ☐ = 17 9+8
                   8+9

55. ☐ + ☐ = 18

56. ☐ + ☐ = 16

57. ☐ + ☐ = 14

58. ☐ + ☐ = 15

Problem solving

EXERCISES

Name	Alex	Terry	Elsa	Sarah	Paige	Katy	Lee	Luis
Rocks found	7	6	8	7	4	5	9	8

1. How many rocks did Terry find?

2. How many rocks did Katy find?

3. Who found the most?

4. Who found the fewest?

5. Who found six rocks?

6. Who found seven rocks?

7. Who found more, Sarah or Paige?

8. Who found fewer, Alex or Luis?

9. How many children found more than seven?

10. How many children found fewer than seven?

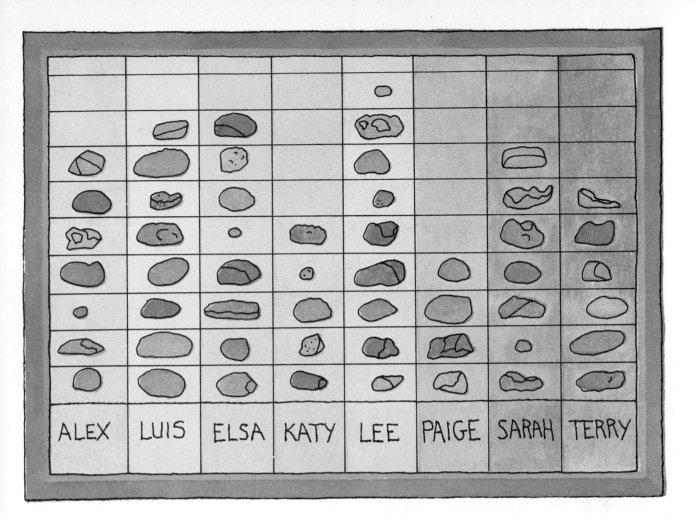

Complete.

11. Luis found $\underline{8}$.
    Katy found $\underline{5}$.
    Together they found $\underline{13}$.

12. Lee found $\underline{?}$.
    Elsa found $\underline{?}$.
    Together they found $\underline{?}$.

13. Alex found $\underline{?}$.
    Terry found $\underline{?}$.
    Together they found $\underline{?}$.

14. Paige found $\underline{?}$.
    Sarah found $\underline{?}$.
    Together they found $\underline{?}$.

★15. Katy found $\underline{?}$.
    Paige found $\underline{?}$.
    Sarah found $\underline{?}$.
    Together they found $\underline{?}$.

★16. Terry found $\underline{?}$.
    Paige found $\underline{?}$.
    Luis found $\underline{?}$.
    Together they found $\underline{?}$.

Subtraction facts

$$\begin{array}{r} 7 \\ -3 \\ \hline 4 \end{array}$$

Difference

EXERCISES

Subtract.

1. $\begin{array}{r} 5 \\ -3 \\ \hline \end{array}$
2. $\begin{array}{r} 6 \\ -2 \\ \hline \end{array}$
3. $\begin{array}{r} 8 \\ -3 \\ \hline \end{array}$

4. $\begin{array}{r} 5 \\ -2 \\ \hline \end{array}$
5. $\begin{array}{r} 5 \\ -0 \\ \hline \end{array}$
6. $\begin{array}{r} 4 \\ -4 \\ \hline \end{array}$

7. $\begin{array}{r} 10 \\ -1 \\ \hline \end{array}$
8. $\begin{array}{r} 6 \\ -6 \\ \hline \end{array}$
9. $\begin{array}{r} 9 \\ -5 \\ \hline \end{array}$
10. $\begin{array}{r} 6 \\ -3 \\ \hline \end{array}$
11. $\begin{array}{r} 8 \\ -4 \\ \hline \end{array}$
12. $\begin{array}{r} 9 \\ -6 \\ \hline \end{array}$

13. $\begin{array}{r} 7 \\ -6 \\ \hline \end{array}$
14. $\begin{array}{r} 8 \\ -5 \\ \hline \end{array}$
15. $\begin{array}{r} 8 \\ -1 \\ \hline \end{array}$
16. $\begin{array}{r} 10 \\ -2 \\ \hline \end{array}$
17. $\begin{array}{r} 8 \\ -2 \\ \hline \end{array}$
18. $\begin{array}{r} 10 \\ -3 \\ \hline \end{array}$

19. $\begin{array}{r} 9 \\ -2 \\ \hline \end{array}$
20. $\begin{array}{r} 10 \\ -4 \\ \hline \end{array}$
21. $\begin{array}{r} 9 \\ -9 \\ \hline \end{array}$
22. $\begin{array}{r} 7 \\ -3 \\ \hline \end{array}$
23. $\begin{array}{r} 10 \\ -5 \\ \hline \end{array}$
24. $\begin{array}{r} 9 \\ -8 \\ \hline \end{array}$

Give each difference.

25. $\begin{array}{r} 2 \\ -0 \\ \hline \end{array}$	26. $\begin{array}{r} 3 \\ -3 \\ \hline \end{array}$	27. $\begin{array}{r} 10 \\ -2 \\ \hline \end{array}$	28. $\begin{array}{r} 6 \\ -0 \\ \hline \end{array}$
29. $\begin{array}{r} 4 \\ -2 \\ \hline \end{array}$	30. $\begin{array}{r} 10 \\ -3 \\ \hline \end{array}$	31. $\begin{array}{r} 7 \\ -5 \\ \hline \end{array}$	32. $\begin{array}{r} 10 \\ -5 \\ \hline \end{array}$
33. $\begin{array}{r} 5 \\ -4 \\ \hline \end{array}$	34. $\begin{array}{r} 8 \\ -6 \\ \hline \end{array}$	35. $\begin{array}{r} 6 \\ -3 \\ \hline \end{array}$	36. $\begin{array}{r} 9 \\ -8 \\ \hline \end{array}$
37. $\begin{array}{r} 9 \\ -2 \\ \hline \end{array}$	38. $\begin{array}{r} 8 \\ -5 \\ \hline \end{array}$	39. $\begin{array}{r} 5 \\ -3 \\ \hline \end{array}$	40. $\begin{array}{r} 8 \\ -8 \\ \hline \end{array}$
41. $\begin{array}{r} 10 \\ -6 \\ \hline \end{array}$	42. $\begin{array}{r} 7 \\ -4 \\ \hline \end{array}$	43. $\begin{array}{r} 6 \\ -4 \\ \hline \end{array}$	44. $\begin{array}{r} 10 \\ -7 \\ \hline \end{array}$
45. $\begin{array}{r} 10 \\ -4 \\ \hline \end{array}$	46. $\begin{array}{r} 9 \\ -4 \\ \hline \end{array}$	47. $\begin{array}{r} 5 \\ -2 \\ \hline \end{array}$	48. $\begin{array}{r} 8 \\ -3 \\ \hline \end{array}$
49. $\begin{array}{r} 9 \\ -5 \\ \hline \end{array}$	50. $\begin{array}{r} 7 \\ -3 \\ \hline \end{array}$	51. $\begin{array}{r} 9 \\ -7 \\ \hline \end{array}$	52. $\begin{array}{r} 6 \\ -2 \\ \hline \end{array}$
53. $\begin{array}{r} 5 \\ -4 \\ \hline \end{array}$	54. $\begin{array}{r} 9 \\ -6 \\ \hline \end{array}$	55. $\begin{array}{r} 8 \\ -1 \\ \hline \end{array}$	56. $\begin{array}{r} 7 \\ -2 \\ \hline \end{array}$
57. $\begin{array}{r} 6 \\ -5 \\ \hline \end{array}$	58. $\begin{array}{r} 10 \\ -8 \\ \hline \end{array}$	59. $\begin{array}{r} 8 \\ -4 \\ \hline \end{array}$	60. $\begin{array}{r} 9 \\ -3 \\ \hline \end{array}$

Who am I?

61. If you subtract me from 9, you get 4.

62. If you subtract me from 10, you get 7.

63. If you subtract me from 6, you get 6.

64. If you subtract me from myself, you get 0.

Addition and subtraction

Addition and subtraction are related.

Family of Facts

3 + 2 = 5

5 − 2 = 3

2 + 3 = 5

5 − 3 = 2

1.

2 + 1 = 3

1 + 2 = 3

3 − 1 = 2

3 − 2 = 1

2.

3.

4.

5.

6.

Use the numbers in two addition equations and two subtraction equations.

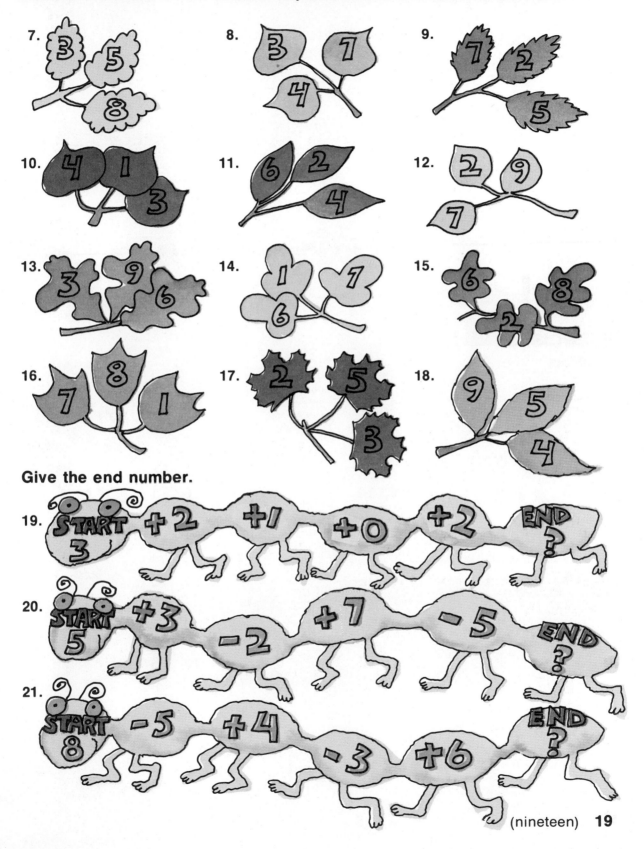

7. 3 5 8

8. 3 7 4

9. 7 2 5

10. 4 1 3

11. 6 2 4

12. 2 9 7

13. 3 9 6

14. 1 7 6

15. 6 8 2

16. 7 8 1

17. 2 5 3

18. 9 5 4

Give the end number.

19. START 3 +2 +1 +0 +2 END ?

20. START 5 +3 -2 +7 -5 END ?

21. START 8 -5 +4 -3 +6 END ?

Subtraction facts

You can subtract by taking away.

You can subtract by finding a missing addend.

13
−6
‾‾
7

13
−6
‾‾
7

?
+6
‾‾
13

EXERCISES
Subtract.

1. 11
  −5

2. 12
  −3

3. 14
  −6

4. 13
  −8

5. 14
  −7

6. 11
  −9

7. 15
  −9
  ?
  +9
  ‾‾
  15

8. 12
  −5
  ?
  +5
  ‾‾
  12

9. 16
  −8
  ?
  +8
  ‾‾
  16

10. 15
  −8
  ?
  +8
  ‾‾
  15

11. 17
  −8
  ?
  +8
  ‾‾
  17

12. 16
  −9
  ?
  +9
  ‾‾
  16

13. 17
  −9
  ?
  +9
  ‾‾
  17

14. 16
  −7
  ?
  +7
  ‾‾
  16

15. 18
  −9
  ?
  +9
  ‾‾
  18

Give each difference.

16. 14
    − 5

17. 12
    − 5

18. 13
    − 8

19. 15
    − 8

20. 10
    − 4

21. 12
    − 6

22. 13
    − 5

23. 15
    − 7

24. 11
    − 2

25. 13
    − 6

26. 11
    − 5

27. 16
    − 7

28. 11
    − 3

29. 12
    − 7

30. 14
    − 9

31. 15
    − 6

32. 13
    − 9

33. 12
    − 9

34. 10
    − 8

35. 17
    − 9

36. 12
    − 8

37. 14
    − 7

38. 12
    − 4

39. 14
    − 8

40. 11
    − 7

41. 13
    − 7

42. 11
    − 6

43. 17
    − 8

44. 13
    − 4

45. 15
    − 9

46. 11
    − 4

47. 13
    − 9

48. 11
    − 8

49. 14
    − 6

50. 12
    − 3

51. 16
    − 8

Keeping Skills Sharp

1. 5
   +9

2. 4
   +9

3. 6
   +9

4. 7
   +8

5. 9
   +7

6. 8
   +6

7. 8
   +5

8. 8
   +8

9. 8
   +7

10. 9
    +9

11. 5
    +8

12. 6
    +8

13. 7
    +9

14. 7
    +7

15. 8
    +9

16. 9
    +5

17. 9
    +6

18. 9
    +8

Subtraction facts

You can subtract by taking away.

You can subtract by finding a missing addend.

$$12 - 3 = \underline{9}$$

Read as "12 minus 3 equals 9."

$$11 - 4 = \underline{7}$$

Read as "11 minus 4 equals 7."

EXERCISES

Subtract.

1. $12 - 5 = \underline{7}$

2. $11 - 5 = \underline{?}$

3. $13 - 4 = \underline{?}$

4. $12 - 7 = \underline{?}$

5. $13 - 8 = \underline{?}$

6. $11 - 9 = \underline{?}$

7. $12 - 8 = \underline{?}$

8. $13 - 6 = \underline{?}$

9. $12 - 6 = \underline{?}$

10. $17 - 8 = \underline{?}$

11. $16 - 8 = \underline{?}$

12. $15 - 9 = \underline{?}$

13. $14 - 8 = \underline{?}$

14. $11 - 8 = \underline{?}$

15. $17 - 9 = \underline{?}$

16. $14 - 9 = \underline{?}$

17. $16 - 7 = \underline{?}$

18. $15 - 8 = \underline{?}$

19. $11 - 6 = \underline{?}$

20. $15 - 7 = \underline{?}$

21. $11 - 7 = \underline{?}$

22. $15 - 6 = \underline{?}$

23. $18 - 9 = \underline{?}$

24. $16 - 9 = \underline{?}$

Subtract.

25. $11 - 5 = \underline{?}$ 26. $13 - 7 = \underline{?}$ 27. $15 - 6 = \underline{?}$

28. $14 - 8 = \underline{?}$ 29. $11 - 6 = \underline{?}$ 30. $12 - 6 = \underline{?}$

31. $11 - 2 = \underline{?}$ 32. $13 - 8 = \underline{?}$ 33. $13 - 6 = \underline{?}$

34. $14 - 7 = \underline{?}$ 35. $12 - 7 = \underline{?}$ 36. $15 - 8 = \underline{?}$

37. $12 - 5 = \underline{?}$ 38. $18 - 9 = \underline{?}$ 39. $11 - 4 = \underline{?}$

40. $15 - 9 = \underline{?}$ 41. $11 - 7 = \underline{?}$ 42. $14 - 6 = \underline{?}$

43. $12 - 4 = \underline{?}$ 44. $14 - 5 = \underline{?}$ 45. $16 - 8 = \underline{?}$

46. $16 - 7 = \underline{?}$ 47. $11 - 9 = \underline{?}$ 48. $12 - 8 = \underline{?}$

49. $12 - 3 = \underline{?}$ 50. $13 - 5 = \underline{?}$ 51. $11 - 3 = \underline{?}$

52. $17 - 8 = \underline{?}$ 53. $12 - 9 = \underline{?}$ 54. $13 - 9 = \underline{?}$

Use each shortcut.

To add 9, I sometimes add 10 and then subtract 1.

55. $\begin{array}{r} 6 \\ +9 \\ \hline \end{array}$ 56. $\begin{array}{r} 9 \\ +9 \\ \hline \end{array}$ 57. $\begin{array}{r} 8 \\ +9 \\ \hline \end{array}$ 58. $\begin{array}{r} 7 \\ +9 \\ \hline \end{array}$

To subtract 9, I sometimes subtract 10 and then add 1.

59. $\begin{array}{r} 15 \\ -9 \\ \hline \end{array}$ 60. $\begin{array}{r} 18 \\ -9 \\ \hline \end{array}$ 61. $\begin{array}{r} 16 \\ -9 \\ \hline \end{array}$ 62. $\begin{array}{r} 17 \\ -9 \\ \hline \end{array}$

Problem solving

1 penny

1 cent

1¢

1 nickel

5 cents

5¢

1 dime

10 cents

10¢

EXERCISES

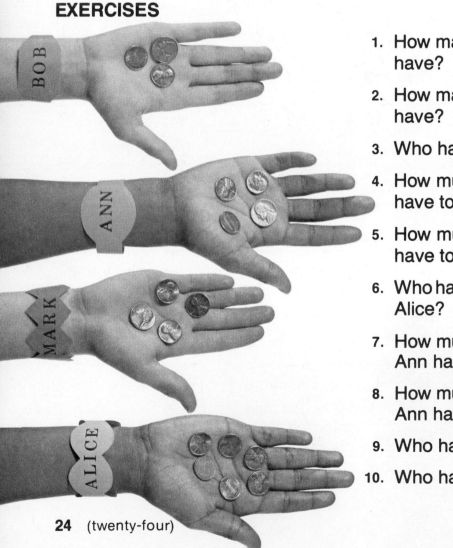

1. How many pennies does Bob have?

2. How many nickels does Mark have?

3. Who has a dime?

4. How much do Bob and Mark have together?

5. How much do Alice and Bob have together?

6. Who has more money, Mark or Alice?

7. How much more money does Ann have than Mark?

8. How much more money does Ann have than Bob?

9. Who has the least money?

10. Who has the most money?

GREATEST SUM WINS

Which sum is greatest?

1. $\begin{array}{r} 5 \\ +2 \\ \hline \end{array}$ $\begin{array}{r} 3 \\ +3 \\ \hline \end{array}$ $\begin{array}{r} 4 \\ +5 \\ \hline \end{array}$
2. $\begin{array}{r} 8 \\ +3 \\ \hline \end{array}$ $\begin{array}{r} 2 \\ +6 \\ \hline \end{array}$ $\begin{array}{r} 7 \\ +2 \\ \hline \end{array}$
3. $\begin{array}{r} 1 \\ +9 \\ \hline \end{array}$ $\begin{array}{r} 8 \\ +5 \\ \hline \end{array}$ $\begin{array}{r} 6 \\ +6 \\ \hline \end{array}$

4. $\begin{array}{r} 5 \\ +9 \\ \hline \end{array}$ $\begin{array}{r} 6 \\ +7 \\ \hline \end{array}$ $\begin{array}{r} 3 \\ +8 \\ \hline \end{array}$
5. $\begin{array}{r} 8 \\ +8 \\ \hline \end{array}$ $\begin{array}{r} 6 \\ +9 \\ \hline \end{array}$ $\begin{array}{r} 8 \\ +6 \\ \hline \end{array}$
6. $\begin{array}{r} 5 \\ +7 \\ \hline \end{array}$ $\begin{array}{r} 3 \\ +8 \\ \hline \end{array}$ $\begin{array}{r} 4 \\ +5 \\ \hline \end{array}$

Play this game.

1. Form groups of three or four. Get some addition flashcards.
2. Mix up the flashcards and put them face down.
3. Each pick a card. The player picking the greatest sum wins the cards.
4. The player who gets the most cards wins!

Problem solving

EXERCISES

1. Jan made 12  .

   She ate 4  .

   How many  did

   she have left?

2. Juan made 14  .

   He ate 5  .

   How many  did

   he have left?

3. Susan made 16  .

   She gave 8  away.

   How many did she have left?

4. Randy made 13  .

   He sold 6  .

   How many

   did he have left?

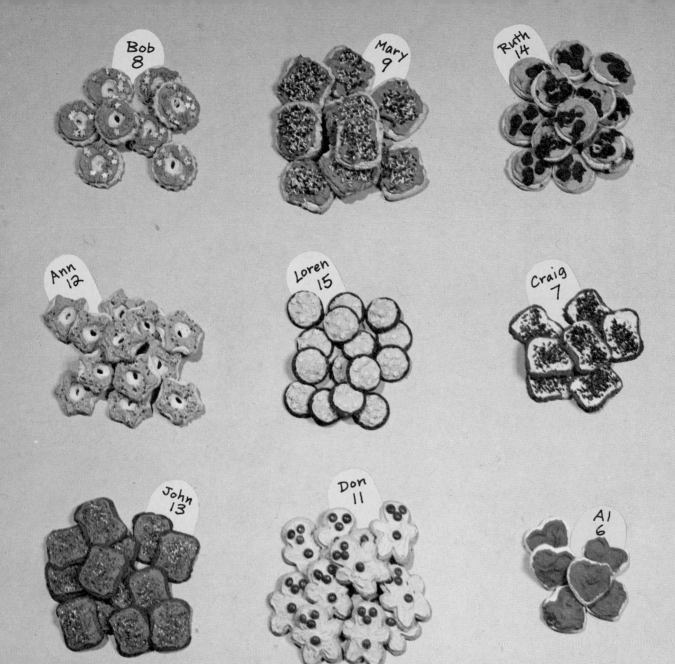

Bob
8

Mary
9

Ruth
14

Ann
12

Loren
15

Craig
7

John
13

Don
11

Al
6

First tell who made more cookies.
Then tell how many more.

5. Bob or Mary
6. Ruth or Craig
7. Ann or Al
8. Don or Mary
9. Loren or Bob
10. Craig or John
11. Ruth or Al
12. Al or Loren

Give each sum. [pages 1–13]

1. 3 +4	2. 4 +4	3. 3 +6	4. 6 +4	5. 0 +6	6. 4 +5
7. 6 +5	8. 7 +7	9. 8 +7	10. 4 +8	11. 8 +9	12. 9 +4
13. 8 +8	14. 5 +7	15. 9 +9	16. 9 +8	17. 6 +6	18. 7 +9

Give each difference. [pages 16–23]

19. 12 −5	20. 7 −0	21. 8 −4	22. 9 −4	23. 8 −8	24. 10 −6
25. 15 −6	26. 15 −8	27. 11 −8	28. 17 −8	29. 13 −8	30. 12 −9
31. 16 −8	32. 17 −9	33. 11 −6	34. 16 −7	35. 13 −9	36. 14 −7

Solve. [pages 14–15, 24, 26–27]

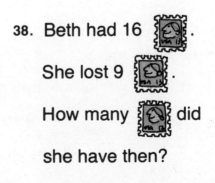

37. Jerry had 6 🔔 .

He bought 9 🔔 .

How many 🔔 did

he have then?

38. Beth had 16 📮 .

She lost 9 📮 .

How many 📮 did

she have then?

You can order 2 addends in 2 ways.

1. Make these number cards:

   Use your cards to see how many ways you can order 3 addends.

2. Make these number cards:

   Use your cards to see how many ways you can order 4 addends.

CHAPTER REVIEW

$$8 \atop +4 \atop \overline{12}$$

Give each sum.

1. $7 \atop +0$	2. $5 \atop +4$	3. $2 \atop +6$	4. $4 \atop +6$	5. $3 \atop +8$	6. $8 \atop +8$
7. $7 \atop +9$	8. $5 \atop +9$	9. $7 \atop +8$	10. $6 \atop +6$	11. $9 \atop +9$	12. $5 \atop +8$
13. $9 \atop +4$	14. $8 \atop +9$	15. $2 \atop +9$	16. $6 \atop +8$	17. $4 \atop +8$	18. $9 \atop +6$

Give each difference.

19. $7 \atop -0$	20. $9 \atop -5$	21. $8 \atop -8$	22. $10 \atop -3$	23. $9 \atop -6$	24. $8 \atop -5$
25. $15 \atop -6$	26. $11 \atop -6$	27. $17 \atop -9$	28. $12 \atop -3$	29. $15 \atop -7$	30. $18 \atop -9$
31. $16 \atop -8$	32. $12 \atop -4$	33. $14 \atop -5$	34. $11 \atop -4$	35. $16 \atop -7$	36. $13 \atop -8$

1. Add the numbers along each side.

Did you get the same sum? When the sums are the same, the triangle is magic.

2. Is this a magic triangle?
   Hint: Add the numbers along each side.

3. Is this a magic triangle?

Form W

13 ... a b c d
14 ... a b c d
15 ...

33 ... a b c d
34 ... a b c d

13 ... a b c d
14 ... a b c d

3 ... a b c d
4 ...

29 ... a b c d
30 ... a b c d
31 ...

MAJOR CHECKUP
Standardized Format

Give the correct letter.

1. Add.

5
$+3$

   a. 7
   b. 2
   c. 8
   d. none of these

2. Add.

$9 + 8$

   a. 17
   b. 1
   c. 16
   d. none of these

3. In $8 + 5 = 13$, 13 is called the

   a. sum
   b. addend
   c. difference
   d. none of these

4. In $9 + 7 = 16$, the addends are

   a. 9 and 16
   b. 9 and 7
   c. 7 and 16
   d. none of these

5. Complete.

$3 + \underline{?} = 8$

   a. 11
   b. 5
   c. 6
   d. none of these

6. Add.

5
3
$+9$

   a. 17
   b. 18
   c. 16
   d. none of these

7. Had: 9 pennies
Found: 6 pennies
How many pennies
in all?

   a. 3
   b. 16
   c. 15
   d. none of these

8. Subtract.

10
-7

   a. 2
   b. 4
   c. 5
   d. none of these

9. Subtract.

$16 - 7$

   a. 8
   b. 7
   c. 9
   d. none of these

10. In $14 - 6 = 8$, 8 is called the

   a. sum
   b. difference
   c. addend
   d. none of these

11. How much money?

1 nickel
3 pennies

   a. 4¢
   b. 12¢
   c. 8¢
   d. none of these

12. Which is the greatest sum?

   a. $6 + 9$
   b. $7 + 9$
   c. $8 + 8$
   d. $9 + 8$

2
Place
Value

Ordinal numbers

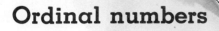

EXERCISES

1. Who is first in line?

2. Who is sixth in line?

3. How many are ahead of the fourth student?

4. How many are behind the third student?

5. What place is Ann in?

6. What place is Dave in?

7. How many students are before Joe?

8. How many students are after Mary?

Complete.

9. The  is <u>eighth</u>.

10. The 🐦 is _____?_____.

11. The 🐦 is _____?_____.

12. The 🐦 is _____?_____.

13. The 🐦 is _____?_____.

14. The 🐦 is _____?_____.

15. The _____?_____ is ninth.

16. The _____?_____ is tenth.

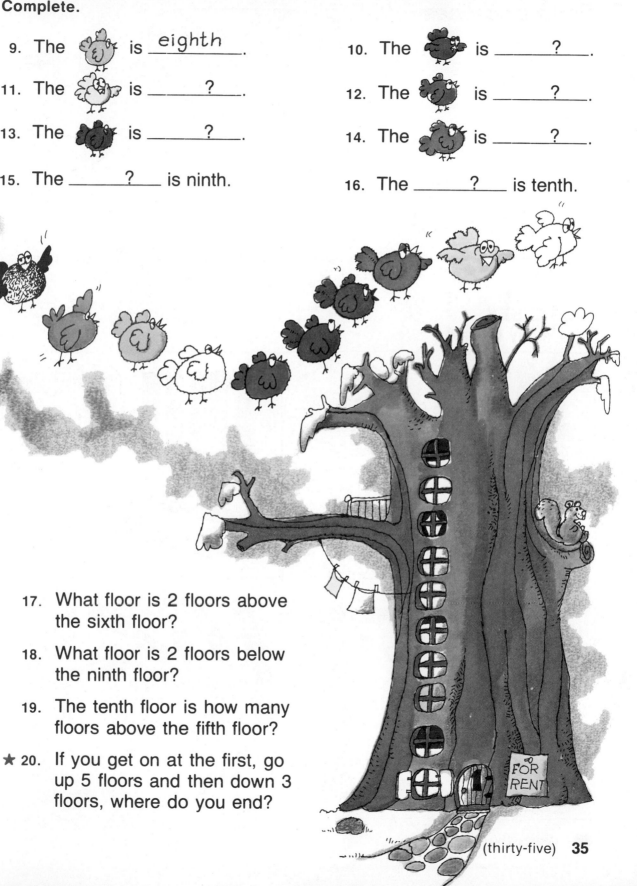

17. What floor is 2 floors above the sixth floor?

18. What floor is 2 floors below the ninth floor?

19. The tenth floor is how many floors above the fifth floor?

★ 20. If you get on at the first, go up 5 floors and then down 3 floors, where do you end?

Tens and ones

These are digits,

0, 1, 2, 3, 4, 5, 6, 7, 8, 9

We use digits to write about larger numbers.

Tens	Ones
3	5

Thirty-five

EXERCISES
How many blocks?

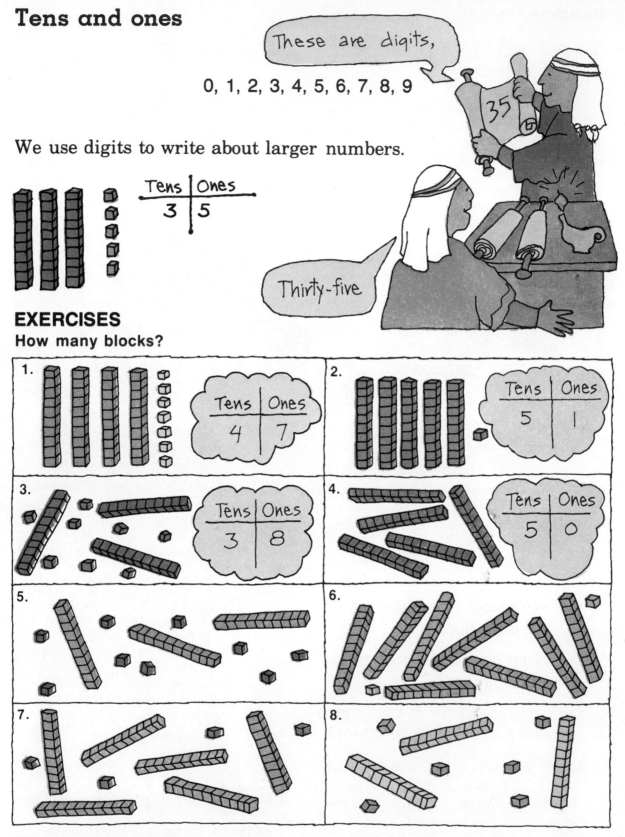

1.

Tens	Ones
4	7

2.

Tens	Ones
5	1

3.

Tens	Ones
3	8

4.

Tens	Ones
5	0

5.

6.

7.

8.

How many balls?

9.

10.

11.

12.

13.

14.

15.

16.

Write the number.

17. forty-seven

18. seventy-four

19. fifty-six

20. sixty-five

21. ninety-three

22. thirty-nine

23. eighty-two

24. twenty-eight

1. 7
    +5

2. 7
    +4

3. 6
    +5

4. 7
    +7

5. 5
    +8

6. 8
    +7

7. 4
    +8

8. 8
    +8

9. 6
    +6

10. 9
    +4

11. 8
    +9

12. 8
    +6

13. 9
    +5

14. 3
    +8

15. 6
    +9

16. 9
    +9

17. 6
    +7

18. 7
    +9

Hundreds

When you put 10 tens together, you get 1 hundred.

10 tens make 1 hundred.

Shown below are 2 hundreds, 3 tens, and 7 ones.

Hundreds	Tens	Ones
2	3	7

237

two hundred thirty-seven

EXERCISES
How many blocks?

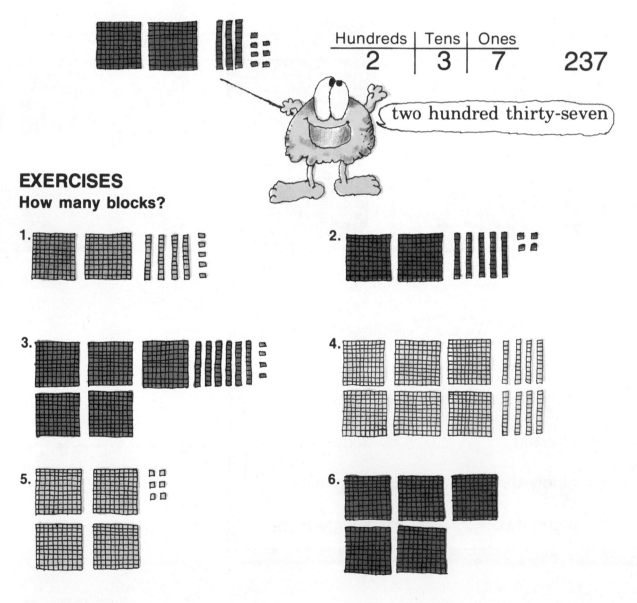

How many marbles?

7.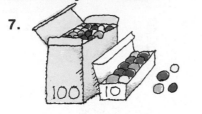

8.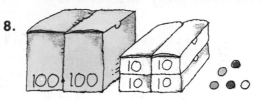

9.

10.

Write each number.

11.
Hundreds	Tens	Ones
9	3	0

12.
Hundreds	Tens	Ones
6	2	5

13.
Hundreds	Tens	Ones
3	0	4

14.
Hundreds	Tens	Ones
5	2	3

15.
Hundreds	Tens	Ones
5	9	0

16.
Hundreds	Tens	Ones
9	0	0

17. four hundred fifty-two

18. seven hundred forty-nine

19. one hundred eighty-seven

20. three hundred sixty

21. nine hundred twelve

22. six hundred eleven

23. five hundred eight

24. nine hundred

These tables have been cut apart.
Write the number.

25.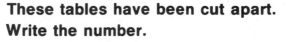

26.

Comparing numbers

fewer blocks

$35 < 40$

35 is less than 40

more blocks

$35 > 26$

35 is greater than 26

EXERCISES

Which number is greater?

1. 24 42
2. 83 38
3. 64 67
4. 53 63
5. 74 34
6. 63 48
7. 49 59
8. 62 60
9. 29 31

34 comes before 35. So, 34 < 35

31 32 33 34 35 36 37 38 39 40 41 42

< or >?
is less than   is greater than

10. 35 (?) 36
11. 48 (?) 35
12. 36 (?) 42

13. 45 (?) 38
14. 37 (?) 43
15. 43 (?) 34

16. 57 (?) 60
17. 40 (?) 37
18. 80 (?) 90

19. 99 (?) 86
20. 58 (?) 77
21. 66 (?) 47

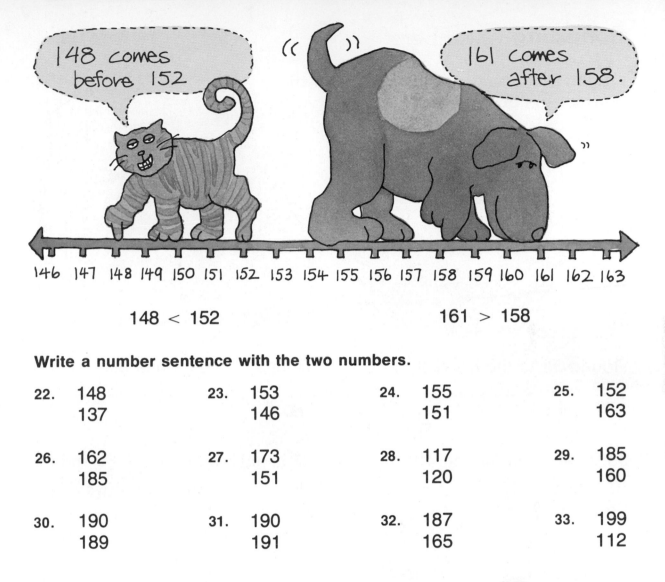

148 < 152   161 > 158

Write a number sentence with the two numbers.

| 22. | 148 | 23. | 153 | 24. | 155 | 25. | 152 |
| | 137 | | 146 | | 151 | | 163 |

| 26. | 162 | 27. | 173 | 28. | 117 | 29. | 185 |
| | 185 | | 151 | | 120 | | 160 |

| 30. | 190 | 31. | 190 | 32. | 187 | 33. | 199 |
| | 189 | | 191 | | 165 | | 112 |

Answer.

34. Jack is 28 years old.
Jill is 52 years old.
Who is older?

35. Joe is 153 centimeters tall.
Ken is 163 centimeters tall.
Who is taller?

36. Rover is 45 centimeters tall.
Duke is 53 centimeters tall.
Which is shorter?

37. Martha scored 116 points.
Charles scored 114 points.
Who scored more?

38. Sandy read 123 pages.
Dennis read 142 pages.
Who read more?

Rounding

Sometimes numbers are rounded to the nearest ten or hundred.

Round 38 to the nearest ten.

38 is between 30 and 40.

It is nearer 40.
So, round to 40.

Round 85 to the nearest ten.

85 is halfway between 80 and 90.

When a number is halfway between two numbers, round to the larger number.
So, round to 90.

Round 246 to the nearest hundred.

246 is between 200 and 300.

It is nearer 200.
So, round to 200.

Round 750 to the nearest hundred.

750 is halfway between 700 and 800.

So, round to 800.

EXERCISES

A rounded number was used in each statement.
Pick the exact number.

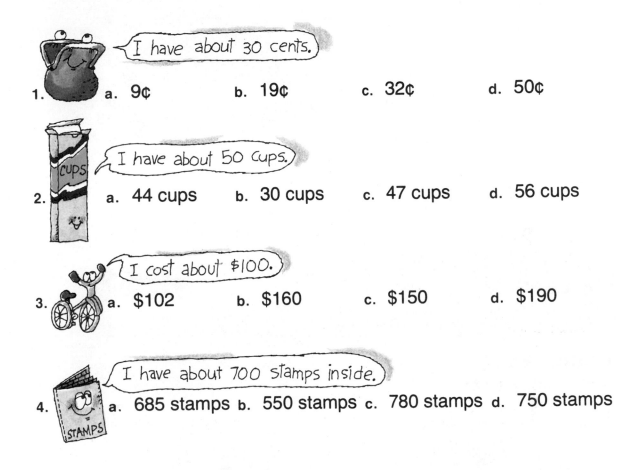

1. **a.** 9¢   **b.** 19¢   **c.** 32¢   **d.** 50¢

2. **a.** 44 cups   **b.** 30 cups   **c.** 47 cups   **d.** 56 cups

3. **a.** $102   **b.** $160   **c.** $150   **d.** $190

4. **a.** 685 stamps   **b.** 550 stamps   **c.** 780 stamps   **d.** 750 stamps

Round to the nearest ten.

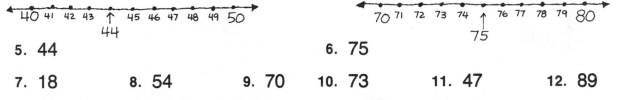

5. 44   6. 75

7. 18   8. 54   9. 70   10. 73   11. 47   12. 89

Round to the nearest hundred.

13. 327   14. 558

15. 309   16. 280   17. 329   18. 450   19. 729   20. 855

Thousands

When you put 10 hundreds together, you
get 1 thousand.

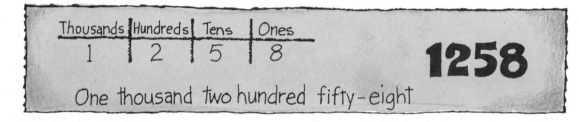

Thousands	Hundreds	Tens	Ones
1	2	5	8

1258

One thousand two hundred fifty-eight

EXERCISES
How many blocks?

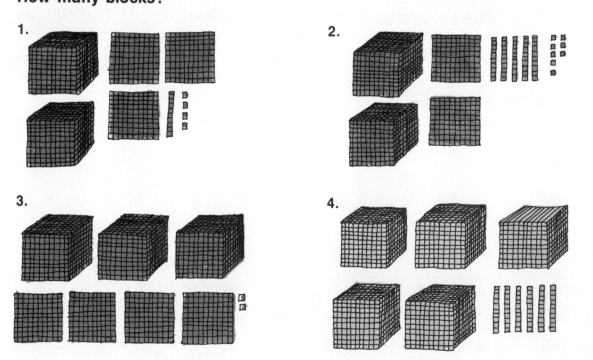

1.

2.

3.

4.

Write each number.

5. 4 thousands, 3 hundreds, 8 tens, 5 ones

6. 9 thousands, 6 hundreds, 4 tens, 6 ones

7. 5 thousands, 0 hundreds, 5 tens, 2 ones

8. 2 thousands, 7 hundreds, 0 tens, 0 ones

9. 6 thousands, 3 hundreds, 0 tens, 2 ones

10. 8 thousands, 0 hundreds, 5 tens, 2 ones

Give the number that is 1000 more.

11. 3842   12. 5617   13. 2314   14. 5638

15. 2915   16. 4623   17. 3514   18. 7283

Give the number that is 100 less.

19. 5634   20. 2847   21. 2956   22. 7291

23. 7403   24. 5620   25. 3817   26. 3605

Give the number that has

27. 5 in the ones place
2 in the hundreds place
8 in the thousands place
3 in the tens place

28. 6 in the hundreds place
3 in the tens place
0 in the ones place
7 in the thousands place

29. 3 in the tens place
6 in the ones place
1 in the thousands place
5 in the hundreds place

30. 9 in the ones place
3 in the thousands place
8 in the hundreds place
7 in the tens place

More about thousands

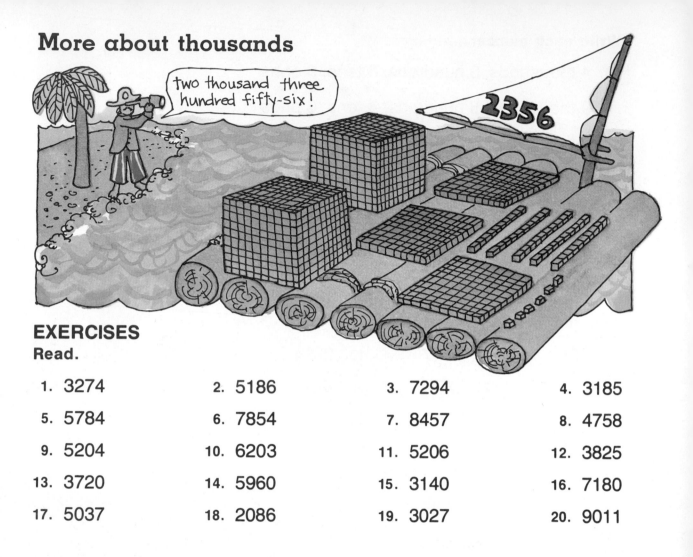

two thousand three hundred fifty-six!

2356

EXERCISES
Read.

1. 3274	2. 5186	3. 7294	4. 3185
5. 5784	6. 7854	7. 8457	8. 4758
9. 5204	10. 6203	11. 5206	12. 3825
13. 3720	14. 5960	15. 3140	16. 7180
17. 5037	18. 2086	19. 3027	20. 9011

Write each number.

21. six thousand two hundred ninety-three

22. five thousand four hundred sixty-one

23. eight thousand seven hundred eleven

24. four thousand three hundred six

25. four thousand two hundred

26. three thousand forty

27. seven thousand

28. seven thousand nine

Give the value of the red digit.

29. 3**2**81
    3000

30. 614**3**

31. **5**731

32. 34**9**6

33. 7**8**14

34. 8**0**61

35. 172**8**

36. **6**205

37. **3**333

38. 3**3**33

39. 33**3**3

40. 333**3**

Give the total score.

Keeping Skills Sharp

1. 13 −8	2. 14 −7	3. 12 −4	4. 15 −9	5. 14 −5	6. 17 −8
7. 16 −8	8. 11 −8	9. 13 −9	10. 18 −9	11. 12 −3	12. 12 −5
13. 11 −4	14. 17 −9	15. 15 −7	16. 14 −6	17. 13 −6	18. 16 −7

Comparing numbers

Which number is greater?

$2432 > 2351$
is greater than

$2351 < 2432$
is less than

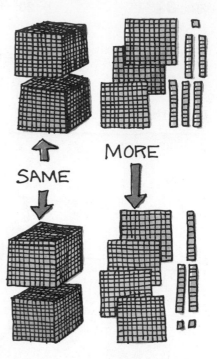

SAME   MORE

EXERCISES

< **or** > ?

is less than   is greater than

1. 5382 ● 6382
2. 4821 ● 2834
3. 6423 ● 6504

4. 9806 ● 9527
5. 4391 ● 4267
6. 8347 ● 8601

7. 5984 ● 5979
8. 6728 ● 6718
9. 7456 ● 7470

10. 8293 ● 8261
11. 2582 ● 2538
12. 7595 ● 7593

13. 9643 ● 9640
14. 3512 ● 3514
15. 1010 ● 1001

Who am I?

16.
I am 1000 greater than 4368.

17.
I am 100 less than 3741.

BUILD-A-NUMBER

1. Draw a table like this:

Th	H	T	O

2. Your teacher will mix up the ten cards.

3. Your teacher will draw a card. Write the digit in *any* place of your table.

4. Repeat step 3 until your table is filled in.

5. The player who builds the greatest number wins!

More about thousands

THOUSANDS					
H	T	O	H	T	O
3	7	4	5	3	6

374,536

three hundred seventy-four thousand, five hundred thirty-six

The red digits tell how many thousands. A comma may be used to set off the thousands.

EXERCISES
Read.

1. The distance around the middle of the earth is about 25,000 miles.

2. The moon is about 250,000 miles from the earth.

3. The Saturn Five can put a load weighing 222,000 pounds into orbit around the earth.

4. To travel from the earth to the moon, a spaceship must reach a speed of 24,500 miles per hour.

5. Neil Armstrong and Buzz Aldrin landed on the moon July 20, 1969.

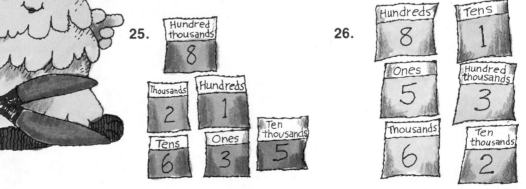

Write the number.

6. forty-two thousand

7. three-hundred thousand

8. five hundred fifty thousand

9. seven hundred forty-two thousand

10. two hundred twelve thousand, three hundred

11. five hundred sixty-two thousand, four hundred eighty

12. twenty-one thousand, five hundred sixty-two

Give the value of the red digit.

13. 62,154   14. 39,074   15. 28,261   16. 36,003

17. 251,207   18. 316,358   19. 508,921   20. 734,629

21. 555,555   22. 555,555   23. 555,555   24. 555,555

★**These tables have been cut apart. Write the number.**

25.
Hundred thousands
8

Thousands	Hundreds
2	1

Tens	Ones	Ten thousands
6	3	5

26.
Hundreds	Tens
8	1

Ones	Hundred thousands
5	3

Thousands	Ten thousands
6	2

Dollars

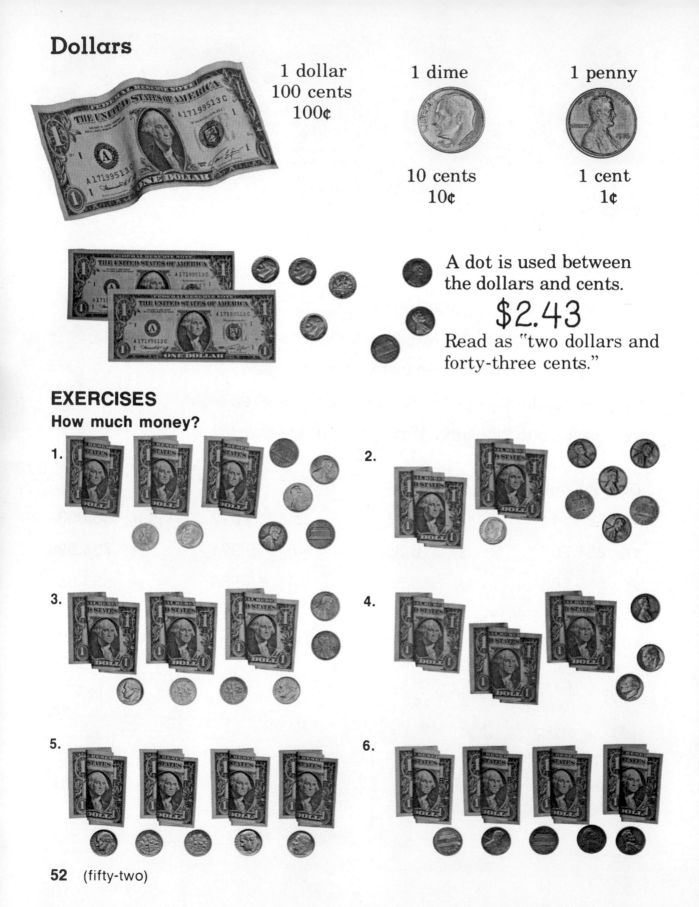

1 dollar
100 cents
100¢

1 dime

10 cents
10¢

1 penny

1 cent
1¢

A dot is used between the dollars and cents.

$2.43

Read as "two dollars and forty-three cents."

EXERCISES

How much money?

1.

2.

3.

4.

5.

6.

Read each price.

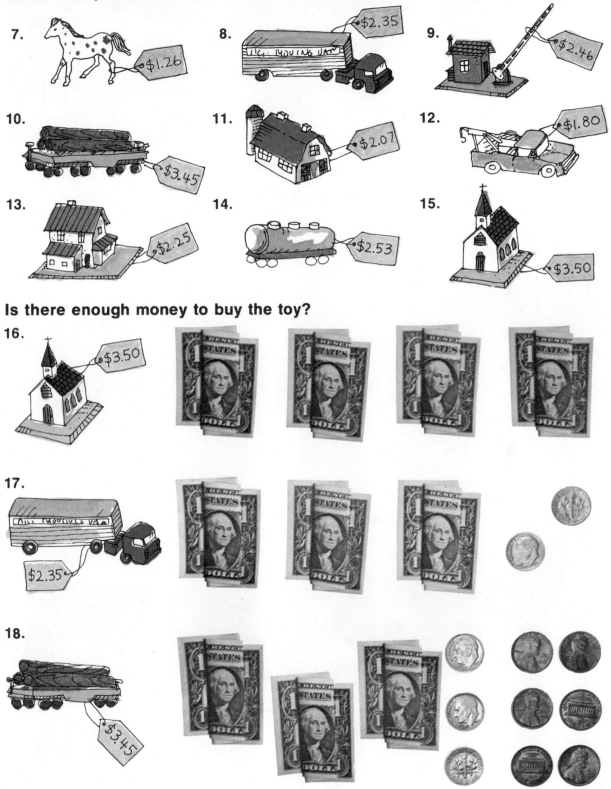

7. $1.26

8. $2.35

9. $2.46

10. $3.45

11. $2.07

12. $1.80

13. $2.25

14. $2.53

15. $3.50

Is there enough money to buy the toy?

16. $3.50

17. $2.35

18. $3.45

CHAPTER CHECKUP

Write the number. [pages 36-39, 44-47]

1.
Tens	Ones
3	6

2.
Hundreds	Tens	Ones
5	2	3

3.
Thousands	Hundreds	Tens	Ones
4	0	1	7

4. sixty-two   5. three hundred eighty   6. two hundred eleven

7. five hundred nine   8. one thousand two hundred sixty-five

9. five thousand forty   10. nine thousand two hundred seven

Give the value of the red digit. [pages 44-47]

11. 3821   12. 4693   13. 5018   14. 9375

< or >?   [pages 40-41, 48-49]
is less than   is greater than

15. 89 (?) 69   16. 281 (?) 316   17. 360 (?) 342

18. 3516 (?) 3543   19. 3824 (?) 3915   20. 8516 (?) 8507

How much money? [pages 52-53]

21.   22.

1. Get a newspaper and cut out some number facts.
2. Make a chart like the one below.
3. Paste your facts in the right boxes.

MY NUMBER FACTS

| 0–9 |
| 10–99 |
| 100–999 |
| 1000–9999 |
| Greater than 9999 |

CHAPTER REVIEW

How many gum drops?

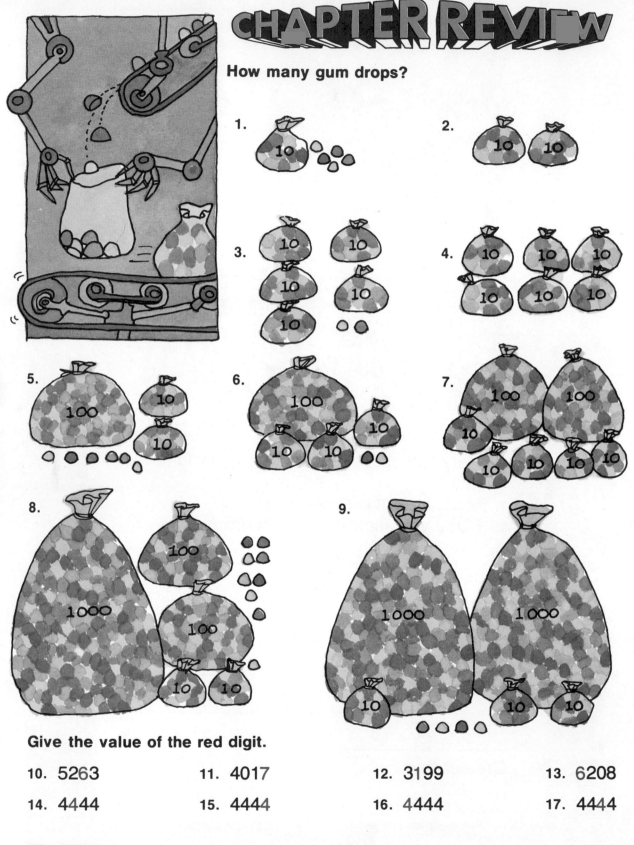

1.

2.

3.

4.

5.

6.

7.

8.

9.

Give the value of the red digit.

10. 5263

11. 4017

12. 3199

13. 6208

14. 4444

15. 4444

16. 4444

17. 4444

What Animal Keeps the Best Time?

SECRET CODE

58	A
99	C
301	D
580	G
999	H
3251	O
2351	T
2531	W

**First give the number.
Then give the letter.
What number is**

1. 10 less than 68?

2. 2 thousands, 5 hundreds, 3 tens, and one?

3. 20 greater than 38?   4. 100 less than 2451?

5. 1 less than 100?   6. 1 less than 1000?

7. 2 thousands less than 2301?

8. 3 hundreds greater than 2951?

9. 2 thousands less than 2580?

NUMBER LETTER

	NUMBER	LETTER
1.	58	A
2.	?	?
3.	?	?
4.	?	?
5.	?	?
6.	?	?
7.	?	?
8.	?	?
9.	?	?

Form W

	a	b	c	d		a	b	c	d		a	b	c	d		a	b	c	d		a	b	c	d
14					34					14					4					30				
15	a	b	c	d							a	b	c	d						31	a	b	c	d

MAJOR CHECKUP
Standardized Format

Give the correct letter.

1. Add.

2
5
+9

    a. 16
    b. 15
    c. 14
    d. 17

2. Subtract.

14
−9

    a. 4
    b. 3
    c. 6
    d. none of these

3. How much money?

2 dimes
2 nickels
3 pennies

    a. 24¢
    b. 28¢
    c. 33¢
    d. 43¢

4. Which is the greatest amount of money?

a. 4 dimes
b. 3 dimes and 1 nickel
c. 3 dimes and 3 pennies
d. 3 dimes and 3 nickels

5. What letter is seventh in this word?

NUMERAL

    a. L
    b. R
    c. A
    d. E

6. Which number is smallest?

    a. sixty-four
    b. forty-six
    c. forty-eight
    d. fifty

7. 76 rounded to the nearest ten is

    a. 70
    b. 77
    c. 80
    d. 100

8. What number is 1 less than 170?

    a. 169
    b. 171
    c. 179
    d. none of these

9. What number is 10 more than 78?

    a. 79
    b. 178
    c. 68
    d. 88

10. Six thousand, four hundred four is

    a. 6440
    b. 6400
    c. 6044
    d. 6404

11. Which number is greatest?

    a. 5683
    b. 5671
    c. 5684
    d. 5646

12. How much money?

1 dollar
3 dimes
4 pennies

    a. $1.34
    b. $1.54
    c. $1.70
    d. $1.52

3
Addition

READY OR NOT !

1. 4
   +5

2. 5
   +8

3. 7
   +8

4. 5
   +6

5. 7
   +7

6. 6
   +6

7. 9
   +8

8. 0
   +8

9. 4
   +8

10. 1
    +7

11. 6
    +0

12. 6
    +7

13. 2
    +7

14. 7
    +9

15. 9
    +4

16. 5
    +9

17. 8
    +8

18. 3
    +7

19. 9
    +6

20. 6
    +8

21. 4
    +6

22. 9
    +9

23. 3
    +8

24. 3
    +9

Adding 2-digit numbers

To find the sum, first we add the ones.

Then we add the tens.

Tens	Ones
3	5
+2	3
	8

Tens	Ones
3	5
+2	3
5	8

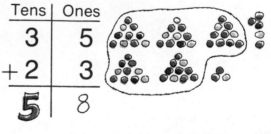

There are 58 marbles in all.

EXERCISES
Add.

1. 24
   +21

2. 22
   +36

3. 30
   +25

60 (sixty)

4. 20
   +18

5. 52
   +30

6. 15
   +32

7. 23
   +45

8. 45
   +23

9. 62
   +21

10. 63
    +22

11. 12
    +30

12. 32
    +32

13. 51
    +16

14. 43
    +22

15. 57
    +32

16. 21
    +70

17. 35
    +41

18. 49
    +50

19. 32
    + 5

20. 43
    + 4

21. 21
    + 7

22. 34
    + 5

23. 40
    + 9

24. 26
    +42

25. 37
    +51

26. 81
    +16

27. 28
    +71

28. 75
    +24

29. 53 + 21 = ?

$$53 \atop +21$$

30. 35 + 14 = ?

31. 14 + 35 = ?

32. 51 + 45 = ?

33. 45 + 51 = ?

Add across. Add down.

34.

30	13	?
24	22	?
?	?	?

35.

21	13	?
14	30	?
?	?	?

Adding with regrouping

Add ones.

$$\begin{array}{r} 25 \\ +18 \\ \hline \end{array}$$

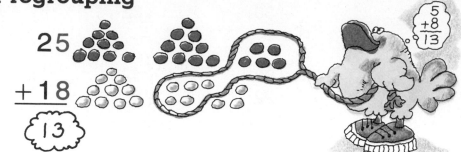

Add ones. (13)

Regroup.

1 ten and 3 ones

$$\begin{array}{r} 1 \\ 25 \\ +18 \\ \hline 3 \end{array}$$

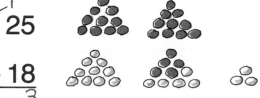

Add tens.

$$\begin{array}{r} 1 \\ 25 \\ +18 \\ \hline 43 \end{array}$$

There are 43 eggs in all.

EXERCISES
Add.

1. $\begin{array}{r} 28 \\ +24 \\ \hline \end{array}$

2. $\begin{array}{r} 35 \\ +29 \\ \hline \end{array}$

3. $\begin{array}{r} 38 \\ +23 \\ \hline \end{array}$

4. $\begin{array}{r} 36 \\ +38 \\ \hline \end{array}$

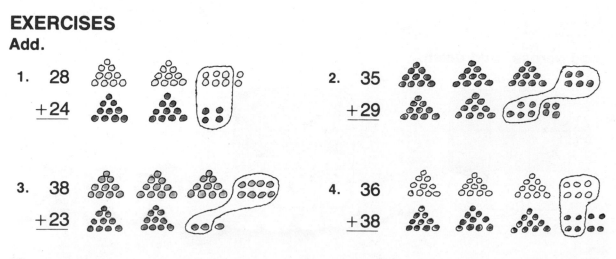

5. 55 + 38	6. 45 + 19	7. 57 + 26	8. 42 + 36	9. 25 + 55
10. 47 + 7	11. 26 + 43	12. 62 + 29	13. 27 + 27	14. 66 + 25
15. 56 + 17	16. 35 + 28	17. 63 + 28	18. 53 + 8	19. 39 + 20
20. 41 + 29	21. 43 + 6	22. 67 + 32	23. 37 + 18	24. 48 + 48
25. 46 + 16	26. 38 + 7	27. 29 + 17	28. 54 + 26	29. 49 + 36
30. 64 + 27	31. 55 + 30			

To add 9,
I can add
10 and
subtract 1.

SHORTCUT

Use the shortcut.

32. 47 + 9 = ?   33. 58 + 9 = ?

34. 65 + 9 = ?   35. 37 + 9 = ?

36. 73 + 9 = ?   37. 84 + 9 = ?

Adding—regrouping tens

Add ones.

$$85$$
$$+63$$
$$\overline{8}$$

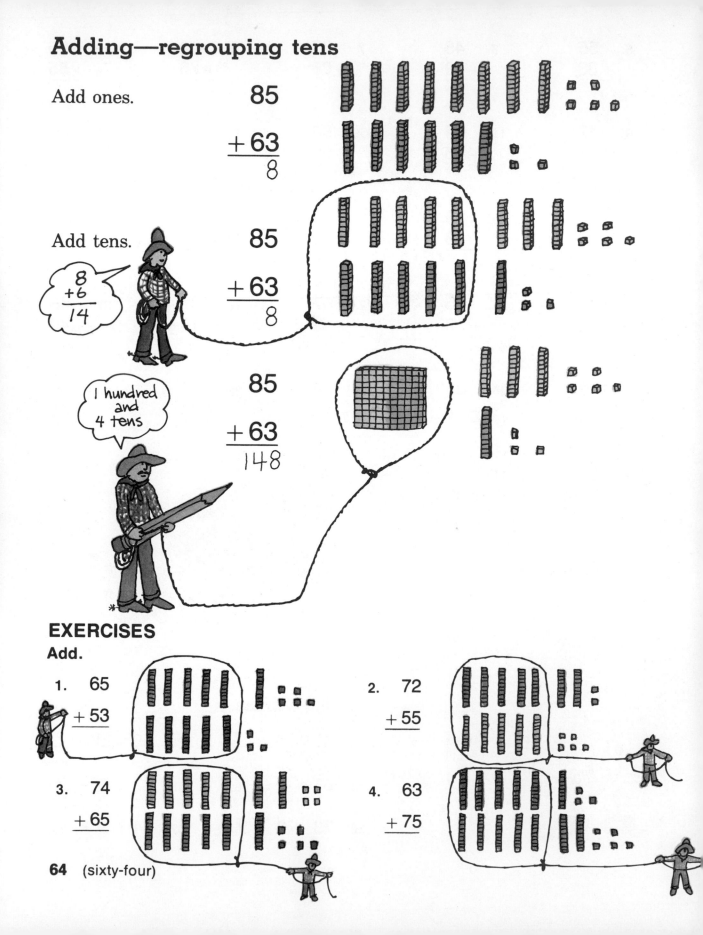

Add tens.

$$\begin{array}{r} 8 \\ +6 \\ \hline 14 \end{array}$$

$$85$$
$$+63$$
$$\overline{8}$$

1 hundred
and
4 tens

$$85$$
$$+63$$
$$\overline{148}$$

EXERCISES
Add.

1. $\begin{array}{r} 65 \\ +53 \\ \hline \end{array}$

2. $\begin{array}{r} 72 \\ +55 \\ \hline \end{array}$

3. $\begin{array}{r} 74 \\ +65 \\ \hline \end{array}$

4. $\begin{array}{r} 63 \\ +75 \\ \hline \end{array}$

5.	56 +83	6.	49 +70	7.	68 +51	8.	85 +73	9.	95 +82
10.	67 +53	11.	67 +55	12.	87 +78	13.	65 +36	14.	83 +59
15.	86 +28	16.	97 +48	17.	78 +83	18.	68 +17	19.	88 +75
20.	$.79 +.66 $1.45	21.	$.84 +.59	22.	$.99 +.38	23.	$.75 +.22	24.	$.69 +.56
25.	$.95 +.95	26.	$.64 +.28	27.	$.76 +.19	28.	$.59 +.95	29.	$.98 +.74
30.	$.77 +.20	31.	$.85 +.28	32.	$.75 +.53	33.	$.80 +.70	34.	$.96 +.19

Who am I?

★35.
I am 10 less than the sum of 65 and 86.

★36.
I am 100 greater than the sum of 79 and 54.

Menu

Hamburger $.85

Superburger $1.19

Hot Dog $.65

French Fries $.49

Hot Pie $.35

Shake $.68

Large Milk $.37

Small Milk $.26

EXERCISES

Give the total price.

1.

2.

3.

4.

5.

6.

7.

8.

Solve.

9. Jan bought  and 🥛 .

   How much did she spend?

10. Alex bought and 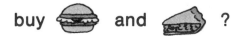 .

    How much did he spend?

11. Jim bought 🍔 🍔 .

    How much did he spend?

12. Sarah has $1.29. Can she

    buy 🍔 and  ?

13. José has $1.06. Can he

    buy 🍔 and 🍔 ?

14. Susan bought 🍟 🍟 🥤 .

    How much did she spend?

More than 2 addends

Add ones.

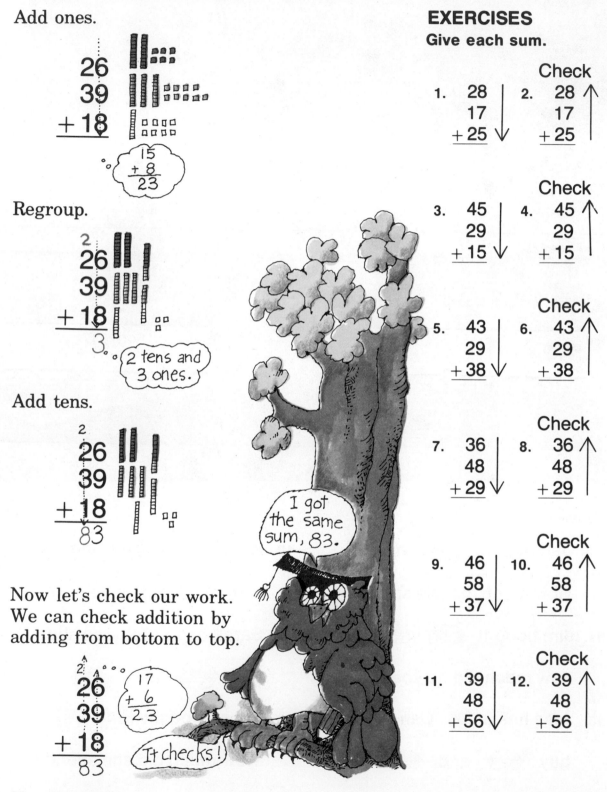

$$\begin{array}{r} 26 \\ 39 \\ +18 \\ \hline \end{array}$$

$$\begin{array}{r} 15 \\ +\ 8 \\ \hline 23 \end{array}$$

Regroup.

$$\begin{array}{r} {\scriptstyle 2} \\ 26 \\ 39 \\ +18 \\ \hline 3 \end{array}$$

2 tens and 3 ones.

Add tens.

$$\begin{array}{r} {\scriptstyle 2} \\ 26 \\ 39 \\ +18 \\ \hline 83 \end{array}$$

I got the same sum, 83.

Now let's check our work. We can check addition by adding from bottom to top.

$$\begin{array}{r} {\scriptstyle 2} \\ 26 \\ 39 \\ +18 \\ \hline 83 \end{array}$$

$$\begin{array}{r} 17 \\ +\ 6 \\ \hline 23 \end{array}$$

It checks!

EXERCISES
Give each sum.

		Check	
1.	28 ↓	2.	28 ↑
	17		17
	+25		+25

		Check	
3.	45 ↓	4.	45 ↑
	29		29
	+15		+15

		Check	
5.	43 ↓	6.	43 ↑
	29		29
	+38		+38

		Check	
7.	36 ↓	8.	36 ↑
	48		48
	+29		+29

		Check	
9.	46 ↓	10.	46 ↑
	58		58
	+37		+37

		Check	
11.	39 ↓	12.	39 ↑
	48		48
	+56		+56

Add.

13.
```
  26
  37
+ 49
```

14.
```
  35
  56
+ 28
```

15.
```
  59
  74
+ 86
```

16.
```
  53
  29
+ 68
```

17.
```
  16
  21
  29
+ 35
```

18.
```
  47
  56
  66
+ 27
```

19.
```
  27
  39
  48
+ 55
```

20.
```
  49
  26
  67
+ 38
```

21.
```
  46
  57
  29
+ 28
```

22.
```
  45
  64
  38
+ 16
```

23.
```
  54
  38
   9
+ 17
```

24.
```
  25
  65
  18
+  7
```

To add 18, I add 20 and subtract 2.

SHORTCUT

Use the shortcut.

25. $47 + 18 = \underline{\ ?\ }$

26. $53 + 18 = \underline{\ ?\ }$

27. $68 + 18 = \underline{\ ?\ }$

28. $59 + 18 = \underline{\ ?\ }$

29. $37 + 18 = \underline{\ ?\ }$

30. $75 + 18 = \underline{\ ?\ }$

31. $63 + 18 = \underline{\ ?\ }$

32. $39 + 18 = \underline{\ ?\ }$

1.
```
  16
－ 8
```

2.
```
   9
－ 6
```

3.
```
  14
－ 8
```

4.
```
  13
－ 8
```

5.
```
  15
－ 8
```

6.
```
  17
－ 9
```

7.
```
  12
－ 6
```

8.
```
  12
－ 9
```

9.
```
  11
－ 4
```

10.
```
  18
－ 9
```

11.
```
   8
－ 8
```

12.
```
  13
－ 9
```

13.
```
  13
－ 7
```

14.
```
  17
－ 8
```

15.
```
  10
－ 8
```

16.
```
  14
－ 7
```

17.
```
  10
－ 3
```

18.
```
  15
－ 6
```

Adding 3-digit numbers

Add ones and regroup.
Add tens.
Add hundreds.

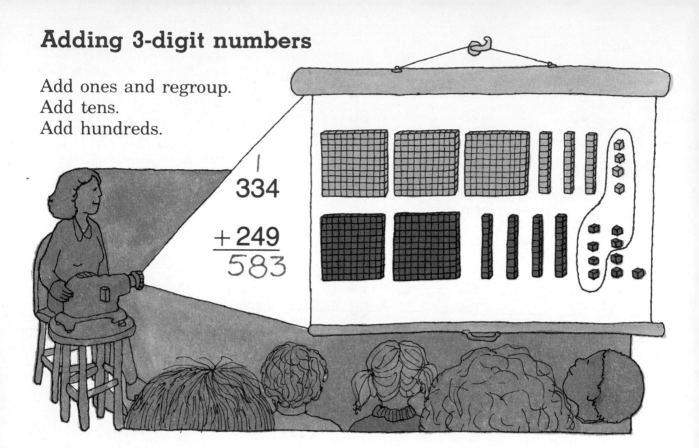

334
+249
583

EXERCISES
Give each sum.

1. 327 +456	2. 214 +328	3. 326 +252	4. 226 +443	5. 418 +226
6. 459 +216	7. 524 +329	8. 238 +401	9. 406 +357	10. 308 +178
11. 352 +531	12. 238 +406	13. 468 +317	14. 342 +342	15. 526 +269
16. 469 +319	17. 254 +439	18. 306 +582	19. 529 +101	20. 348 +317

TICKETS SOLD	FIRST WEEK	SECOND WEEK
FIRST GRADE	123	105
SECOND GRADE	96	89
THIRD GRADE	108	95
FOURTH GRADE	119	125
FIFTH GRADE	98	98
SIXTH GRADE	89	105

Solve.

21. How many tickets did the first grade sell?

22. How many tickets did the third grade sell?

23. How many tickets did the fourth grade sell?

24. Did the second grade sell fewer than 200 tickets?

25. Who sold more tickets, the fifth grade or the sixth grade?

Addition— regrouping ones and tens

Add ones.

285
+376
11

Regroup.

285
+376
1

Add tens.

285
+376
161

Regroup.

285
+376
61

Add hundreds.

285
+376
661

EXERCISES
Add.

1. 295
+376

2. 378
+256

3. 467
+384

4. 275
+468

5. 593
+247

6. 384
+229

7. 508
+296

8. 352
+580

9. 392
+341

10. 524
+168

11. 395
+271

12. 458
+458

13. 729
+158

14. 476
+258

15. 258
+476

16. 592 +324	17. 759 +216	18. 388 +456	19. 297 +629	20. 629 +297

21. 153 68 + 53	22. 253 24 +145	23. 138 54 + 95	24. 536 129 + 43	25. 206 58 + 8

26. 316 208 54 + 19	27. 158 74 130 + 87	28. 156 241 58 +267	29. 374 29 162 + 6	30. 593 106 86 + 7

Complete.

31.

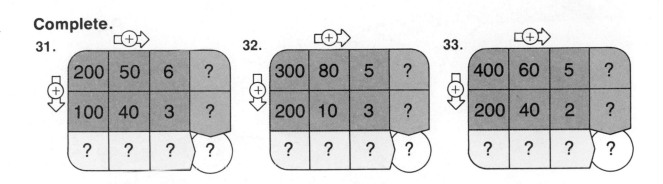

200	50	6	?
100	40	3	?
?	?	?	?

32.

300	80	5	?
200	10	3	?
?	?	?	?

33.

400	60	5	?
200	40	2	?
?	?	?	?

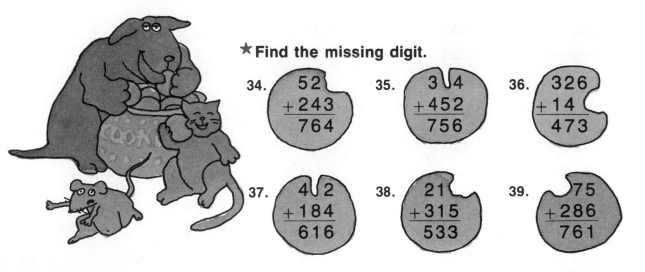

★ **Find the missing digit.**

34. 52⬚
+243
764

35. 3⬚4
+452
756

36. 326
+14⬚
473

37. 4⬚2
+184
616

38. 21⬚
+315
533

39. ⬚75
+286
761

Addition—regrouping ones, tens, and hundreds

Add ones.

$$\begin{array}{r} 849 \\ +276 \\ \hline 15 \end{array}$$

Regroup.

$$\begin{array}{r} \overset{1}{8}49 \\ +276 \\ \hline 5 \end{array}$$

Add tens.

$$\begin{array}{r} \overset{1}{8}49 \\ +276 \\ \hline 12\;5 \end{array}$$

Regroup.

$$\begin{array}{r} \overset{1}{8}\overset{1}{4}9 \\ +276 \\ \hline 25 \end{array}$$

Add hundreds.

$$\begin{array}{r} \overset{1}{8}\overset{1}{4}9 \\ +276 \\ \hline 11\;25 \end{array}$$

1 thousand and 1 hundred

EXERCISES
Add.

1. 594
+960

2. 683
+821

3. 752
+659

4. 829
+374

5. 456
+597

6. 729
+308

7. 835
+214

8. 653
+378

9. 514
+795

10. 953
+689

11. 695
+546

12. 747
+859

13. 513
+358

14. 829
+173

15. 382
+956

16. 584 +592	17. 959 +386	18. 626 +958	19. 846 +759	20. 758 +279
21. 738 +497	22. 675 +386	23. 890 +278	24. 853 +589	25. 629 +296
26. 752 +651	27. 259 +958	28. 914 +759	29. 374 +680	30. 829 +358

31. 829 + 370 = _?_

32. 596 + 748 = _?_

33. 785 + 391 = _?_

34. 593 + 278 = _?_

35. 605 + 597 = _?_

36. 665 + 487 = _?_

37. 856 + 856 = _?_

38. 958 + 796 = _?_

39. 674 + 795 = _?_

Solve.

40. Tire: $5.69
    Horn: $3.75
    How much for both?

★41. Bicycle: $98.50
    Light: $4.59
    How much for both?

★42. Tube: $3.25
    Tire: $5.69
    Bell: $1.85
    How much for all?

Estimating sums

Sometimes you do not need an exact answer. Then you can **estimate**. One way to estimate a sum is to round each addend.

To estimate
this sum:

29	round to	30
+ 54	round to	+ 50
		80

The sum is about 80.

To estimate
this sum:

227	round to	200
+ 584	round to	+ 600
		800

The sum is about 800.

40 + 20 = 60
The answer should be around 60. I must have made a mistake.

Estimating can help you find mistakes, too. Can you help him find his mistake?

37
+18
45

EXERCISES
**First estimate the sum.
Then add and compare.**

1.	48 +17	2.	39 +49	3.	52 +21	4.	63 +17	5.	74 +15
6.	39 +38	7.	42 +27	8.	51 +38	9.	42 +59	10.	37 +63
11.	327 +318	12.	219 +478	13.	421 +308	14.	524 +389	15.	275 +190

Which sum is greater?

1.

H	T	O
3	8	5
6	5	9

H	T	O
5	3	6
5	8	9

10 4 4

2.

H	T	O
7	4	3
8	5	9

H	T	O
7	5	8
9	3	4

3.

H	T	O
9	6	7
5	3	8

H	T	O
7	9	3
6	8	5

4.

H	T	O
7	4	8
6	5	9

H	T	O
6	9	5
8	7	4

Play the game.

H	T	O

1. Draw a table like this one.

2. As your teacher picks a card, write the digit in any place in your table.

3. After six digits have been picked, add your numbers.

4. The player who gets the greatest sum wins!

Adding larger numbers

Large numbers can be added in the same way as smaller numbers.

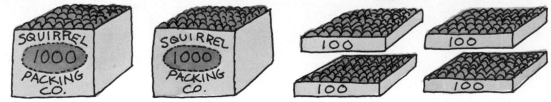

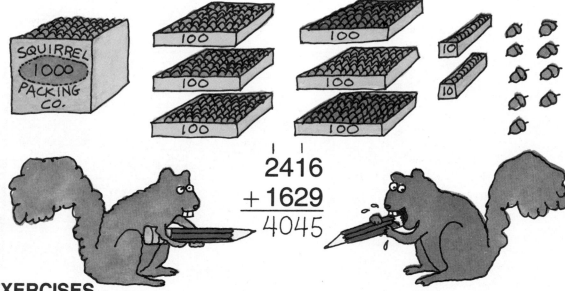

$$2416$$
$$+1629$$
$$\overline{4045}$$

EXERCISES
Add.

1. 3278
    +4125

2. 7463
    +1282

3. 5067
    +3543

4. 3333
    +1586

5. 2654
    +3528

6. 3614
    +2537

7. 2579
    +5426

8. 5426
    +2579

9. 2718
    +3295

10. 5583
    +2978

11. 4729
    +4873

12. 5979
    +3864

| 13. 5785
+2336 | 14. 6157
+1289 | 15. 3859
+4675 | 16. 2856
+2344 |

| 17. 7825
+ 358 | 18. 3650
+ 799 | 19. 5368
+ 754 | 20. 526
+4859 |

21. 7218 + 1395 = _?_   22. 6284 + 2593 = _?_

23. 4706 + 395 = _?_   24. 467 + 2953 = _?_

Who am I?

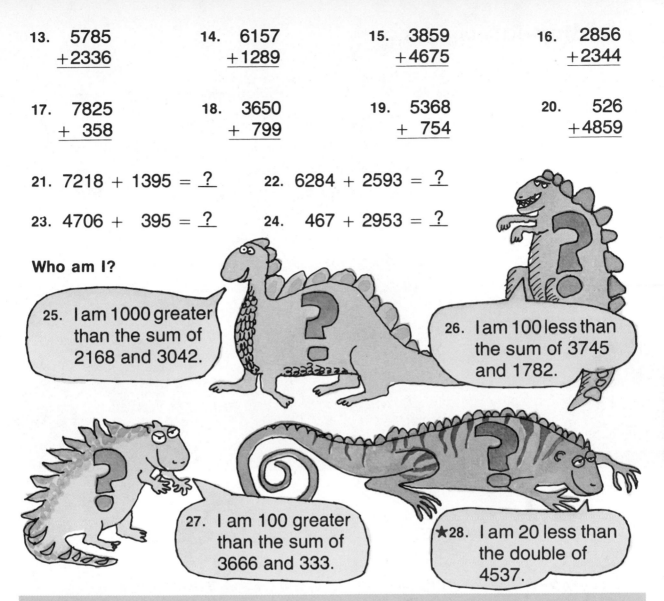

25. I am 1000 greater than the sum of 2168 and 3042.

26. I am 100 less than the sum of 3745 and 1782.

27. I am 100 greater than the sum of 3666 and 333.

★28. I am 20 less than the double of 4537.

Keeping Skills Sharp

Write the number.

1. fifty-six
2. ninety
3. one hundred three
4. one hundred sixty-seven
5. two thousand three hundred
6. six thousand two hundred eleven
7. four thousand one hundred forty
8. five thousand forty-six
9. nine thousand two hundred fifteen
10. eight thousand five

Problem solving

Solve.

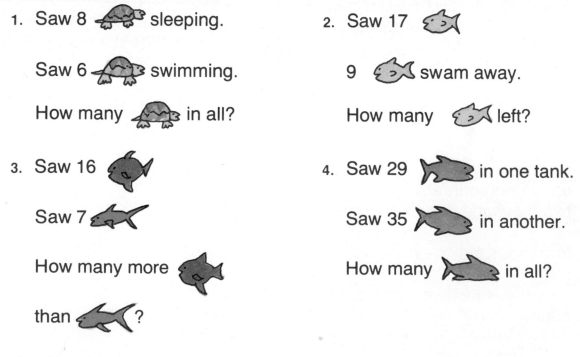

1. Saw 8 sleeping.

   Saw 6 swimming.

   How many in all?

2. Saw 17

   9 swam away.

   How many left?

3. Saw 16

   Saw 7

   How many more

   than ?

4. Saw 29 in one tank.

   Saw 35 in another.

   How many in all?

Solve.

5. Which day were there the fewest visitors?

6. Which day were there the most visitors?

7. How many people visited during the first two days of the week?

8. How many visitors were there during the last two days of the week?

★ 9. What was the total number of visitors on Monday, Wednesday, and Friday?

★ 10. How many visitors came in all during the week?

DAY	VISITORS
Monday	1128
Tuesday	1606
Wednesday	1042
Thursday	1542
Friday	1629
Saturday	1837

CHAPTER CHECKUP

Give each sum. [pages 59–65, 68–70, 72–77]

1. 56 +28	2. 37 + 6	3. 75 +18	4. 23 + 8	5. 47 +39
6. 76 +35	7. 84 +76	8. 59 +57	9. 75 +69	10. 57 +75
11. 25 38 +29	12. 42 18 + 6	13. 59 7 +26	14. 25 53 +18	15. 29 30 +31
16. 352 +594	17. 635 +281	18. 734 +586	19. 598 +275	20. 659 +748

21. $23 + 36 = \underline{\ ?\ }$ 22. $58 + 29 = \underline{\ ?\ }$

23. $19 + 38 = \underline{\ ?\ }$ 24. $87 + 69 = \underline{\ ?\ }$

25. $159 + 283 = \underline{\ ?\ }$ 26. $325 + 875 = \underline{\ ?\ }$

Give the total price. [pages 66–67, 71, 80–81]

27.

28.

Project

2 3 4 5 6 7 8 9 10 11 12

1. Get two blocks and label the faces 1 through 6.

2. Get a piece of graph paper and number it as shown above.

3. Roll your blocks and graph the sum of the "up" numbers.

4. Repeat step 3 about 50 times.

5. Tell some things that your graph shows.

Add.

TRAVEL WITH CARE

1. 53
+ 21

2. 74
+ 15

3. 61
+ 6

REGROUP 10 ONES FOR 1 TEN

45
+ 27
72

4. 36
+ 28

5. 47
+ 7

6. 18
+ 65

REGROUP ONES AND TENS

68
+ 59
127

7. 59
+ 68

8. 74
+ 36

9. 65
+ 57

REGROUP 20 ONES FOR 2 TENS

35
28
+ 39
102

10. 49
13
+ 28

11. 36
29
+ 18

12. 27
59
+ 8

REGROUP ONES AND TENS

395
+ 246
641

13. 259
+ 386

14. 758
+ 165

15. 387
+ 546

REGROUP ONES, TENS, AND HUNDREDS

578
+ 943
1521

16. 674
+ 829

17. 253
+ 978

18. 768
+ 697

This is a magic square because all the sums are the same.

8	1	6	→ 15
3	5	7	→ 15
4	9	2	→ 15

15 15 15 15 15

Are these magic squares?

1.

16	2	12
6	10	14
8	18	4

2.

80	10	60
30	50	70
40	90	20

3.

30	23	28
25	27	29
26	31	24

4.

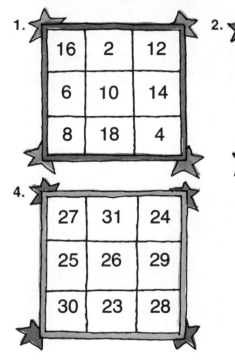

27	31	24
25	26	29
30	23	28

5. Start with the magic square shown at the top of the page. Make a new square by adding 10 to each number.

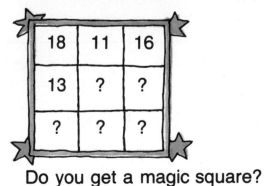

18	11	16
13	?	?
?	?	?

Do you get a magic square?

Give the correct letter.

1. Add.

9
+8

a. 16
b. 17
c. 18
d. 15

2. Complete.

6 + ? = 9

a. 15
b. 13
c. 14
d. none of these

3. Subtract.

16
−7

a. 9
b. 7
c. 8
d. none of these

4. A related subtraction fact for
8 + 5 = 13 is

a. 5 + 8 = 13
b. 13 − 6 = 7
c. 13 − 5 = 8
d. none of these

5. How much money?

2 dimes
3 nickels
3 pennies

a. 34¢
b. 42¢
c. 43¢
d. 38¢

6. The 8 in 583 stands for

a. 8 ones
b. 8 hundreds
c. 8 tens
d. none of these

7. 342 rounded to the nearest hundred is

a. 340
b. 350
c. 400
d. 300

8. In 7958, which digit is in the thousands place?

a. 8
b. 9
c. 7
d. 5

9. Which is the most money?

a. $2.56
b. $1.65
c. $2.65
d. $1.56

10. Add.
38 + 27

a. 65
b. 55
c. 75
d. none of these

11. Add.

659
+245

a. 894
b. 804
c. 904
d. none of these

12. Add.

7826
+1935

a. 9761
b. 9751
c. 8761
d. none of these

4
Subtraction

READY OR NOT !

1. 14
 − 6

2. 13
 − 9

3. 15
 − 6

4. 9
 − 9

5. 14
 − 7

6. 16
 − 8

7. 11
 − 9

8. 17
 − 9

9. 11
 − 8

10. 18
 − 9

11. 12
 − 9

12. 10
 − 6

Subtracting 2-digit numbers

To find the difference, we
first subtract the ones.

Tens	Ones
3	8
−1	5
	3

Then we subtract the tens.

Tens	Ones
3	8
−1	5
2	3

There are 23 eggs left.

EXERCISES
Subtract.

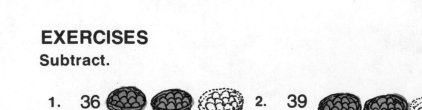

1. 36
 − 12

2. 39
 − 16

3. 43
 − 20

4. 48 − 23	5. 47 − 15	6. 38 − 16	7. 59 − 25	8. 28 − 25
9. 59 − 35	10. 39 − 29	11. 57 − 52	12. 65 − 11	13. 60 − 10
14. 46 − 15	15. 79 − 63	16. 44 − 12	17. 77 − 71	18. 53 − 32
19. 85 − 45	20. 86 − 53	21. 65 − 40	22. 56 − 21	23. 74 − 74
24. 75 − 31	25. 88 − 46	26. 69 − 25	27. 78 − 63	28. 96 − 30

29. 68 − 24 = ?

30. 80 − 20 = ?

31. 95 − 25 = ?

32. 76 − 33 = ?

33. 87 − 45 = ?

Give the end number.

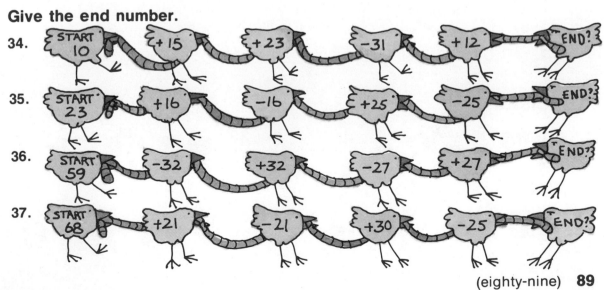

34. START 10 + 15 + 23 − 31 + 12 END?

35. START 23 + 16 − 16 + 25 − 25 END?

36. START 59 − 32 + 32 − 27 + 27 END?

37. START 68 + 21 − 21 + 30 − 25 END?

(eighty-nine) **89**

Subtracting with regrouping

When there are not enough ones, you
have to regroup.

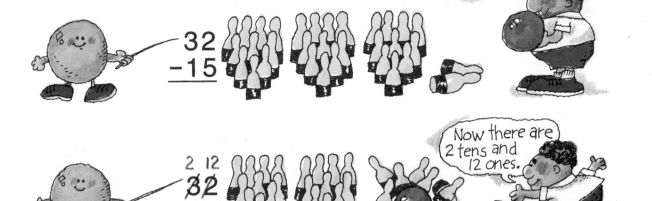

$$\begin{array}{r} 32 \\ -15 \end{array}$$

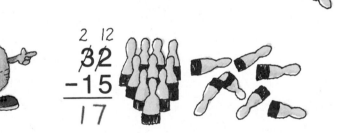

$$\begin{array}{r} {}^{2}\,{}^{12} \\ \cancel{3}\cancel{2} \\ -15 \\ \hline 17 \end{array}$$

There are 17 pins left.

EXERCISES

1.
$$\begin{array}{r} 31 \\ -18 \end{array}$$

2.
$$\begin{array}{r} 33 \\ -15 \end{array}$$

3.
$$\begin{array}{r} 44 \\ -19 \end{array}$$

4.
$$\begin{array}{r} 45 \\ -28 \end{array}$$

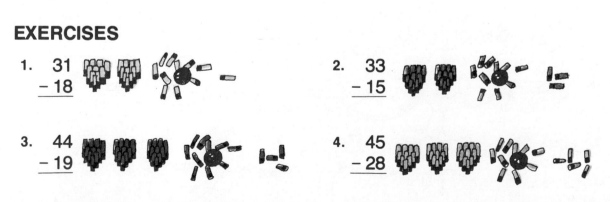

5. 50
  − 32

6. 33
  − 12

7. 41
  − 23

8. 65
  − 18

9. 54
  − 45

10. 82
  − 25

11. 64
  − 32

12. 81
  − 26

13. 52
  − 39

14. 40
  − 18

15. 53
  − 36

16. 70
  − 49

17. 80
  − 35

18. 63
  − 22

19. 71
  − 65

To subtract 9, I can subtract 10 and then add 1.

SHORTCUT

Use the shortcut.

32. 66 − 9 = ?

33. 53 − 9 = ?

34. 72 − 9 = ?

35. 45 − 9 = ?

36. 91 − 9 = ?

37. 80 − 9 = ?

38. 38 − 9 = ?

39. 57 − 9 = ?

40. 85 − 9 = ?

20. 74
  − 58

21. 62
  − 31

22. 80
  − 63

23. 51
  − 46

24. 90
  − 42

25. 44
  − 32

26. 42
  − 16

27. 50
  − 35

28. 61
  − 58

29. 43
  − 21

30. 60
  − 28

31. 73
  − 69

More about subtracting 2-digit numbers

When there are not enough ones, regroup.

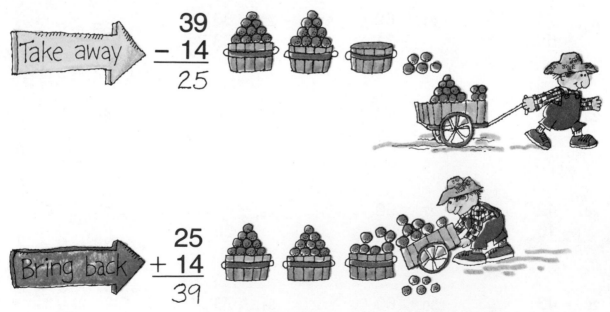

$$\begin{array}{r} \overset{513}{\cancel{6}\cancel{3}} \\ -\ 28 \\ \hline 35 \end{array}$$

You can check subtraction by addition.

Take away
$$\begin{array}{r} 39 \\ -\ 14 \\ \hline 25 \end{array}$$

Bring back
$$\begin{array}{r} 25 \\ +\ 14 \\ \hline 39 \end{array}$$

We got back to 39, the number we started with. It checks!

EXERCISES

Give each difference.

1. 78
 − 23

2. 59
 − 16

3. 72
 − 25

4. 60
 − 38

5. 51
 − 38

6. 73
 − 58

7. 81
 − 6

8. 90
 − 30

9. 86
 − 79

10. 58
 − 25

11. 40
 − 7

12. 61
 − 52

13. 83
 − 50

14. 92
 − 57

15. 92
 − 58

Check each subtraction by adding.

16. 58
 − 25
 33

17. 49
 − 16
 32

18. 97
 − 35
 52

19. 75
 − 25
 50

20. 5 13
 6̸3̸
 − 38
 25

21. 6 12
 7̸2̸
 − 38
 44

Give the missing digits.

22. 7 4
 − 2 ☐
 5 2

*23. 8 3
 − 5 ☐
 2 6

*24. ☐ 5
 − 3 ☐
 5 6

Subtracting 3-digit numbers

Subtract ones.

$$\begin{array}{r} 453 \\ -182 \\ \end{array}$$

Regroup 1 hundred for 10 tens.

$$\begin{array}{r} \overset{3}{\cancel{4}}\overset{15}{5}3 \\ -182 \\ \hline 1 \end{array}$$

Subtract tens and then hundreds.

$$\begin{array}{r} \overset{3}{\cancel{4}}\overset{15}{5}3 \\ -182 \\ \hline 271 \end{array}$$

EXERCISES
Subtract.

1. 538 − 213	2. 827 − 301	3. 658 − 283	4. 742 − 592	5. 553 − 172
6. 757 − 166	7. 926 − 315	8. 608 − 246	9. 591 − 300	10. 826 − 256
11. 718 − 52	12. 655 − 85	13. 529 − 46	14. 658 − 73	15. 704 − 91
16. $5.67 − 3.18	17. $6.23 − 2.09	18. $7.40 − 3.28	19. $9.58 − 6.29	20. $6.25 − 5.09
21. $6.92 − 6.58	22. $7.29 − 6.84	23. $6.08 − 4.92	24. $8.67 − 7.59	25. $5.63 − 4.91

26. 819 − 306 = ?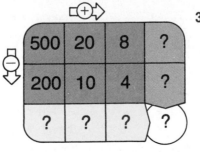

27. 729 − 508 = ?

28. 952 − 372 = ?

Add across. Subtract down.

29.

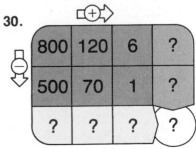

⊕→			
500	20	8	?
200	10	4	?
?	?	?	?

30.

⊕→			
800	120	6	?
500	70	1	?
?	?	?	?

Problem solving

These steps can help you solve problems.

1. Read the problem and find the question.

    David saw 11 black horses. He saw 8 white horses. <u>How many did he see in all?</u>

2. What are the facts?

    11 black horses
    8 white horses

3. Decide what to do.

    <u>Add</u> or subtract?

4. Answer the question.

    $$\begin{array}{r} 11 \\ +\ 8 \\ \hline 19 \end{array}$$ There were 19 horses in all.

5. Does your answer seem right?

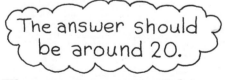

The answer should be around 20.

The answer seems right.

EXERCISES
Add or subtract? Decide what to do.

1. There were 23 clowns on a truck.
   8 clowns jumped off.
   How many were left?

2. Alice counted 105 people in one band and 84 people in another.
   How many were there in all?

3. Jerry saw 43 balloons. 18 of them blew away. How many were left?

4. There were 186 girl scouts and 149 boy scouts. How many were there in all?

Solve.

5. Marty saw 59 old cars and 38 new cars. How many did he see in all?

6. There were 93 on one drill team and 78 on another. How many in all?

7. There were 108 people in a horse club. 75 rode in the parade. How many did not ride in the parade?

8. A clown had 93 pieces of candy. She threw 18 pieces to some children. How many pieces did she have left?

9. There were 342 children in the parade and 219 adults. How many were there in all?

10. There were 342 children in the parade and 219 adults. How many more children were in the parade?

11. Paul bought a snow cone for $.65 and some peanuts for $.45. How much did he spend?

12. Mary had $1.30. She bought some cotton candy for $.85. How much money did she have left?

Tell a story.

Sam's book has 138 pages.
He read 45 pages.
He has 93 pages left to read.

STORY PROBLEMS

NUMBER ★NEWS★

138 − 45 = 93

War and Peas

Problem solving

A veterinarian is a doctor for animals. A
"vet" can tell you how much you should
feed your dog. How much a dog should eat
depends on the dog's weight and age.

Saint Bernard
80 kilograms

Irish terrier
13 kilograms

Siberian husky
21 kilograms

The questions refer to the dogs on pages 98 and 99.

1. Which dog weighs the most?

2. Which dog weighs the least?

3. How many dogs weigh more than 40 kilograms?

4. How many dogs weigh less than 30 kilograms?

5. How much more does the husky weigh than the Irish terrier?

6. How much more does the Saint Bernard weigh than the husky?

7. How much more does the German shepherd weigh than the beagle?

8. What is the total weight of the husky and the Irish terrier?

| Golden retriever | Collie | Lhasa apso | Dalmatian |
| 39 kilograms | 34 kilograms | 7 kilograms | 24 kilograms |

| Poodle | Beagle | German shepherd |
| 25 kilograms | 16 kilograms | 46 kilograms |

9. How much heavier is the dalmatian than the Lhasa apso?

10. What is the difference in weight between the heaviest dog and the lightest dog?

Subtracting 3-digit numbers

Sometimes you have to regroup more than once.

Not enough ones.

$$\begin{array}{r} 542 \\ -277 \\ \hline \end{array}$$

Regroup.

$$\begin{array}{r} 5\overset{3}{\cancel{4}}\overset{12}{\cancel{2}} \\ -277 \\ \hline \end{array}$$

Subtract ones.

$$\begin{array}{r} 5\overset{3}{\cancel{4}}\overset{12}{\cancel{2}} \\ -277 \\ \hline 5 \end{array}$$

Regroup.

$$\begin{array}{r} \overset{4}{\cancel{5}}\overset{13}{\cancel{4}}\overset{12}{\cancel{2}} \\ -277 \\ \hline 5 \end{array}$$

Subtract tens.

$$\begin{array}{r} \overset{4}{\cancel{5}}\overset{13}{\cancel{4}}\overset{12}{\cancel{2}} \\ -277 \\ \hline 65 \end{array}$$

Subtract hundreds.

$$\begin{array}{r} \overset{4}{\cancel{5}}\overset{13}{\cancel{4}}\overset{12}{\cancel{2}} \\ -277 \\ \hline 265 \end{array}$$

EXERCISES
Subtract.

1. $\begin{array}{r} 346 \\ -159 \\ \hline \end{array}$
2. $\begin{array}{r} 437 \\ -289 \\ \hline \end{array}$
3. $\begin{array}{r} 520 \\ -157 \\ \hline \end{array}$
4. $\begin{array}{r} 638 \\ -349 \\ \hline \end{array}$
5. $\begin{array}{r} 725 \\ -558 \\ \hline \end{array}$

6. $\begin{array}{r} 836 \\ -597 \\ \hline \end{array}$
7. $\begin{array}{r} 952 \\ -386 \\ \hline \end{array}$
8. $\begin{array}{r} 735 \\ -259 \\ \hline \end{array}$
9. $\begin{array}{r} 943 \\ -478 \\ \hline \end{array}$
10. $\begin{array}{r} 525 \\ -269 \\ \hline \end{array}$

11. 762 − 348	12. 403 − 152	13. 571 − 329	14. 629 − 252	15. 629 − 375
16. 558 − 269	17. 856 − 589	18. 482 − 194	19. 946 − 379	20. 754 − 596
21. 418 − 302	22. 629 − 461	23. 753 − 48	24. 666 − 283	25. 726 − 489

Solve.

26. How much do the boxes weigh together?

27. How much heavier is the yellow box?

156 Kilograms

225 Kilograms

For ME

(one hundred one) **101**

Subtracting 3-digit numbers

Sometimes you will need to regroup twice before subtracting ones.

Need to regroup.

$$\begin{array}{r} 603 \\ -258 \\ \hline \end{array}$$

No tens here.

Regroup 1 hundred for 10 tens.

$$\begin{array}{r} {\scriptstyle 5\ 10} \\ \cancel{6}\cancel{0}3 \\ -258 \\ \hline \end{array}$$

Regroup 1 ten for 10 ones.

$$\begin{array}{r} {\scriptstyle 5\ \cancel{10}\ 13} \\ {\scriptstyle 9} \\ \cancel{6}\cancel{0}\cancel{3} \\ -258 \\ \hline \end{array}$$

Subtract.

$$\begin{array}{r} {\scriptstyle 5\ \cancel{10}\ 13} \\ {\scriptstyle 9} \\ \cancel{6}\cancel{0}\cancel{3} \\ -258 \\ \hline 345 \end{array}$$

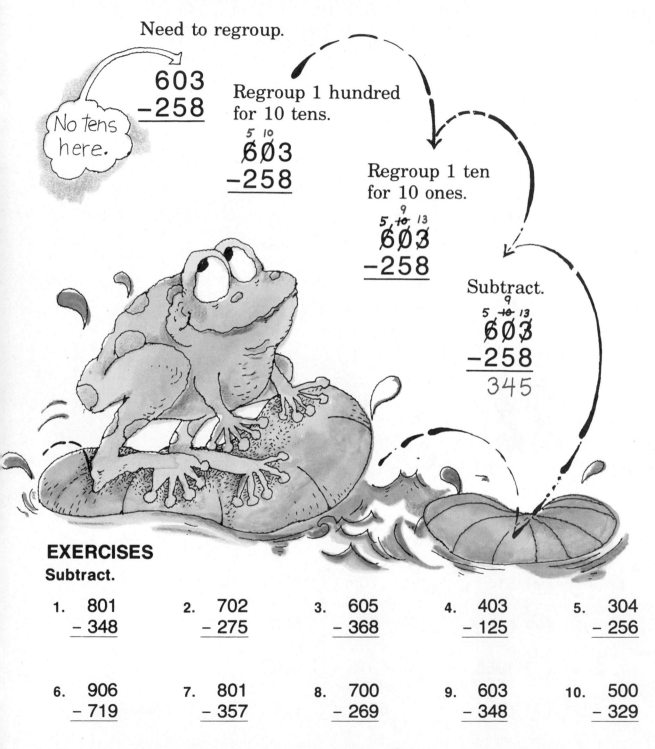

EXERCISES
Subtract.

1. $\begin{array}{r} 801 \\ -348 \\ \hline \end{array}$
2. $\begin{array}{r} 702 \\ -275 \\ \hline \end{array}$
3. $\begin{array}{r} 605 \\ -368 \\ \hline \end{array}$
4. $\begin{array}{r} 403 \\ -125 \\ \hline \end{array}$
5. $\begin{array}{r} 304 \\ -256 \\ \hline \end{array}$

6. $\begin{array}{r} 906 \\ -719 \\ \hline \end{array}$
7. $\begin{array}{r} 801 \\ -357 \\ \hline \end{array}$
8. $\begin{array}{r} 700 \\ -269 \\ \hline \end{array}$
9. $\begin{array}{r} 603 \\ -348 \\ \hline \end{array}$
10. $\begin{array}{r} 500 \\ -329 \\ \hline \end{array}$

11. 594
−211

12. 628
−319

13. 605
−453

To subtract 28, I subtract 30 and then add 2.

14. 725
−438

15. 403
−248

16. 301
−158

17. 935
−616

18. 728
−359

19. 654
−277

20. 701
−358

21. 896
−423

22. 604
−241

SHORTCUT

23. 753
−289

24. 653
−289

25. 507
−358

26. 752
− 84

27. 609
−258

28. 358
−299

Use the shortcut.

29. 802
−246

30. 746
−358

31. 501
−216

38. 70 − 28 = ?

39. 60 − 28 = ?

40. 90 − 28 = ?

32. 563
−467

33. 900
−527

34. 489
−325

41. 100 − 28 = ?

42. 150 − 28 = ?

35. 634
−349

36. 873
−496

37. 958
−659

43. 170 − 28 = ?

44. 260 − 28 = ?

45. 350 − 28 = ?

Estimating differences

You can use rounding to help estimate a difference. An estimate can help you find mistakes.

Each number is rounded to the nearest ten.

Each number is rounded to the nearest hundred.

79 rounds to 80
−23 rounds to −20
60

The difference is about 60.

598 rounds to 600
−223 rounds to −200
400

The difference is about 400.

EXERCISES

**First estimate the difference.
Then subtract and compare.**

1.	92 − 28	2.	87 − 46	3.	63 − 31	4.	74 − 20	5.	93 − 62
6.	59 − 15	7.	74 − 23	8.	58 − 37	9.	65 − 49	10.	94 − 27
11.	598 − 326	12.	614 − 195	13.	874 − 229	14.	769 − 255	15.	893 − 374
16.	808 − 299	17.	701 − 519	18.	902 − 385	19.	500 − 218	20.	900 − 196

Add or subtract.

21. 584
   +326

22. 584
   − 326

23. 715
   +482

24. 715
   − 482

25. 623
   +587

26. 623
   − 587

27. 906
   +758

28. 906
   − 758

29. 596
   +379

30. 629
   − 583

31. 648
   +856

32. 593
   − 407

33. 753
   − 278

34. 641
   − 384

35. 906
   +539

36. 537 − 288 = ?

37. 653 + 269 = ?

38. 706 + 816 = ?

39. 903 − 775 = ?

Solve.

40. Who sold the most tickets?

41. How many tickets did Anita and Brian sell together?

42. How many tickets did Carl, David, and Jeanne sell together?

43. How many more tickets did Susan sell than Anita?

44. How many more tickets did David sell than Wilma?

Rock Concert

Name	Tickets sold
Anita	46
Brian	38
Carl	53
David	76
Jeanne	59
Mike	35
Susan	68
Wilma	47

Problem solving

Solve.

1. Alex wants to buy and .

   How much money does he need?

2. Ruth wants to buy and .

   How much money does she need?

3. Carla has $5.00. She wants to buy

    .

   How much money will she have left?

4. Tom has $4.50. He wants to buy .

   How much money will he have left?

5. How much more does

   cost than ?

6. How much more do

   cost than ?

7. Terry wants to buy

   and .

   How much money does
   she need?

8. Sarah has $8.54.

   She wants to buy .

   How much money will she
   have left?

9. Robert has $3.88.

   He wants to buy .

   How much more money
   does he need?

10. Janet has $2.63.

   She wants to buy .

   How much more money
   does she need?

11. Mary wants to buy  ,

   , and .

   How much money does
   she need?

12. Larry has $9.00.

   He wants to buy

   and .

   How much money will he
   have left?

Subtracting 4-digit numbers

Regroup 1 ten for 10 ones.
Subtract ones.

$$\begin{array}{r} {}^{2}9\overset{12}{\cancel{3}}2 \\ -2587 \\ \hline 5 \end{array}$$

Regroup 1 hundred for 10 tens.
Subtract tens.

$$\begin{array}{r} {}^{0}9\overset{12}{\cancel{1}}\overset{12}{\cancel{3}}2 \\ -2587 \\ \hline 45 \end{array}$$

Regroup 1 thousand for 10 hundreds.
Subtract hundreds.

$$\begin{array}{r} {}^{8}\cancel{9}\overset{10}{\cancel{1}}\overset{12}{\cancel{3}}\overset{12}{2} \\ -2587 \\ \hline 545 \end{array}$$

Subtract thousands.

$$\begin{array}{r} {}^{8}\cancel{9}\overset{10}{\cancel{1}}\overset{12}{\cancel{3}}\overset{12}{2} \\ -2587 \\ \hline 6545 \end{array}$$

EXERCISES
Subtract.

1.	8973 − 2546	2.	6543 − 2170
3.	5432 − 1856	4.	7345 − 2286
5.	9386 − 2559	6.	6258 − 2079
7.	5763 − 1694	8.	3940 − 1583
9.	9637 − 2749	10.	7635 − 3958
11.	5824 − 1786	12.	8863 − 4597
13.	7593 − 6650	14.	2473 − 1278
15.	8812 − 3960	16.	6813 − 1796

17. 7128 − 3452	18. 9604 − 2358	19. 8300 − 2564	20. 4674 − 1295
21. 5963 − 2874	22. 6208 − 3169	23. 5342 − 2658	24. 9375 − 4897

Give the end number.

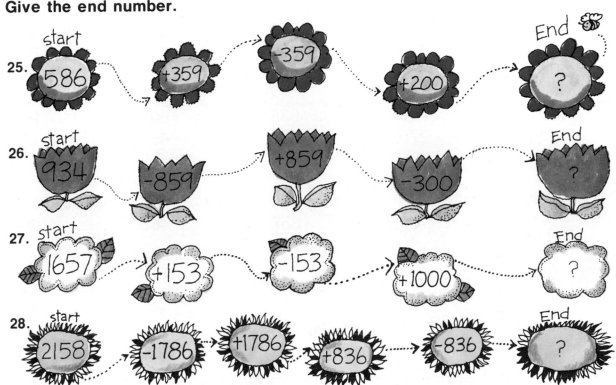

25. start 586 → +359 → −359 → +200 → End ?
26. start 934 → −859 → +859 → −300 → End ?
27. start 1657 → +153 → −153 → +1000 → End ?
28. start 2158 → −1786 → +1786 → +836 → −836 → End ?

Keeping Skills Sharp

1. 526 +348	2. 719 +154	3. 836 +291	4. 637 +567	5. 567 +637
6. 75 28 +39	7. 74 64 +78	8. 75 56 +88	9. 79 86 +35	10. 58 76 +64

Give each difference. [pages 87–95, 100–105]

1. $\begin{array}{r} 59 \\ -23 \\ \hline \end{array}$	2. $\begin{array}{r} 78 \\ -35 \\ \hline \end{array}$	3. $\begin{array}{r} 92 \\ -38 \\ \hline \end{array}$	4. $\begin{array}{r} 75 \\ -49 \\ \hline \end{array}$	5. $\begin{array}{r} 80 \\ -53 \\ \hline \end{array}$
6. $\begin{array}{r} 562 \\ -348 \\ \hline \end{array}$	7. $\begin{array}{r} 709 \\ -254 \\ \hline \end{array}$	8. $\begin{array}{r} 653 \\ -429 \\ \hline \end{array}$	9. $\begin{array}{r} 842 \\ -290 \\ \hline \end{array}$	10. $\begin{array}{r} 625 \\ -552 \\ \hline \end{array}$
11. $\begin{array}{r} 524 \\ -458 \\ \hline \end{array}$	12. $\begin{array}{r} 752 \\ -275 \\ \hline \end{array}$	13. $\begin{array}{r} 835 \\ -368 \\ \hline \end{array}$	14. $\begin{array}{r} 621 \\ -459 \\ \hline \end{array}$	15. $\begin{array}{r} 920 \\ -275 \\ \hline \end{array}$
16. $\begin{array}{r} 504 \\ -375 \\ \hline \end{array}$	17. $\begin{array}{r} 306 \\ -169 \\ \hline \end{array}$	18. $\begin{array}{r} 400 \\ -358 \\ \hline \end{array}$	19. $\begin{array}{r} 702 \\ -465 \\ \hline \end{array}$	20. $\begin{array}{r} 801 \\ -397 \\ \hline \end{array}$

21. $68 - 42 = \underline{?}$ 22. $92 - 57 = \underline{?}$

23. $593 - 158 = \underline{?}$ 24. $628 - 354 = \underline{?}$

25. $721 - 347 = \underline{?}$ 26. $815 - 456 = \underline{?}$

27. $902 - 529 = \underline{?}$ 28. $401 - 357 = \underline{?}$

Solve. [pages 96–99, 106–107]

29. How many more cookies in the larger box?

30. How much more does the larger box cost?

Project

1. List all the children in your class.

2. Next to each name, write the age of the child.

3. Add all the ages. This is your **class life sum.**

4. What will your class life sum be 1 year from now?

5. What was your class life sum 1 year ago?

6. What was your class life sum 3 years ago?

7. What was your class life sum 5 years ago?

CHAPTER REVIEW

Subtract.

1. 78
    −24

2. 69
    −35

3. 98
    −43

REGROUP
I TEN FOR
10 ONES

4 12
5̸2̸
−23
29

4. 63
    −38

5. 82
    −45

6. 90
    −67

REGROUP
I TEN FOR
10 ONES

3 13
6̸4̸3̸
−228
415

7. 562
    −349

8. 780
    −259

9. 865
    −457

REGROUP
I HUNDRED FOR
10 TENS

4 14
5̸4̸8
−352
196

10. 748
    −392

11. 926
    −451

12. 837
    −263

REGROUP
TWICE

6 11 15
7̸2̸5̸
−256
469

13. 523
    −258

14. 735
    −386

15. 947
    −268

REGROUP
TWICE

9
6 10 11
7̸0̸1̸
−345
356

16. 804
    −259

17. 602
    −354

18. 500
    −276

CHAPTER CHALLENGE

Complete this addition table.
Hint: You can find a missing addend by subtracting.

+	58	93	?	?	?	408
94	152	?	?	233	?	?
?	?	160	226	?	?	?
185	?	?	?	?	?	?
?	?	?	586	?	?	?
658	?	?	?	?	1194	?
?	?	?	?	?	?	784

	a	b	c	d		a	b	c	d		a	b	c	d		a	b	c	d		a	b	c	d
14					34					14					4					30				
15	a	b	c	d														c	d	31	a	b	c	d

MAJOR CHECKUP
Standardized Format

Give the correct letter.

1. In $5 + 8 = 13$, 13 is called the

    a. addend
    b. difference
    c. sum
    d. none of these

2. Complete.

    $5 + \underline{?} = 8$

    a. 13
    b. 3
    c. 14
    d. none of these

3. Add.

    6
    2
    $+9$

    a. 17
    b. 18
    c. 16
    d. 15

4. Which numeral has a 6 in the hundreds place?

    a. 586
    b. 643
    c. 760
    d. none of these

5. Five hundred nine is

    a. 509
    b. 590
    c. 905
    d. none of these

6. In 3896, what digit is in the thousands place?

    a. 6
    b. 8
    c. 9
    d. 3

7. Which number is 10 more than 136?

    a. 126
    b. 236
    c. 137
    d. 146

8. Which totals $1.56?

    a. 1 dollar and 6 dimes
    b. 5 dimes and 6 pennies
    c. 1 dollar, 6 dimes, and 5 pennies
    d. none of these

9. Add.

    73
    68
    $+95$

    a. 236
    b. 226
    c. 235
    d. 237

10. Add.

    5829
    $+3648$

    a. 9467
    b. 8467
    c. 9477
    d. none of these

11. Subtract.

    716
    -493

    a. 323
    b. 383
    c. 223
    d. 283

12. Subtract.

    9603
    -2945

    a. 7658
    b. 6668
    c. 6758
    d. 6658

5
Time
and
Money

Hour and half hour

The short hand is the hour hand.
The long hand is the minute hand.

These two clocks both show 4:00.
We read 4:00 as "four o'clock."

These two clocks both show 8:30.
We read 8:30 as "eight-thirty."

EXERCISES
Give the time.

1.

2.

3.

4.

5.

6.

7.

8.

9.

Give the time.

10. one hour
    later than

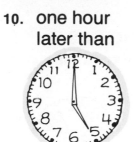

11. one hour
    earlier than

12. two hours
    earlier than

13. one hour
    earlier than

14. two hours
    later than

15. one hour
    later than

Complete.

	Time in	Baking time	Time out
16.	7:00	1 hour	?
17.	8:00	2 hours	?
18.	9:30	2 hours	?
19.	10:30	1 hour	?
20.	2:30	2 hours	?
★ 21.	3:30	?	5:30
★ 22.	?	2 hours	7:30

(one hundred seventeen) **117**

Minutes

There are 60 minutes in 1 hour. There are 24 hours in 1 day. The hour hand goes around the clock 2 times in a day.

A.M. is used for time after 12:00 midnight and before 12:00 noon. Dolores' school starts at 8:45 A.M.

P.M. is used for times after 12:00 noon and before 12:00 midnight. Dolores' school is out at 3:10 P.M.

The time is 9:08, or eight minutes after nine.

The time is 5:48, or twelve minutes before six.

1.

2.

3.

4.

5.

6.

Match.

7. 11 minutes after 8

8. 11 minutes before 8

9. 8 minutes after 11

10. 8 minutes before 11

a.

b.

c.

d.

Give each time in two ways.

11.

12.

13.

A.M. or P.M.?

14. When does the sun rise?

15. When does the sun set?

16. When do you get home from school?

17. When do you go to bed?

18. When do you get up?

19. When do you eat supper?

Give each time.
Be sure to give A.M. or P.M.

cock-a-dooodle-dooo...

20. one hour after 12:00 midnight

21. three hours after 12:00 midnight

22. two hours before 12:00 noon

23. one hour and 20 minutes before midnight

24. two hours and 30 minutes before noon

More about time

Beth is waiting for a morning train. It is 7:50. The next train is due at 8:15. How long will she have to wait?

From 7:50 to 8:00 is 10 minutes.
From 8:00 to 8:15 is 15 minutes.
She will have to wait 25 minutes.

EXERCISES
Complete.

	1.	2.	3.	4.	5.	6.
Time						
Next train due	2:30	3:09	5:05	6:10	7:15	8:30
Waiting time	?	?	?	?	?	?

Bus drivers take people many places. They take people to and from work and school. They also take people from city to city. Bus drivers try to stay on schedule.

BUS SCHEDULE

CITY	TIME
Elm City	10:00 A.M.
Springfield	10:40 A.M.
Redlands	11:30 A.M.
Willow	12:40 P.M.
Seaside	1:25 P.M.
Oakville	1:50 P.M.

EXERCISES

Use the schedule to solve the problems.

7. When does the bus arrive at Seaside?

8. How long does it take to go from Willow to Seaside?

9. How long does it take to go from Springfield to Redlands?

10. How many minutes does it take to go from Elm City to Springfield?

11. The bus was 15 minutes early getting to Seaside. What time did it get to Seaside?

12. The bus was 20 minutes late getting to Oakville. When did it get to Oakville?

Keeping Skills Sharp

1. 378
  − 259

2. 746
  − 350

3. 827
  − 562

4. 750
  − 132

5. 962
  − 870

6. 642
  − 254

7. 823
  − 165

8. 964
  − 487

9. 760
  − 385

10. 955
  − 697

11. 402
  − 159

12. 703
  − 376

13. 501
  − 268

14. 600
  − 436

15. 800
  − 751

Money

penny	nickel	dime
1¢	5¢	10¢
$.01	$.05	$.10

quarter	half-dollar	dollar
25¢	50¢	100¢
$.25	$.50	$1.00

EXERCISES

Give the total value in dollars.

1.
2.
3.
4.

How much change?

5.

6.

7.

8.

Solve.

9. Bill had a half-dollar, a quarter, and 3 pennies. How much did he have in all?

10. Joan had 2 quarters. She found a dime and 2 nickels. How much did she have in all?

11. Leon had a half-dollar, 2 quarters, and 3 dimes. He spent the half-dollar. How much was left?

12. Sarah had a half-dollar and 3 quarters. She spent $.67. How much did she have left?

Study the clues.
Tell what coins are in the bag.

13.

There are 5 coins.

$.61

More about money

Clerks work with money.
They tell you how
much something costs.
They also make change.

EXERCISES
Tell what coins you would give the clerk.

You have	You buy	You give the clerk

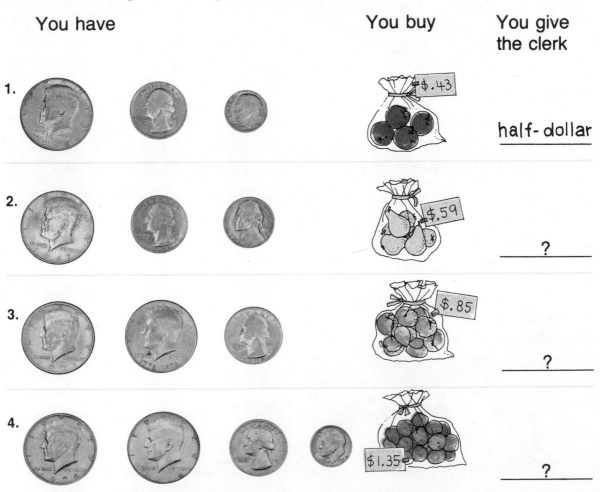

1. $.43 — half-dollar

2. $.59 — ?

3. $.85 — ?

4. $1.35 — ?

Tell what money you would give the clerk.

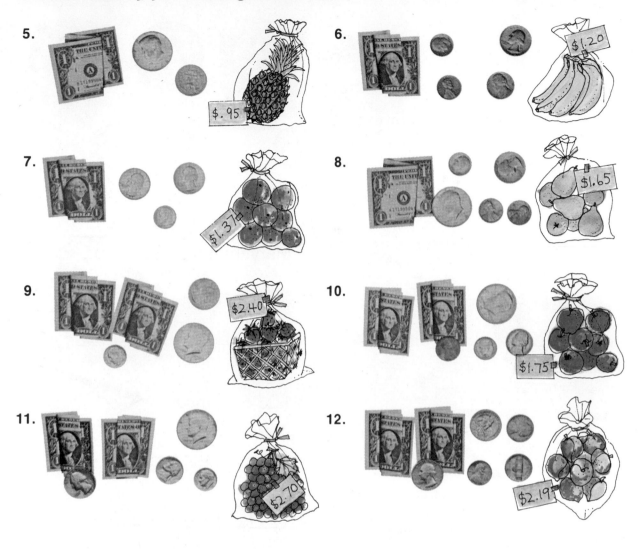

5. $.95

6. $1.20

7. $1.37

8. $1.65

9. $2.40

10. $1.75

11. $2.70

12. $2.19

Study the clues.
Tell what is in each bag.

13. There are 6 coins. $.76

✶14. $1.16

✶15. $1.16

Earning and spending

Complete.

Mary had this money in her purse.

1. Mary had ?.

Earned two quarters.

2. Mary then had ?.

Spent 54¢ on ice cream.

3. Mary then had ?.

Spent $1.25 on a movie.

4. Mary then had ?.

Earned one half-dollar.

5. Then Mary had ?.

LEMONADE 5¢

BIJOU THEATRE
MATINÉE TODAY
NOW SHOWING

MARY'S DELIVERY SERVICE

Gave a dime and a quarter to her brother.

6. Then Mary had ?.

Complete.

Hugh had $2.76. He earned one dollar, one quarter, and one nickel.

7. Hugh had __?__.

Spent two quarters and one nickel.

8. Then Hugh had __?__.

Bought a candle for $.75.

9. Then he had __?__.

For his birthday he got two dollars, one half-dollar, and three quarters.

10. Then Hugh had __?__.

Lost a quarter and a penny.

11. Then Hugh had __?__.

Gave $1.50 to the United Fund.

12. Then he had __?__.

What time is shown? [pages 115–117]

1.

2.

3.

A.M. or P.M.? [pages 118–121]

4. one hour after midnight

5. 3:47 in the afternoon

6. one hour after 11:30 A.M.

7. two hours after 10:30 P.M.

Give the total value in dollars. [pages 122–125]

8.

9.

Solve. [pages 123, 126–127]

10. Alex had $3.45. He earned one half-dollar and three dimes. How much did he have then?

11. Elaine had $3.08. She spent a dollar and a quarter. How much did she have then?

Mr. Mahoney's class made this graph. It shows what time the students go to bed before a school day.

1. How many go to bed at 8:00?

2. How many go to bed before 8:00?

3. How many go to bed after 9:00?

4. How many students are in the class?

5. Make a graph of the bedtimes of your class.

6. Tell some things about your graph.

CHAPTER REVIEW

It's 8:15 and I haven't made my first rescue today!

Match.

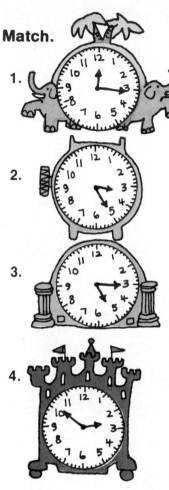

1.  a. 3:25

2.  b. 2:51

3.  c. 12:16

4.  d. 5:15

Give the total value in dollars.

5.

6.

7. one dollar
   two quarters
   one dime

8. two dollars
   two half-dollars
   three dimes
   four pennies

CHAPTER CHALLENGE

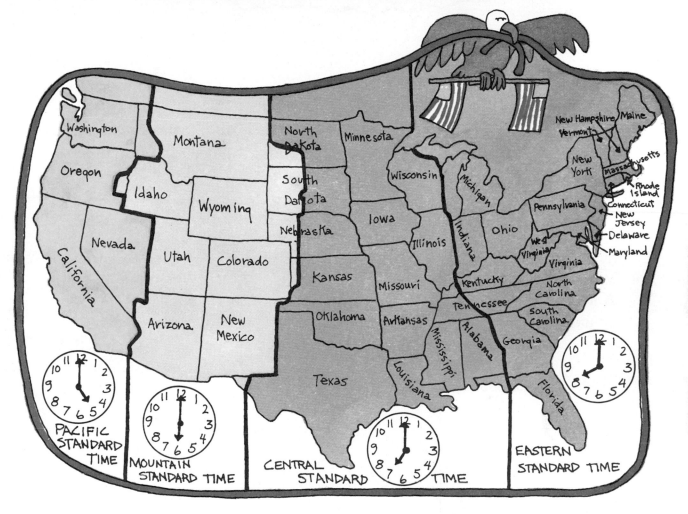

1. It is 5:00 A.M. in California. What time is it in Colorado?

2. What time is it in Missouri when it is 3:00 P.M. in Ohio?

3. It is 11:00 A.M. in Arizona. What time is it in New York?

4. It is 10:00 P.M. in Nevada. What time is it in Maryland?

5. When it is noon in Georgia, what time is it in the state of Washington?

6. A jet flew from Chicago, Illinois, to New York City. It took 1 hour and 50 minutes. If it left Chicago at 11:45 A.M., what time did it arrive in New York?

7. Find out what time zones Alaska and Hawaii are in.

Form W

| a | b | c | d | | a | b | c | d | | a | b | c | d | | a | b | c | d | | a | b | c | d | | a | b | c | d |
14 | | | | | 34 | | | | | 14 | | | | | 4 | | | | | 30 | | | | | | | | |
| a | b | c | d | | a | b | c | d | | | | c | d | | | | | | | a | b | c | d |
15 | | | | | | | | | | | | | | | 31 | | | |

MAJOR CHECKUP
Standardized Format

Give the correct letter.

1. In $6 + 4 = 10$, 6 is called

    a. a sum
    b. an addend
    c. a difference
    d. none of these

2. Add.

  3
  5
$+6$

    a. 13
    b. 15
    c. 14
    d. 16

3. Which of these facts is related to $6 + 8 = 14$?

    a. $6 + 4 = 10$
    b. $7 + 8 = 15$
    c. $14 - 8 = 6$
    d. none of these

4. Which numeral has a 6 in the hundreds place?

    a. 346
    b. 680
    c. 568
    d. none of these

5. Which number is 1 more than 169?

    a. 168
    b. 179
    c. 269
    d. 170

6. Which number is the smallest?

    a. 3782
    b. 3827
    c. 3278
    d. 3287

7. Add.

  37
  29
$+48$

    a. 104
    b. 94
    c. 114
    d. 113

8. Add.

  368
$+249$

    a. 617
    b. 507
    c. 607
    d. none of these

9. Subtract.

  800
-347

    a. 453
    b. 563
    c. 543
    d. 547

10. What time is shown?

    a. 11:55
    b. 12:55
    c. 11:00
    d. none of these

11. Which time is in the afternoon?

    a. noon
    b. 2:30 A.M.
    c. 4:45 P.M.
    d. none of these

12. How much money?

1 dollar
1 half-dollar
2 dimes
1 nickel
3 pennies

    a. $1.78
    b. $1.83
    c. $2.28
    d. $2.03

6

Multiplication Facts through 9 × 5

Addition and multiplication

The total number of buttons
can be found by adding.

$$2 + 2 + 2 + 2 + 2 + 2 = 12$$

There are 6 sets of two.

EXERCISES
How many?

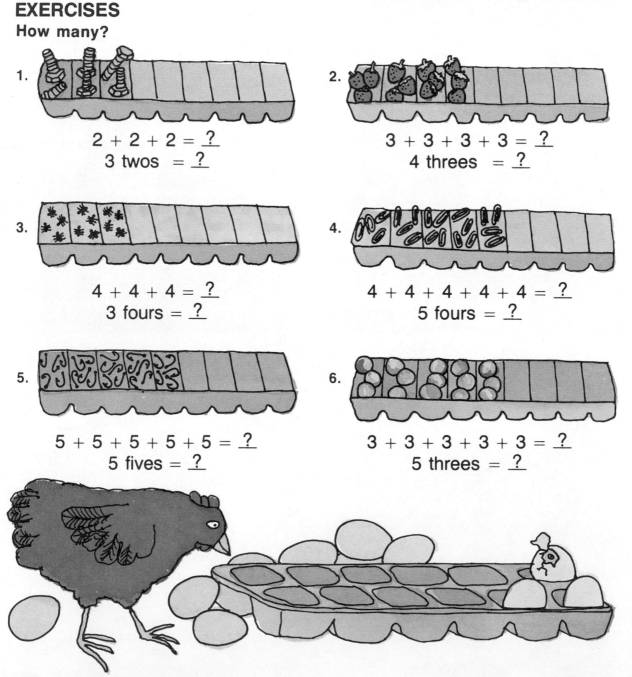

1.

$$2 + 2 + 2 = \underline{?}$$
$$3 \text{ twos } = \underline{?}$$

2.

$$3 + 3 + 3 + 3 = \underline{?}$$
$$4 \text{ threes } = \underline{?}$$

3.

$$4 + 4 + 4 = \underline{?}$$
$$3 \text{ fours } = \underline{?}$$

4.

$$4 + 4 + 4 + 4 + 4 = \underline{?}$$
$$5 \text{ fours } = \underline{?}$$

5.

$$5 + 5 + 5 + 5 + 5 = \underline{?}$$
$$5 \text{ fives } = \underline{?}$$

6.

$$3 + 3 + 3 + 3 + 3 = \underline{?}$$
$$5 \text{ threes } = \underline{?}$$

How many?

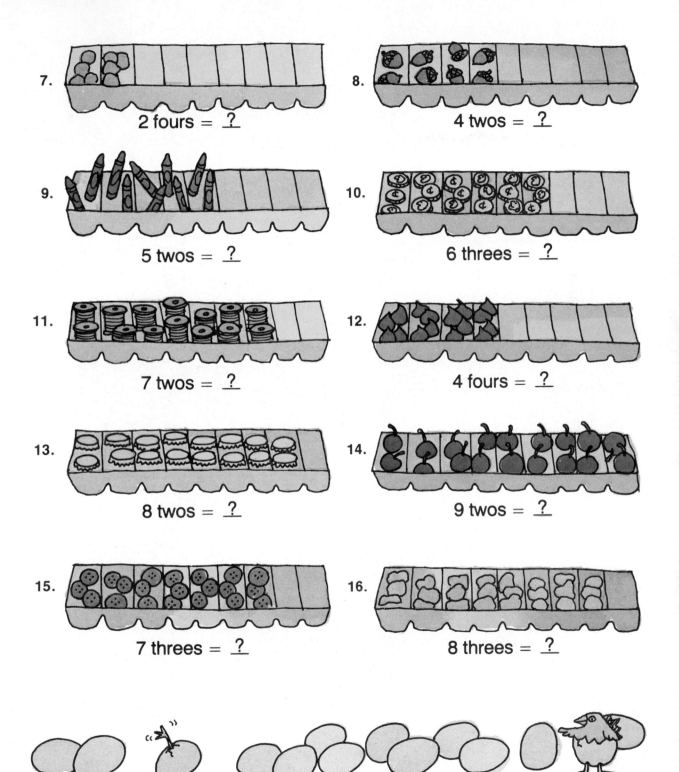

7.   2 fours = ?

8.   4 twos = ?

9.   5 twos = ?

10.   6 threes = ?

11.   7 twos = ?

12.   4 fours = ?

13.   8 twos = ?

14.   9 twos = ?

15.   7 threes = ?

16.   8 threes = ?

2 as a factor

There are 3 sets of two.

We can multiply to find the total.

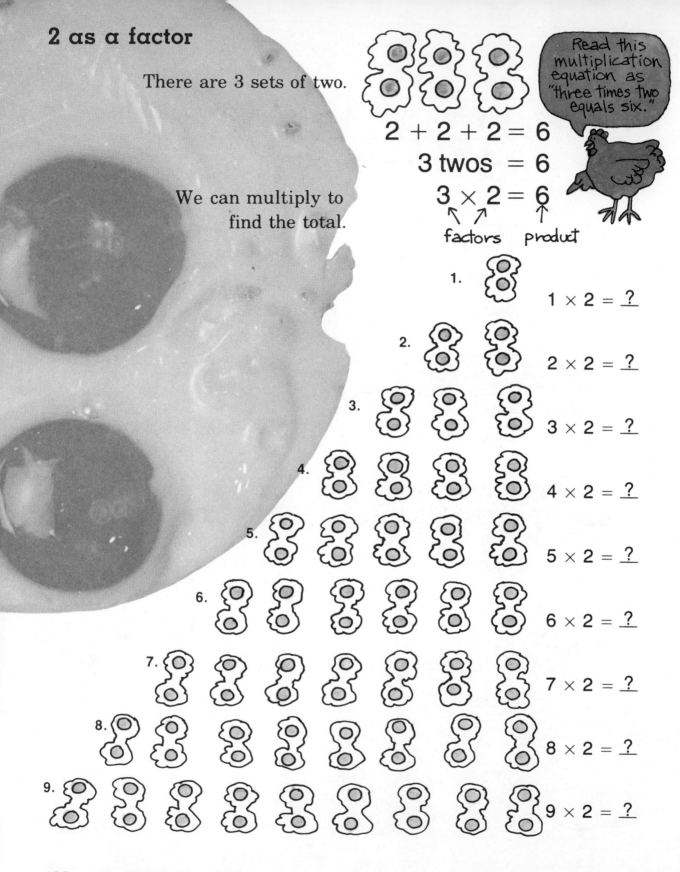

$2 + 2 + 2 = 6$

3 twos $= 6$

$3 \times 2 = 6$

factors   product

Read this multiplication equation as "three times two equals six."

1. $1 \times 2 = \underline{?}$

2. $2 \times 2 = \underline{?}$

3. $3 \times 2 = \underline{?}$

4. $4 \times 2 = \underline{?}$

5. $5 \times 2 = \underline{?}$

6. $6 \times 2 = \underline{?}$

7. $7 \times 2 = \underline{?}$

8. $8 \times 2 = \underline{?}$

9. $9 \times 2 = \underline{?}$

Multiply.

10. 2 in each set
    × 3 sets
    ? in all

11. 2 in each set
    × 5 sets
    ? in all

12. 2	13. 2	14. 2	15. 2	16. 2	17. 2
×1	×2	×3	×4	×5	×6

18. 2	19. 2	20. 2	21. 2	22. 2	23. 2
×7	×8	×9	×8	×6	×2

24. 2	25. 2	26. 2	27. 2	28. 2	29. 2
×4	×7	×9	×5	×8	×7

30. 2	31. 2	32. 2	33. 2	34. 2	35. 2
×9	×3	×8	×4	×1	×9

Complete.

36.

$$\begin{array}{ccccc} 2 & 2 & 2 & 2 & 2 \\ \times 1 & \times 2 & \times 3 & \times 4 & \times 5 \\ \hline 2 & \boxed{?} & \boxed{?} & \boxed{?} & \boxed{?} \end{array}$$

0 1 2 3 5 7 9

37. Even numbers: 2, 4, 6, 8, 10, ?, ?, ?, ?

38. Odd numbers: 1, 3, 5, ?, ?, 11, ?, ?, ?

3 as a factor

$$4 \times 3 = 12$$

EXERCISES
Give each product.

1. $1 \times 3 = \underline{?}$

2. $2 \times 3 = \underline{?}$

3. $3 \times 3 = \underline{?}$

4. $4 \times 3 = \underline{?}$

5. $5 \times 3 = \underline{?}$

6. $6 \times 3 = \underline{?}$

7. $7 \times 3 = \underline{?}$

8. $8 \times 3 = \underline{?}$

9. $9 \times 3 = \underline{?}$

19. 3
    ×6

20. 3
    ×4

21. 2
    ×8

22. 3
    ×5

23. 2
    ×9

24. 2
    ×7

25. 3
    ×2

26. 3
    ×1

27. 2
    ×6

28. 3
    ×9

29. 2
    ×8

30. 3
    ×6

31. 2
    ×4

32. 3
    ×4

33. 2
    ×9

34. 3
    ×3

35. 2
    ×5

36. 3
    ×7

37. 3
    ×8

38. 2
    ×1

39. 3
    ×5

40. 2
    ×9

41. 3
    ×7

42. 2
    ×8

43. 2
    ×7

44. 3
    ×2

45. 3
    ×3

46. 3
    ×9

47. 2
    ×2

48. 2
    ×7

Keeping Skills Sharp

1. 558
   +306

2. 737
   +128

3. 246
   +316

4. 409
   +258

5. 346
   +327

6. 596
   +351

7. 435
   +294

8. 652
   +973

9. 941
   +674

10. 872
    +573

11. 948
    +359

12. 755
    +275

13. 695
    +876

14. 284
    +597

15. 527
    +773

4 as a factor

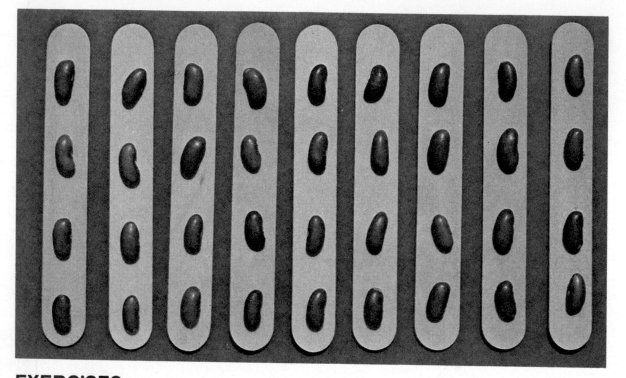

EXERCISES
Give each product. If you need to, use the picture above.

1. $1 \times 4 = \underline{?}$

2. $2 \times 4 = \underline{?}$

3. $3 \times 4 = \underline{?}$

4. $4 \times 4 = \underline{?}$

5. $5 \times 4 = \underline{?}$

6. $6 \times 4 = \underline{?}$

7. $7 \times 4 = \underline{?}$

8. $8 \times 4 = \underline{?}$

9. $9 \times 4 = \underline{?}$

10. $4 \times 4 = \underline{?}$

11. $6 \times 4 = \underline{?}$

12. $8 \times 4 = \underline{?}$

13. $2 \times 4 = \underline{?}$

14. $9 \times 4 = \underline{?}$

15. $3 \times 4 = \underline{?}$

16. $8 \times 4 = \underline{?}$

17. $5 \times 4 = \underline{?}$

18. $9 \times 4 = \underline{?}$

19. $1 \times 4 = \underline{?}$

20. $7 \times 4 = \underline{?}$

21. $6 \times 4 = \underline{?}$

22. $5 \times 4 = \underline{?}$

23. $3 \times 4 = \underline{?}$

24. $4 \times 4 = \underline{?}$

Multiply.

25. 4
    ×1

26. 4
    ×2

27. 4
    ×3

28. 4
    ×4

29. 4
    ×5

30. 4
    ×6

31. 4
    ×7

32. 4
    ×8

33. 4
    ×9

34. 3
    ×1

35. 3
    ×5

36. 4
    ×6

37. 4
    ×7

38. 4
    ×1

39. 3
    ×8

40. 4
    ×2

41. 2
    ×9

42. 3
    ×6

43. 4
    ×3

44. 3
    ×9

45. 4
    ×8

46. 3
    ×4

47. 4
    ×9

48. 3
    ×3

49. 4
    ×5

50. 2
    ×7

51. 2
    ×8

52. 3
    ×7

53. 2
    ×6

54. 4
    ×4

Solve.

55. 6

How many wheels?

56. 7

How many wheels?

57. 8

How many wheels?

58. 9

How many wheels?

5 as a factor

EXERCISES

Give each product. If you need to, use
the picture above.

1. $1 \times 5 = \underline{?}$

2. $2 \times 5 = \underline{?}$

3. $3 \times 5 = \underline{?}$

4. $4 \times 5 = \underline{?}$

5. $5 \times 5 = \underline{?}$

6. $6 \times 5 = \underline{?}$

7. $7 \times 5 = \underline{?}$

8. $8 \times 5 = \underline{?}$

9. $9 \times 5 = \underline{?}$

10. $4 \times 5 = \underline{?}$

11. $5 \times 5 = \underline{?}$

12. $6 \times 5 = \underline{?}$

13. $8 \times 5 = \underline{?}$

14. $9 \times 5 = \underline{?}$

15. $1 \times 5 = \underline{?}$

16. $4 \times 5 = \underline{?}$

17. $3 \times 5 = \underline{?}$

18. $2 \times 5 = \underline{?}$

19. $3 \times 5 = \underline{?}$

20. $5 \times 5 = \underline{?}$

21. $7 \times 5 = \underline{?}$

22. $8 \times 5 = \underline{?}$

23. $6 \times 5 = \underline{?}$

24. $9 \times 5 = \underline{?}$

Multiply.

25. $\begin{array}{r}5\\ \times 1\\ \hline\end{array}$	26. $\begin{array}{r}5\\ \times 2\\ \hline\end{array}$	27. $\begin{array}{r}5\\ \times 3\\ \hline\end{array}$	28. $\begin{array}{r}5\\ \times 4\\ \hline\end{array}$	29. $\begin{array}{r}5\\ \times 5\\ \hline\end{array}$	30. $\begin{array}{r}5\\ \times 6\\ \hline\end{array}$
31. $\begin{array}{r}5\\ \times 7\\ \hline\end{array}$	32. $\begin{array}{r}5\\ \times 8\\ \hline\end{array}$	33. $\begin{array}{r}5\\ \times 9\\ \hline\end{array}$	34. $\begin{array}{r}3\\ \times 7\\ \hline\end{array}$	35. $\begin{array}{r}3\\ \times 5\\ \hline\end{array}$	36. $\begin{array}{r}4\\ \times 3\\ \hline\end{array}$
37. $\begin{array}{r}2\\ \times 9\\ \hline\end{array}$	38. $\begin{array}{r}2\\ \times 7\\ \hline\end{array}$	39. $\begin{array}{r}4\\ \times 4\\ \hline\end{array}$	40. $\begin{array}{r}3\\ \times 4\\ \hline\end{array}$	41. $\begin{array}{r}5\\ \times 6\\ \hline\end{array}$	42. $\begin{array}{r}4\\ \times 9\\ \hline\end{array}$
43. $\begin{array}{r}5\\ \times 7\\ \hline\end{array}$	44. $\begin{array}{r}3\\ \times 3\\ \hline\end{array}$	45. $\begin{array}{r}5\\ \times 8\\ \hline\end{array}$	46. $\begin{array}{r}4\\ \times 6\\ \hline\end{array}$	47. $\begin{array}{r}5\\ \times 9\\ \hline\end{array}$	48. $\begin{array}{r}3\\ \times 6\\ \hline\end{array}$
49. $\begin{array}{r}3\\ \times 8\\ \hline\end{array}$	50. $\begin{array}{r}4\\ \times 7\\ \hline\end{array}$	51. $\begin{array}{r}4\\ \times 8\\ \hline\end{array}$	52. $\begin{array}{r}4\\ \times 5\\ \hline\end{array}$	53. $\begin{array}{r}3\\ \times 9\\ \hline\end{array}$	54. $\begin{array}{r}5\\ \times 5\\ \hline\end{array}$

Give the end number.

55. START 3 ×5 −9 +5 ? END

56. START 8 ×2 −7 +8 ? END

57. START 6 ×3 −9 +7 ? END

Problem solving

EXERCISES
Complete.

1. 2 🏠 cost _?_ ¢.

2. 2 🚗 cost _?_ ¢.

3. 4 🍄 cost _?_ ¢.

4. 5 🚗 cost _?_ ¢.

5. 8 🪁 cost _?_ ¢.

6. 6 🍄 cost _?_ ¢.

7. 9 🍄 cost _?_ ¢.

8. 8 🚗 cost _?_ ¢.

9. 7 🪁 cost _?_ ¢.

10. 7 🍄 cost _?_ ¢.

11. 9 🪁 cost _?_ ¢.

12. 8 🏠 cost _?_ ¢.

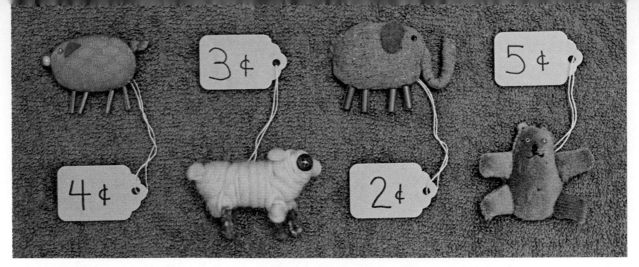

Complete.

13. 4  cost ? ¢.

14. 6 🐘 cost ? ¢.

15. 5 🐑 cost ? ¢.

16. 8 🐻 cost ? ¢.

17. 9 🐘 cost ? ¢.

18. 7 🐑 cost ? ¢.

19. 6 🐻 cost ? ¢.

20. 9 🐷 cost ? ¢.

Solve.

21. How much do

    4  and 2 🐻

    cost?

22. How much do 8 🐘

    and 5 🐷 cost?

23. Luis had 50¢.

    He bought 9 🐘.

    How much money
    did he have left?

24. Lisa had 3 quarters.

    She bought 6 🐷.

    How much money
    did she have left?

1 and 0 as factors

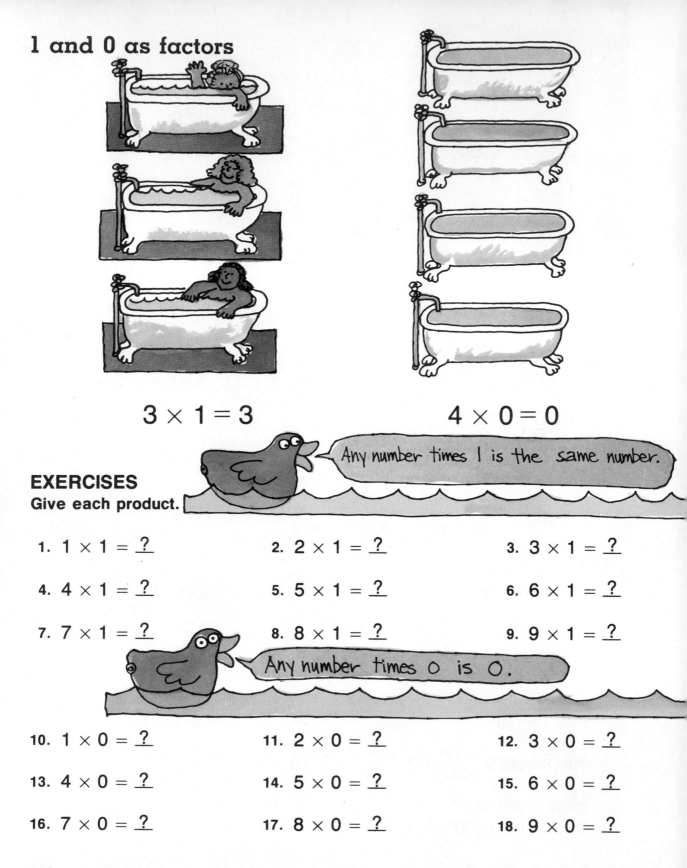

$$3 \times 1 = 3 \qquad\qquad 4 \times 0 = 0$$

Any number times 1 is the same number.

EXERCISES
Give each product.

1. $1 \times 1 = \underline{?}$ 2. $2 \times 1 = \underline{?}$ 3. $3 \times 1 = \underline{?}$

4. $4 \times 1 = \underline{?}$ 5. $5 \times 1 = \underline{?}$ 6. $6 \times 1 = \underline{?}$

7. $7 \times 1 = \underline{?}$ 8. $8 \times 1 = \underline{?}$ 9. $9 \times 1 = \underline{?}$

Any number times 0 is 0.

10. $1 \times 0 = \underline{?}$ 11. $2 \times 0 = \underline{?}$ 12. $3 \times 0 = \underline{?}$

13. $4 \times 0 = \underline{?}$ 14. $5 \times 0 = \underline{?}$ 15. $6 \times 0 = \underline{?}$

16. $7 \times 0 = \underline{?}$ 17. $8 \times 0 = \underline{?}$ 18. $9 \times 0 = \underline{?}$

Multiply.

19. 4
   ×7

20. 0
   ×1

21. 1
   ×6

22. 3
   ×7

23. 0
   ×6

24. 2
   ×7

25. 1
   ×3

26. 0
   ×9

27. 2
   ×8

28. 3
   ×8

29. 4
   ×8

30. 3
   ×4

31. 1
   ×7

32. 1
   ×2

33. 1
   ×9

34. 2
   ×5

35. 5
   ×9

36. 0
   ×3

37. 2
   ×6

38. 5
   ×6

39. 3
   ×9

40. 5
   ×7

41. 0
   ×8

42. 5
   ×4

43. 3
   ×6

44. 0
   ×7

45. 4
   ×9

46. 0
   ×2

47. 4
   ×5

48. 1
   ×5

49. 4
   ×6

50. 1
   ×1

51. 1
   ×8

52. 2
   ×9

53. 5
   ×8

54. 2
   ×3

Who am I?

55. If you multiply a number by me, you get 0.

56. If you multiply a number by me, you get the same number.

57. If you multiply me by 9, you get 27.

★58. If you multiply me by 2 and then add 1 to the product, you get 9.

(one hundred forty-nine) **149**

More about multiplication

You can change the order of the factors without changing the product.

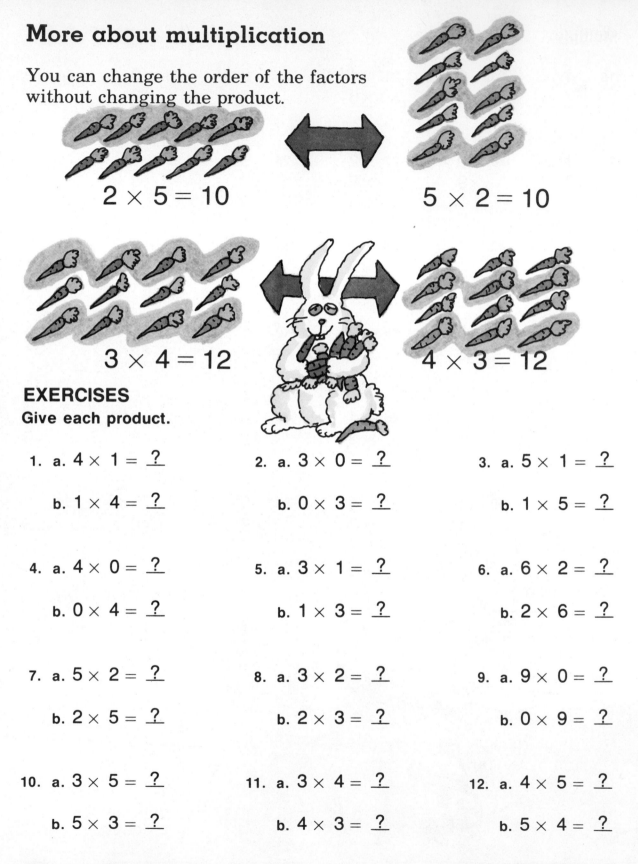

$2 \times 5 = 10$

$5 \times 2 = 10$

$3 \times 4 = 12$

$4 \times 3 = 12$

EXERCISES
Give each product.

1. a. $4 \times 1 = \underline{?}$

   b. $1 \times 4 = \underline{?}$

2. a. $3 \times 0 = \underline{?}$

   b. $0 \times 3 = \underline{?}$

3. a. $5 \times 1 = \underline{?}$

   b. $1 \times 5 = \underline{?}$

4. a. $4 \times 0 = \underline{?}$

   b. $0 \times 4 = \underline{?}$

5. a. $3 \times 1 = \underline{?}$

   b. $1 \times 3 = \underline{?}$

6. a. $6 \times 2 = \underline{?}$

   b. $2 \times 6 = \underline{?}$

7. a. $5 \times 2 = \underline{?}$

   b. $2 \times 5 = \underline{?}$

8. a. $3 \times 2 = \underline{?}$

   b. $2 \times 3 = \underline{?}$

9. a. $9 \times 0 = \underline{?}$

   b. $0 \times 9 = \underline{?}$

10. a. $3 \times 5 = \underline{?}$

    b. $5 \times 3 = \underline{?}$

11. a. $3 \times 4 = \underline{?}$

    b. $4 \times 3 = \underline{?}$

12. a. $4 \times 5 = \underline{?}$

    b. $5 \times 4 = \underline{?}$

Multiply.

13. 3
    ×5

14. 5
    ×8

15. 5
    ×4

16. 4
    ×4

17. 5
    ×6

18. 5
    ×1

19. 4
    ×6

20. 3
    ×7

21. 4
    ×3

22. 3
    ×4

23. 3
    ×9

24. 4
    ×7

25. 3
    ×6

26. 5
    ×3

27. 4
    ×8

28. 5
    ×2

29. 5
    ×7

30. 3
    ×3

How many blocks?

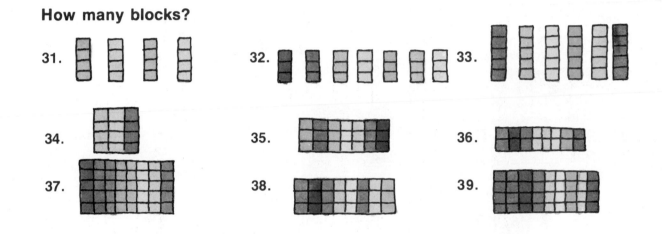

31.

32.

33.

34.

35.

36.

37.

38.

39.

1.   572
   − 158

2.   621
   − 249

3.   430
   − 228

4.   852
   − 343

5.   934
   − 628

6.   743
   − 358

7.   628
   − 249

8.   413
   − 179

9.   525
   − 259

10.   610
    − 258

11.   203
    − 159

12.   506
    − 258

13.   703
    − 375

14.   800
    − 453

15.   900
    − 267

Practice

On your mark! Get set! GO!

1. $\begin{array}{r} 0 \\ \times 7 \\ \hline \end{array}$
2. $\begin{array}{r} 5 \\ \times 5 \\ \hline \end{array}$
3. $\begin{array}{r} 3 \\ \times 2 \\ \hline \end{array}$
4. $\begin{array}{r} 4 \\ \times 6 \\ \hline \end{array}$

5. $\begin{array}{r} 4 \\ \times 3 \\ \hline \end{array}$
6. $\begin{array}{r} 2 \\ \times 3 \\ \hline \end{array}$
7. $\begin{array}{r} 5 \\ \times 6 \\ \hline \end{array}$
8. $\begin{array}{r} 4 \\ \times 2 \\ \hline \end{array}$

9. $\begin{array}{r} 2 \\ \times 2 \\ \hline \end{array}$
10. $\begin{array}{r} 5 \\ \times 1 \\ \hline \end{array}$
11. $\begin{array}{r} 2 \\ \times 4 \\ \hline \end{array}$
12. $\begin{array}{r} 4 \\ \times 7 \\ \hline \end{array}$
13. $\begin{array}{r} 3 \\ \times 3 \\ \hline \end{array}$
14. $\begin{array}{r} 5 \\ \times 3 \\ \hline \end{array}$

15. $\begin{array}{r} 3 \\ \times 4 \\ \hline \end{array}$
16. $\begin{array}{r} 0 \\ \times 0 \\ \hline \end{array}$
17. $\begin{array}{r} 5 \\ \times 7 \\ \hline \end{array}$
18. $\begin{array}{r} 3 \\ \times 6 \\ \hline \end{array}$
19. $\begin{array}{r} 4 \\ \times 8 \\ \hline \end{array}$
20. $\begin{array}{r} 3 \\ \times 9 \\ \hline \end{array}$

21. $\begin{array}{r} 2 \\ \times 7 \\ \hline \end{array}$
22. $\begin{array}{r} 3 \\ \times 5 \\ \hline \end{array}$
23. $\begin{array}{r} 2 \\ \times 5 \\ \hline \end{array}$
24. $\begin{array}{r} 4 \\ \times 5 \\ \hline \end{array}$
25. $\begin{array}{r} 5 \\ \times 8 \\ \hline \end{array}$
26. $\begin{array}{r} 5 \\ \times 2 \\ \hline \end{array}$

27. $\begin{array}{r} 2 \\ \times 1 \\ \hline \end{array}$
28. $\begin{array}{r} 5 \\ \times 4 \\ \hline \end{array}$
29. $\begin{array}{r} 3 \\ \times 7 \\ \hline \end{array}$
30. $\begin{array}{r} 3 \\ \times 1 \\ \hline \end{array}$
31. $\begin{array}{r} 4 \\ \times 1 \\ \hline \end{array}$
32. $\begin{array}{r} 2 \\ \times 9 \\ \hline \end{array}$

33. $\begin{array}{r} 2 \\ \times 6 \\ \hline \end{array}$
34. $\begin{array}{r} 4 \\ \times 4 \\ \hline \end{array}$
35. $\begin{array}{r} 2 \\ \times 8 \\ \hline \end{array}$
36. $\begin{array}{r} 5 \\ \times 9 \\ \hline \end{array}$
37. $\begin{array}{r} 3 \\ \times 8 \\ \hline \end{array}$
38. $\begin{array}{r} 4 \\ \times 9 \\ \hline \end{array}$

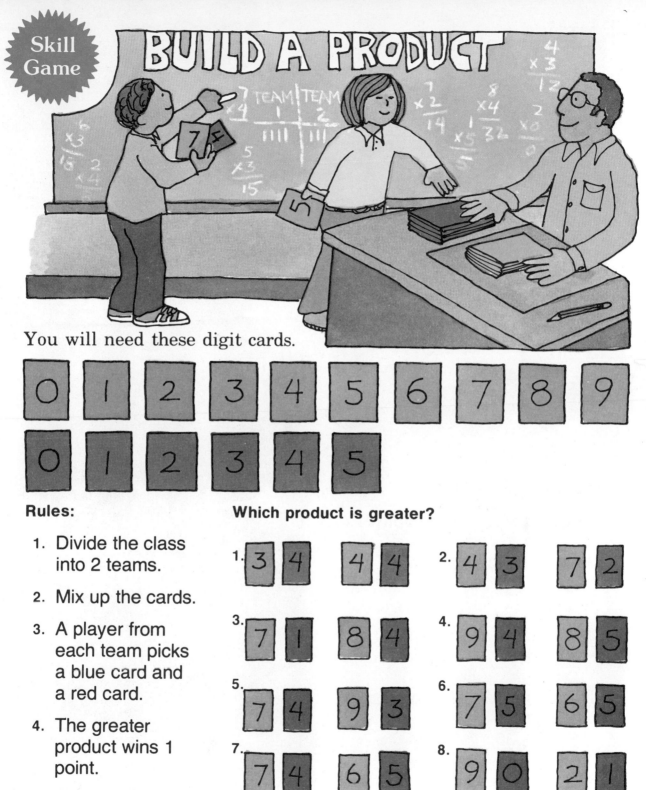

BUILD A PRODUCT

Skill Game

You will need these digit cards.

| 0 | 1 | 2 | 3 | 4 | 5 | 6 | 7 | 8 | 9 |

| 0 | 1 | 2 | 3 | 4 | 5 |

Rules:

1. Divide the class into 2 teams.

2. Mix up the cards.

3. A player from each team picks a blue card and a red card.

4. The greater product wins 1 point.

5. First team to get 12 points wins!

Which product is greater?

1. 3 4   4 4
2. 4 3   7 2
3. 7 1   8 4
4. 9 4   8 5
5. 7 4   9 3
6. 7 5   6 5
7. 7 4   6 5
8. 9 0   2 1

Problem solving

These steps can help you solve problems.

1. Read the problem and find the question.

   3 boxes of apples.
   8 apples in each box.
   How many apples in all?

2. What are the facts?

   3 boxes
   8 apples in each

3. Decide what to do.

   Add, subtract, or multiply?

4. Answer the question.

   $$\begin{array}{r} 8 \\ \times 3 \\ \hline 24 \end{array}$$ There are 24 apples in all.

5. Does your answer seem right?

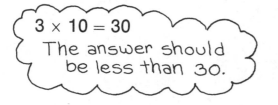

   3 × 10 = 30
   The answer should be less than 30.

   The answer seems right.

Solve.

1. 3 cars.
   6 more cars.
   How many cars?

2. 3 cars.
   6 people in each car.
   How many people?

3. 3 cars.
   6 trucks.
   How many more trucks?

4. 8 pieces of candy.
   5 pieces of gum.
   How many pieces in all?

5. 8 pieces of candy.
   5 pieces of gum.
   How many fewer pieces of gum?

6. 8 packs of gum.
   5 pieces in each pack.
   How many pieces in all?

7.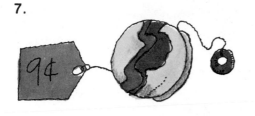

   How much for 5 toys?

8.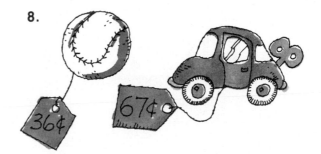

   How much for both?

9. 3 banks.
   7¢ in each bank.
   How much money?

10. 2 banks.
    27¢ in each bank.
    How much money?

Tell a story.

Problem solving

Solve.

1.

   How many candles
   in 8 ?

2.

   How many buttons
   in 7  ?

3.

   How many marbles
   in 6 ⬡ ?

4.

   How many cookies
   in 9 ⬟ ?

5.

   How much for both?

6.

   How much more does
   the red one cost?

Solve.

7. 4 trees in a row.
   7 rows.
   How many trees?

8. 5 candies in a box.
   8 boxes.
   How many candies?

9. 3 shells in one box.
   9 shells in another box.
   How many shells?

10. 8 birds on a fence.
    2 birds flew away.
    How many birds were left?

11. Had $1.17.
    Spent a quarter.
    How much money was left?

12. Had $2.06.
    Earned 3 quarters and 1 dime.
    How much money then?

The picture graph shows how the students
in our class come to school.

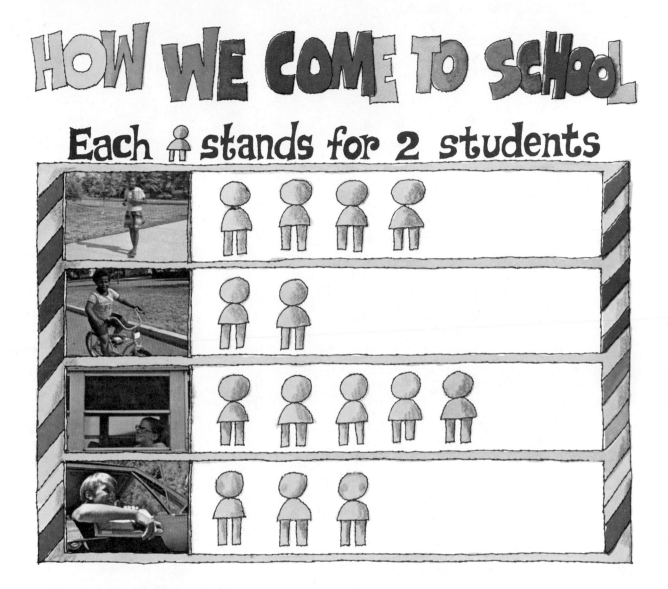

HOW WE COME TO SCHOOL

Each 👤 stands for 2 students

How many students

13. walk?

14. ride a bus?

15. ride a bicycle?

16. ride in a car?

17. How many more ride a bus than ride a bicycle?

18. How many students either walk or ride in a car?

19. How many students in the class?

20. How many students do not walk to school?

Multiply. [pages 133–145, 148–152]

1. 4 ×2	2. 2 ×7	3. 4 ×5	4. 3 ×7	5. 5 ×1	6. 2 ×1
7. 5 ×2	8. 3 ×1	9. 4 ×7	10. 0 ×5	11. 3 ×3	12. 5 ×4
13. 0 ×8	14. 0 ×0	15. 2 ×5	16. 5 ×9	17. 2 ×2	18. 3 ×2
19. 2 ×4	20. 5 ×6	21. 2 ×9	22. 2 ×3	23. 4 ×4	24. 4 ×3
25. 4 ×6	26. 3 ×9	27. 3 ×4	28. 4 ×9	29. 2 ×8	30. 5 ×8

31. $3 \times 5 = $ _?_　　　32. $6 \times 3 = $ _?_　　　33. $7 \times 5 = $ _?_

34. $1 \times 3 = $ _?_　　　35. $6 \times 2 = $ _?_　　　36. $4 \times 4 = $ _?_

Solve. [pages 146–147, 154–157]

37.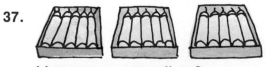

How many candles?

38.

How many pencils?

39. One 🧁 costs 3¢.
How much do 8 🧁
cost?

40. One 🖊 costs 5¢.
How much do 7 🖊
cost?

158 (one hundred fifty-eight)

Favorite Television Program
each 🧍 stands for 3 friends

Electric Co.	🧍 🧍 🧍
Star Trek	🧍 🧍 🧍 🧍 🧍
World of Disney	🧍 🧍 🧍
Creature Feature	🧍
Superman	

1. List your five favorite television programs.

2. Show your list to some friends. Have them tell which program on your list they like best.

3. Make a picture graph. *Hint:* You may want to let 🧍 represent more than one friend, as in the example.

4. Tell what your graph shows.

CHAPTER REVIEW

Multiply.

1. $1 \times 2 = $?
2. $2 \times 2 = $?
3. $3 \times 2 = $?

4. $4 \times 2 = $?
5. $5 \times 2 = $?
6. $6 \times 2 = $?

7. $7 \times 2 = $?
8. $8 \times 2 = $?
9. $9 \times 2 = $?

10. $1 \times 3 = $?
11. $2 \times 3 = $?
12. $3 \times 3 = $?

13. $4 \times 3 = $?
14. $5 \times 3 = $?
15. $6 \times 3 = $?

16. $7 \times 3 = $?
17. $8 \times 3 = $?
18. $9 \times 3 = $?

19. $1 \times 4 = $?
20. $2 \times 4 = $?
21. $3 \times 4 = $?

22. $4 \times 4 = $?
23. $5 \times 4 = $?
24. $6 \times 4 = $?

25. $7 \times 4 = $?
26. $8 \times 4 = $?
27. $9 \times 4 = $?

28. $1 \times 5 = $?
29. $2 \times 5 = $?
30. $3 \times 5 = $?

31. $4 \times 5 = $?
32. $5 \times 5 = $?
33. $6 \times 5 = $?

34. $7 \times 5 = $?
35. $8 \times 5 = $?
36. $9 \times 5 = $?

Complete each puzzle.

Multiply the "corner" numbers to fill in the circle.

Give the correct letter.

1. Complete.

   4 + ? = 7

   a. 11
   b. 5
   c. 3
   d. none of these

2. In 17 − 9 = 8,
   8 is called the

   a. sum
   b. difference
   c. product
   d. none of these

3. Six hundred five is

   a. 650
   b. 605
   c. 665
   d. none of these

4. 66 rounded to the
   nearest ten is

   a. 100
   b. 60
   c. 70
   d. 67

5. What number is 10
   more than 340?

   a. 440
   b. 330
   c. 400
   d. none of these

6. Which number is
   the greatest?

   a. 3504
   b. 4350
   c. 4530
   d. 4503

7. Add.
   79
   68
   +35

   a. 182
   b. 162
   c. 172
   d. none of these

8. Add.
   7691
   +1442

   a. 9143
   b. 9133
   c. 8033
   d. none of these

9. Subtract.
   603
   −275

   a. 332
   b. 338
   c. 328
   d. 428

10. Subtract.
   5263
   −1746

   a. 4517
   b. 4523
   c. 3527
   d. 3517

11. How many minutes
   in one hour?

   a. 50
   b. 30
   c. 100
   d. 60

12. How much money?

   1 dollar
   1 half-dollar
   1 dime
   1 nickel
   2 pennies

   a. $1.42
   b. $1.67
   c. $1.76
   d. none of these

162 (one hundred sixty-two)

7
Division Facts

Division

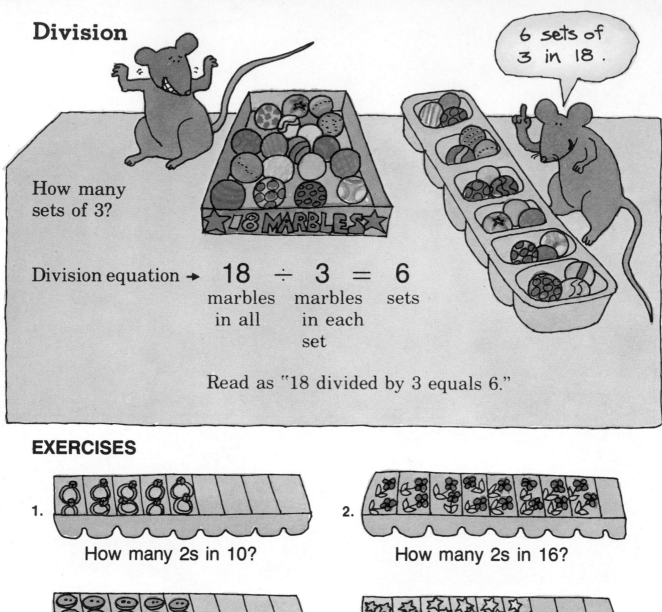

6 sets of 3 in 18.

How many sets of 3?

Division equation → **18 ÷ 3 = 6**

marbles in all · marbles in each set · sets

Read as "18 divided by 3 equals 6."

EXERCISES

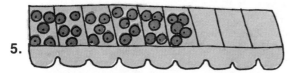

1. How many 2s in 10?

2. How many 2s in 16?

3. How many 3s in 15?

4. How many 4s in 24?

5. How many 5s in 30?

6. How many 3s in 27?

Give each quotient.

7.

$$20 \div 5 = \underline{?}$$

8.

$$18 \div 3 = \underline{?}$$

9.

$$16 \div 4 = \underline{?}$$

10.

$$12 \div 4 = \underline{?}$$

11.
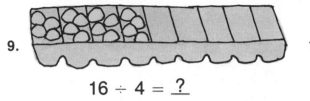

$$18 \div 2 = \underline{?}$$

12.
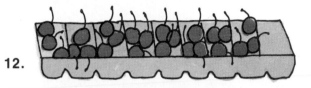

$$24 \div 3 = \underline{?}$$

13.
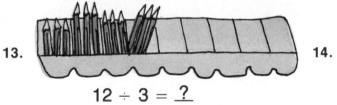

$$12 \div 3 = \underline{?}$$

14.
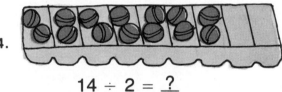

$$14 \div 2 = \underline{?}$$

15.
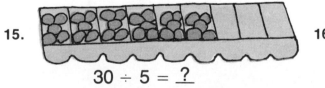

$$30 \div 5 = \underline{?}$$

16.
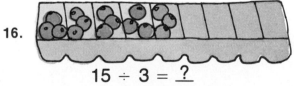

$$15 \div 3 = \underline{?}$$

17.
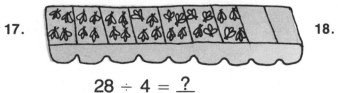

$$28 \div 4 = \underline{?}$$

18.
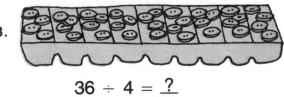

$$36 \div 4 = \underline{?}$$

Dividing by 2 and 3

EXERCISES
Give each quotient.

1. $3 \div 3 = \underline{?}$

2. $4 \div 2 = \underline{?}$

3. $6 \div 3 = \underline{?}$

4. $10 \div 2 = \underline{?}$

5. $2 \div 2 = \underline{?}$

6. $18 \div 2 = \underline{?}$

7. $9 \div 3 = \underline{?}$

8. $12 \div 3 = \underline{?}$

9. $8 \div 2 = \underline{?}$

10. $15 \div 3 = \underline{?}$

11. $16 \div 2 = \underline{?}$

12. $24 \div 3 = \underline{?}$

13. $6 \div 2 = \underline{?}$

14. $21 \div 3 = \underline{?}$

15. $18 \div 3 = \underline{?}$

16. $12 \div 2 = \underline{?}$

17. $27 \div 3 = \underline{?}$

$21 \div 3 = 7$

18. $6 \div 2 = \underline{?}$ 19. $12 \div 3 = \underline{?}$ 20. $2 \div 2 = \underline{?}$

21. $6 \div 3 = \underline{?}$ 22. $3 \div 3 = \underline{?}$ 23. $16 \div 2 = \underline{?}$

24. $8 \div 2 = \underline{?}$ 25. $4 \div 2 = \underline{?}$ 26. $18 \div 3 = \underline{?}$

27. $18 \div 2 = \underline{?}$ 28. $9 \div 3 = \underline{?}$ 29. $12 \div 2 = \underline{?}$

30. $15 \div 3 = \underline{?}$ 31. $21 \div 3 = \underline{?}$ 32. $10 \div 2 = \underline{?}$

33. $27 \div 3 = \underline{?}$ 34. $14 \div 2 = \underline{?}$ 35. $24 \div 3 = \underline{?}$

Solve.

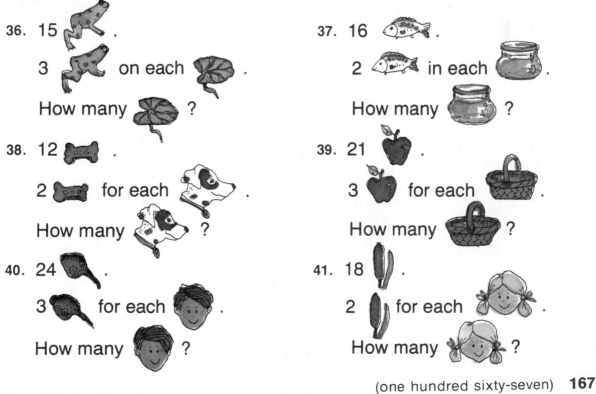

36. 15 .

   3 on each .

   How many ?

37. 16 .

   2 in each .

   How many ?

38. 12 .

   2 for each .

   How many ?

39. 21 .

   3 for each .

   How many ?

40. 24 .

   3 for each .

   How many ?

41. 18 .

   2 for each .

   How many ?

(one hundred sixty-seven) **167**

Dividing by 4 and 5

$$12 \div 4 = 3$$

EXERCISES
Give each quotient.

1. $10 \div 5 = \underline{?}$
2. $4 \div 4 = \underline{?}$
3. $32 \div 4 = \underline{?}$

4. $24 \div 4 = \underline{?}$
5. $5 \div 5 = \underline{?}$
6. $35 \div 5 = \underline{?}$

7. $40 \div 5 = \underline{?}$
8. $20 \div 4 = \underline{?}$
9. $20 \div 5 = \underline{?}$

10. $25 \div 5 = \underline{?}$
11. $15 \div 5 = \underline{?}$
12. $8 \div 4 = \underline{?}$

13. $12 \div 4 = \underline{?}$
14. $30 \div 5 = \underline{?}$
15. $45 \div 5 = \underline{?}$

16. $36 \div 4 = \underline{?}$
17. $16 \div 4 = \underline{?}$
18. $28 \div 4 = \underline{?}$

19. $16 \div 4 = \underline{?}$ 20. $3 \div 3 = \underline{?}$ 21. $4 \div 2 = \underline{?}$

22. $6 \div 2 = \underline{?}$ 23. $10 \div 5 = \underline{?}$ 24. $5 \div 5 = \underline{?}$

25. $12 \div 3 = \underline{?}$ 26. $6 \div 3 = \underline{?}$ 27. $8 \div 2 = \underline{?}$

28. $15 \div 5 = \underline{?}$ 29. $35 \div 5 = \underline{?}$ 30. $21 \div 3 = \underline{?}$

31. $10 \div 2 = \underline{?}$ 32. $20 \div 4 = \underline{?}$ 33. $12 \div 4 = \underline{?}$

34. $20 \div 5 = \underline{?}$ 35. $4 \div 4 = \underline{?}$ 36. $16 \div 2 = \underline{?}$

37. $24 \div 4 = \underline{?}$ 38. $24 \div 3 = \underline{?}$ 39. $32 \div 4 = \underline{?}$

40. $14 \div 2 = \underline{?}$ 41. $25 \div 5 = \underline{?}$ 42. $15 \div 3 = \underline{?}$

43. $40 \div 5 = \underline{?}$ 44. $8 \div 4 = \underline{?}$ 45. $27 \div 3 = \underline{?}$

46. $18 \div 3 = \underline{?}$ 47. $18 \div 2 = \underline{?}$ 48. $28 \div 4 = \underline{?}$

49. $36 \div 4 = \underline{?}$ 50. $30 \div 5 = \underline{?}$ 51. $45 \div 5 = \underline{?}$

52. $2 \div 2 = \underline{?}$ 53. $9 \div 3 = \underline{?}$ 54. $12 \div 2 = \underline{?}$

Give the end number.

55. Start 7 | +9 | ÷2 | −3 | ×4 | End ?

56. Start 6 | +8 | −8 | ×4 | ÷4 | ? End

(one hundred sixty-nine) **169**

Problem solving

EXERCISES

Solve.

1. Left at 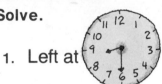 in the morning. Arrived 2 hours later. What time did they arrive?

2. Rode the 🚌 27 miles. Walked 4 miles. How far did they travel?

3. Ruth's 🎒 weighed 12 pounds. John's 🎒 weighed 11 pounds. How much did the 🎒🎒 weigh together?

4. They saw 23 🐥 and 18 🐤. How many more 🐥 than 🐤 did they see?

Solve.

5. They saw 4 🪺.

   Each nest had 3 🥚.

   How many 🥚 did they see?

6. Saw 27 🦆 swimming and

   19 🐤 flying.

   How many 🐦 did they see?

7. They took 36 🌭.

   There were 4 🌭 in each
   package.
   How many packages did
   they take?

8. They took 40 🍪.

   There were 5 🍪 in each
   package.
   How many packages did
   they take?

9. Each package had 4 🥖.

   They took 8 packages. How

   many 🥖 did they take?

10. Each package had 2 🧁.

    They took 16 🧁. How

    many packages did they take?

11. Took 45 🥤.

    Put 5 on a 🥢.

    How many 🥢 did they use?

12. Got home at 🕖 that
    evening.

    How long were they away?
    (*Hint:* See Exercise 1).

Division in vertical form

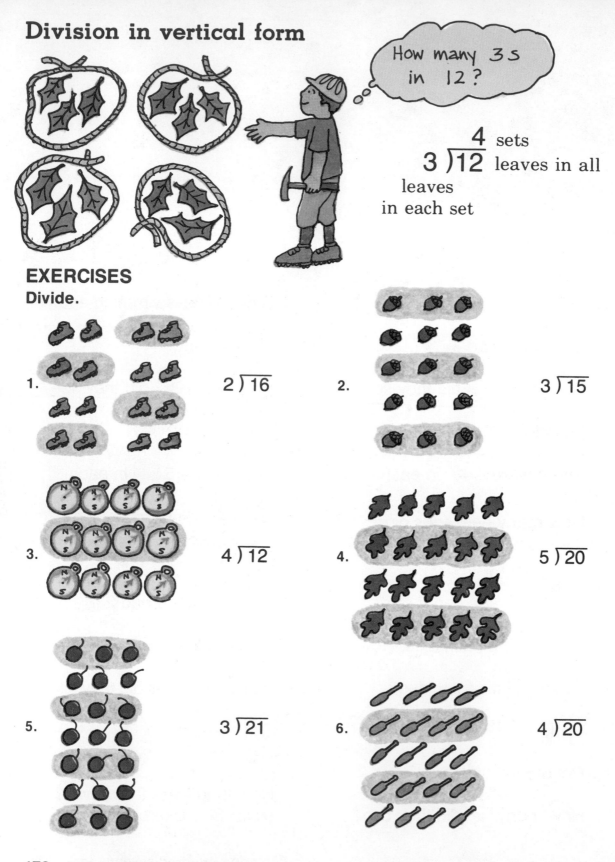

How many 3s in 12 ?

$$\begin{array}{r} 4 \\ 3\overline{)12} \end{array}$$ sets
leaves in all
leaves
in each set

EXERCISES
Divide.

1. $2\overline{)16}$

2. $3\overline{)15}$

3. $4\overline{)12}$

4. $5\overline{)20}$

5. $3\overline{)21}$

6. $4\overline{)20}$

How many
3s in 9?

How many
2s in 8?

How many
5s in 10?

7. $3\overline{)9}$ 8. $2\overline{)8}$ 9. $5\overline{)10}$

10. $5\overline{)5}$ 11. $2\overline{)10}$ 12. $3\overline{)12}$

13. $5\overline{)40}$ 14. $4\overline{)24}$ 15. $2\overline{)4}$

16. $2\overline{)12}$ 17. $3\overline{)24}$ 18. $3\overline{)3}$

19. $4\overline{)8}$ 20. $4\overline{)32}$ 21. $5\overline{)35}$

22. $4\overline{)28}$ 23. $2\overline{)14}$ 24. $5\overline{)15}$

25. $3\overline{)18}$ 26. $5\overline{)30}$ 27. $4\overline{)12}$

28. $4\overline{)28}$ 29. $4\overline{)36}$ 30. $3\overline{)27}$

Give the correct sign, $+$, $-$, $\times$, or $\div$.

31. $4 \ ? \ 3 = 12$ 32. $14 \ ? \ 5 = 9$

33. $16 \ ? \ 4 = 4$ 34. $6 \ ? \ 8 = 14$

35. $8 \ ? \ 2 = 6$ 36. $8 \ ? \ 2 = 16$

37. $8 \ ? \ 2 = 4$ 38. $8 \ ? \ 2 = 10$

Keeping Skills Sharp

Give the value of the red digit.

1. 63 2. 45

3. 821 4. 759

5. 983 6. 2906

7. 9421 8. 7083

9. 7777 10. 7777

11. 7777 12. 7777

13. 9086 14. 3140

15. 3104

(one hundred seventy-three) **173**

Practice

How many 4's in 20?

How many 5's in 20?

$$4\overline{)20}^{\,5}$$

$$5\overline{)20}^{\,4}$$

EXERCISES
Divide.

1. $2\overline{)8}$
2. $3\overline{)15}$
3. $4\overline{)8}$
4. $3\overline{)6}$
5. $3\overline{)12}$

6. $4\overline{)12}$
7. $5\overline{)10}$
8. $3\overline{)9}$
9. $5\overline{)20}$
10. $4\overline{)16}$

11. $4\overline{)20}$
12. $2\overline{)12}$
13. $3\overline{)18}$
14. $2\overline{)10}$
15. $5\overline{)30}$

16. $5\overline{)15}$
17. $4\overline{)32}$
18. $5\overline{)45}$
19. $3\overline{)27}$
20. $4\overline{)36}$

21. $3\overline{)24}$
22. $2\overline{)18}$
23. $4\overline{)24}$
24. $2\overline{)16}$
25. $5\overline{)40}$

26. $2\overline{)14}$
27. $5\overline{)35}$
28. $5\overline{)25}$
29. $3\overline{)21}$
30. $4\overline{)28}$

Solve.

31. 18 cupcakes.
    2 cupcakes in a package.
    How many packages?

32. 35 sticks of gum.
    5 sticks in a package.
    How many packages?

33. 24 oranges.
    3 oranges in a package.
    How many packages?

34. 36 apples.
    4 apples in a package.
    How many packages?

35. 32 buttons.
    4 buttons on a card.
    How many cards?

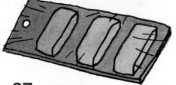

36. 27 erasers.
    3 erasers on a card.
    How many cards?

37. 40 pencils.
    5 pencils in a package.
    How many packages?

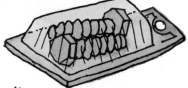

38. 14 bolts.
    2 bolts in a package.
    How many packages?

39. 24 children.
    4 children in each car.
    How many cars?

40. 18 cookies.
    3 cookies on each plate.
    How many plates?

41. 16 ears of corn.
    2 ears in each package.
    How many packages?

42. 45 crayons.
    5 crayons in each box.
    How many boxes?

Multiplication and division

Multiplication and division are related.

$3 \times 2 = 6$
$6 \div 2 = 3$

$2 \times 3 = 6$
$6 \div 3 = 2$

EXERCISES
Complete.

1.

$3 \times 2 = \underline{?}$

$6 \div 2 = \underline{?}$

2.

$4 \times 3 = \underline{?}$

$12 \div 3 = \underline{?}$

3.

$3 \times 4 = \underline{?}$

$12 \div 4 = \underline{?}$

4.

$5 \times 4 = \underline{?}$

$20 \div 4 = \underline{?}$

Use the numbers. Write two multiplication equations and two division equations.

5.  3 12 4

6.  20 4 5

7.  24 4 6

8.  3 7 21

9.  7 14 2

10.  27 3 9

11.  36 9 4

12.  7 28 4

13.  16 2 8

14. 18 9 2

15. 24 8 3

16. 4 8 32

Find the end number.

17. START 5   +8   −5   ×3   ÷4   END ?

18. 4 START   +2   ×3   ÷2   −4   ? END

19. 8 START   +5   −5   ×4   ÷4   ? END

20. START 7   ×5   ÷5   +4   −3   ? END

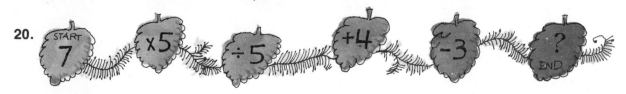

(one hundred seventy-seven) **177**

More about division

Division is finding a missing factor.

$? \times 3 = 24$

$3\overline{)24}$

$? \times 1 = 5$

$1\overline{)5}$

$? \times 5 = 0$

$5\overline{)0}$

$? \times 0 = 4$
There is no number times 0 that equals 4.

We don't divide by 0.

$0\overline{)4}$

EXERCISES
Divide.

1. $4\overline{)4}$ 2. $1\overline{)6}$ 3. $5\overline{)0}$ 4. $2\overline{)12}$ 5. $5\overline{)30}$

6. $1\overline{)9}$ 7. $4\overline{)16}$ 8. $3\overline{)18}$ 9. $3\overline{)21}$ 10. $1\overline{)8}$

11. $5\overline{)45}$ 12. $3\overline{)0}$ 13. $4\overline{)28}$ 14. $4\overline{)0}$ 15. $5\overline{)5}$

16. $2\overline{)16}$ 17. $4\overline{)24}$ 18. $3\overline{)15}$ 19. $2\overline{)14}$ 20. $5\overline{)15}$

21. $4\overline{)20}$ 22. $5\overline{)20}$ 23. $2\overline{)18}$ 24. $5\overline{)35}$ 25. $3\overline{)12}$

26. $5\overline{)40}$ 27. $4\overline{)32}$ 28. $3\overline{)27}$ 29. $4\overline{)36}$ 30. $5\overline{)25}$

The numbers have been covered. Tell what you would do (+, −, ×, ÷) to solve the problem.

31. ● apples in one bag.
    ● apples in another bag.
    How many apples in all?

32. ● people in each car.
    ● cars.
    How many people in all?

33. ● ¢ for a malt.
    ● ¢ for a cone.
    How much more for the malt?

34. ● ¢ in all.
    ● ¢ for each lollipop.
    How many lollipops?

35. $● for each record.
    ● records.
    What is the total cost?

36. ● marbles in a bag.
    ● marbles were lost.
    How many marbles were left?

37. ● dogs in one ring.
    ● dogs in another ring.
    How many dogs in all?

38. ● books in all.
    ● packages.
    How many books in each package?

Keeping Skills Sharp

1. 83 +57	2. 79 +68	3. 47 +95	4. 86 +37	5. 94 +57
6. 26 35 +24	7. 53 85 +72	8. 63 89 +75	9. 57 69 +18	10. 27 48 +68
11. 374 +586	12. 586 +374	13. 327 +486	14. 592 +379	15. 674 +158

Problem solving

These steps can help you solve problems.

1. Read the problem and find the question.

There were 36 jars of paste. Julie put 4 jars in each box. <u>How many boxes did she use?</u>

2. What are the facts?

36 jars in all
4 jars in each box

3. Decide what to do.

Add, subtract, multiply, or <u>divide?</u>

4. Answer the question.

$$4 \overline{)36}^{\,9}$$ She used 9 boxes.

5. Does your answer seem right?

It would take 10 boxes for 40 jars.

The answer seems right.

Solve.

1. 8 crayons.
   4 crayons in each box.

   How many boxes?

2. 8 boxes.
   4 crayons in each box.

   How many crayons in all?

3. 8 crayons in one box.
   4 crayons in another box.

   How many crayons in all?

4. 8 crayons in one box.
   4 crayons in another box.

   How many more crayons in the first box?

5. 21 paint brushes in all.
   3 in each glass.

   How many glasses?

6. 9 children.
   4 pieces of paper for each.

   How many pieces of paper?

7. 19 jars of red finger paint.
   13 jars of blue finger paint.

   How many more jars of red finger paint?

8. 19 jars of red finger paint.
   13 jars of blue finger paint.

   How many jars in all?

9. 9 children.
   Each child drew 3 pictures.

   How many pictures?

10. 32 scissors.
    9 got lost.

    How many were left?

Tell a story.

Problem solving

Postal workers pick up and deliver our mail. We buy stamps to pay for the service.

EXERCISES
Give the total cost of the stamps.

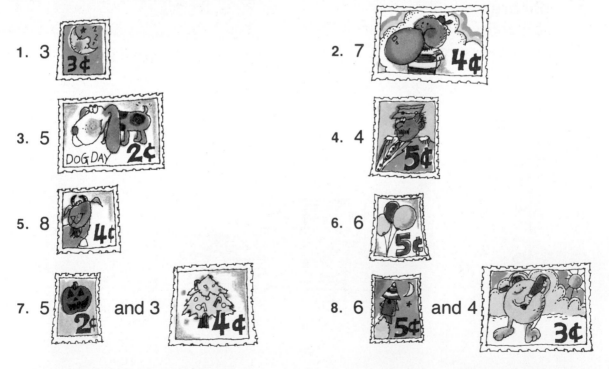

1. 3

2. 7

3. 5

4. 4

5. 8

6. 6

7. 5 and 3

8. 6 and 4

Solve.

9. How many 5¢ can you buy for (coin) ?

10. How many 4¢ can you buy with (coins) ?

11. How many 3¢ can you buy with (coins) ?

12. How many 2¢ can you buy with (coins) ?

13. You have (coins) . You buy 8 5¢ . How much is left?

14. You have (coins) . You buy 9 4¢ . How much is left?

15. You have (bills) . You buy $1.39 . How much is left?

16. You have (bills) . You buy $2.08 . How much is left?

Here's how I add 99 in my head. I add 100. Then I subtract 1.

75 + 100 = 175
175 − 1 = 174

75
+99
———
174

SHORTCUT

Try the shortcut with these exercises.

56	38	143	267	483	638
+99	+99	+99	+99	+99	+99

Division with remainder

Make sets of 4.

There are 2 left over.

quotient

$$4\overline{)22}$$

$$\begin{array}{r} 5 \text{R2} \\ 4\overline{)22} \\ -20 \\ \hline 2 \end{array}$$

remainder

Write the remainder here.

EXERCISES
Divide.

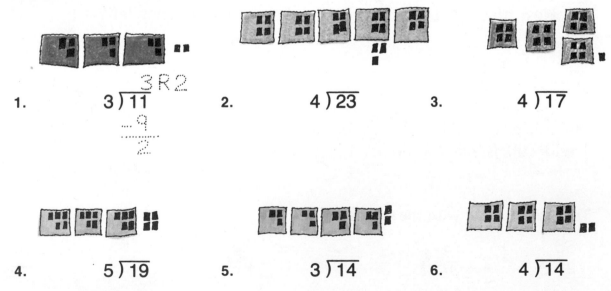

1. $$\begin{array}{r} 3\text{R2} \\ 3\overline{)11} \\ -9 \\ \hline 2 \end{array}$$

2. $4\overline{)23}$

3. $4\overline{)17}$

4. $5\overline{)19}$

5. $3\overline{)14}$

6. $4\overline{)14}$

Divide.

7. $3\overline{)7}$ 8. $5\overline{)12}$ 9. $3\overline{)8}$ 10. $4\overline{)18}$ 11. $2\overline{)7}$

12. $5\overline{)31}$ 13. $4\overline{)29}$ 14. $5\overline{)18}$ 15. $3\overline{)10}$ 16. $4\overline{)21}$

17. $5\overline{)27}$ 18. $4\overline{)35}$ 19. $2\overline{)9}$ 20. $3\overline{)20}$ 21. $5\overline{)29}$

22. $5\overline{)48}$ 23. $2\overline{)11}$ 24. $4\overline{)34}$ 25. $5\overline{)42}$ 26. $3\overline{)22}$

27. $3\overline{)25}$ 28. $5\overline{)37}$ 29. $2\overline{)13}$ 30. $4\overline{)33}$ 31. $2\overline{)19}$

32. $5\overline{)36}$ 33. $3\overline{)28}$ 34. $3\overline{)26}$ 35. $4\overline{)38}$ 36. $2\overline{)15}$

Who am I?

37. If you divide me by 5, you get 4.

38. If you divide me by 4, you get 7.

★39. If you divide me by 2 and then add 3, you get 11

★40. If you divide me by 3 and then subtract 4, you get 1.

★41. If you divide me by 5, you get a quotient of 4 and a remainder of 2.

★42. If you divide me by 3, you get a quotient of 8 and a remainder of 1.

(one hundred eighty-five) **185**

Give each quotient. [pages 163–169]

1. $8 \div 2 = \underline{?}$ 2. $20 \div 5 = \underline{?}$ 3. $18 \div 3 = \underline{?}$

4. $10 \div 5 = \underline{?}$ 5. $16 \div 2 = \underline{?}$ 6. $35 \div 5 = \underline{?}$

7. $12 \div 4 = \underline{?}$ 8. $8 \div 4 = \underline{?}$ 9. $20 \div 4 = \underline{?}$

10. $15 \div 3 = \underline{?}$ 11. $32 \div 4 = \underline{?}$ 12. $14 \div 2 = \underline{?}$

Divide. [pages 172–174, 178]

13. $2\overline{)6}$ 14. $3\overline{)3}$ 15. $3\overline{)9}$ 16. $5\overline{)25}$ 17. $3\overline{)24}$

18. $5\overline{)15}$ 19. $5\overline{)30}$ 20. $2\overline{)18}$ 21. $4\overline{)36}$ 22. $4\overline{)24}$

23. $3\overline{)12}$ 24. $4\overline{)28}$ 25. $5\overline{)0}$ 26. $5\overline{)45}$ 27. $3\overline{)21}$

Solve. [pages 170–171, 175, 179–183]

28. 15 🐢.

3 🐢 in each box.

How many boxes?

29. 24 🐞.

4 🐞 in each bag.

How many bags?

30. 12 🐛.

3 🐛 in each basket.

How many baskets?

31. 18 🐜

2 🐜 in each tray.

How many trays?

Project

Alice kept a tally of the traffic that passed her school.

1. Tell some things about her tally.

2. Make your own tally of the traffic by your school.

3. Make a bar graph.

4. Tell what your graph shows.

Traffic that passed by	
beetles	ЖЖ ЖЖ ЖЖ II
flies	ЖЖ II
frogs	ЖЖ ЖЖ II
flying fish	ЖЖ I
bumble bees	ЖЖ III

Divide.

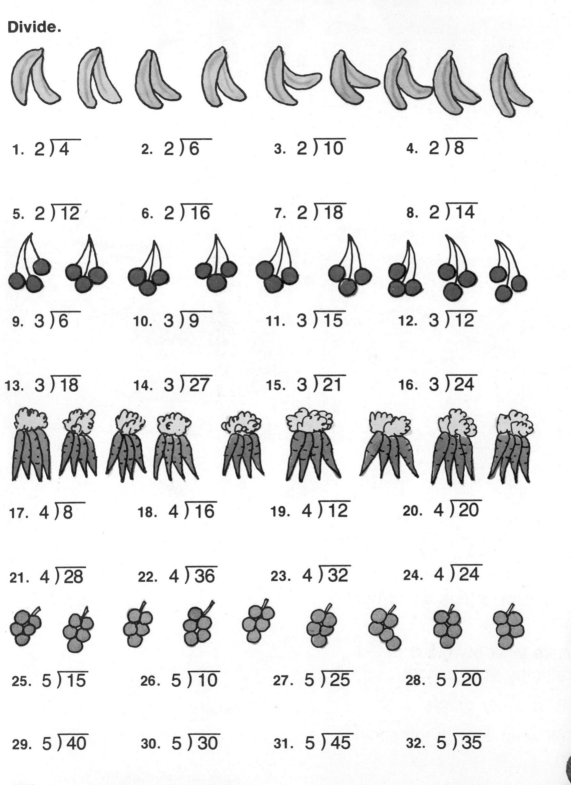

1. 2)4̄

2. 2)6̄

3. 2)1̄0̄

4. 2)8̄

5. 2)1̄2̄

6. 2)1̄6̄

7. 2)1̄8̄

8. 2)1̄4̄

9. 3)6̄

10. 3)9̄

11. 3)1̄5̄

12. 3)1̄2̄

13. 3)1̄8̄

14. 3)2̄7̄

15. 3)2̄1̄

16. 3)2̄4̄

17. 4)8̄

18. 4)1̄6̄

19. 4)1̄2̄

20. 4)2̄0̄

21. 4)2̄8̄

22. 4)3̄6̄

23. 4)3̄2̄

24. 4)2̄4̄

25. 5)1̄5̄

26. 5)1̄0̄

27. 5)2̄5̄

28. 5)2̄0̄

29. 5)4̄0̄

30. 5)3̄0̄

31. 5)4̄5̄

32. 5)3̄5̄

Give the correct signs.

1. $5 \oplus 3 = 2 \otimes 4$
2. $9 \, ? \, 3 = 1 \, ? \, 2$
3. $16 \, ? \, 4 = 10 \, ? \, 6$
4. $3 \, ? \, 2 = 13 \, ? \, 7$
5. $15 \, ? \, 3 = 13 \, ? \, 8$
6. $12 \, ? \, 3 = 3 \, ? \, 1$
7. $8 \, ? \, 0 = 6 \, ? \, 6$
8. $8 \, ? \, 2 = 0 \, ? \, 4$
9. $11 \, ? \, 4 = 28 \, ? \, 4$
10. $6 \, ? \, 6 = 5 \, ? \, 0$
11. $3 \, ? \, 5 = 9 \, ? \, 1$
12. $5 \, ? \, 3 = 2 \, ? \, 4$
13. $27 \, ? \, 3 = 14 \, ? \, 5$
14. $11 \, ? \, 3 = 1 \, ? \, 7$
15. $18 \, ? \, 3 = 9 \, ? \, 3$
16. $36 \, ? \, 4 = 18 \, ? \, 9$
17. $24 \, ? \, 3 = 2 \, ? \, 4$
18. $4 \, ? \, 3 = 10 \, ? \, 3$
19. $8 \, ? \, 8 = 9 \, ? \, 0$
20. $6 \, ? \, 6 = 3 \, ? \, 4$

a b c d   a b c d   a b c d   a b c d   a b c d
14   34   14   4   30
a b c d   c d   a b c d
15   31
a b c Standardized Format   a b c   a b c d

MAJOR CHECKUP

Give the correct letter.

1. In 5 + 3 = 8, the sum is

a. 5
b. 3
c. 8
d. none of these

2. Complete.

6 + ? = 9

a. 15
b. 6
c. 3
d. none of these

3. Add.

4
3
+8

a. 16
b. 15
c. 17
d. 18

4. The 6 in 368 stands for what number?

a. 6
b. 600
c. 60
d. none of these

5. Which number is the smallest?

a. 794
b. 749
c. 947
d. 479

6. 274 rounded to the nearest hundred is

a. 270
b. 200
c. 300
d. none of these

7. Six hundred six is

a. 6660
b. 6606
c. 6066
d. none of these

8. How much money?

1 dollar
2 dimes
3 pennies

a. $1.50
b. $1.05
c. $1.23
d. none of these

9. Add.

729
+386

a. 1115
b. 1005
c. 1015
d. none of these

10. What time is shown?

a. 10:30
b. 6:50
c. 11:30
d. none of these

11. Which is the most money?

a. 2 quarters and 2 dimes
b. 6 dimes
c. 3 quarters
d. 7 dimes and 2 nickels

12. In 4 × 3 = 12, 12 is called the

a. addend
b. sum
c. product
d. none of these

190 (one hundred ninety)

8
Fractions

Fractions and regions

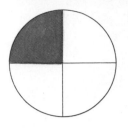

1 part is blue.
4 equal parts.

$\frac{1}{4}$ is blue.
One fourth is blue.

5 parts are red.
6 equal parts.

$\frac{5}{6}$ is red.
Five sixths is red.

EXERCISES
What fraction is shaded?

1.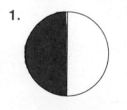

2.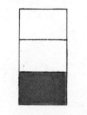

3.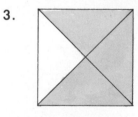

4.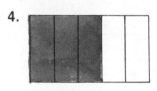

5.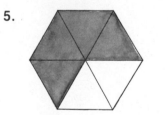

6.

7.

8.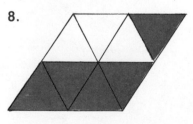

9.

What fraction is red?

10.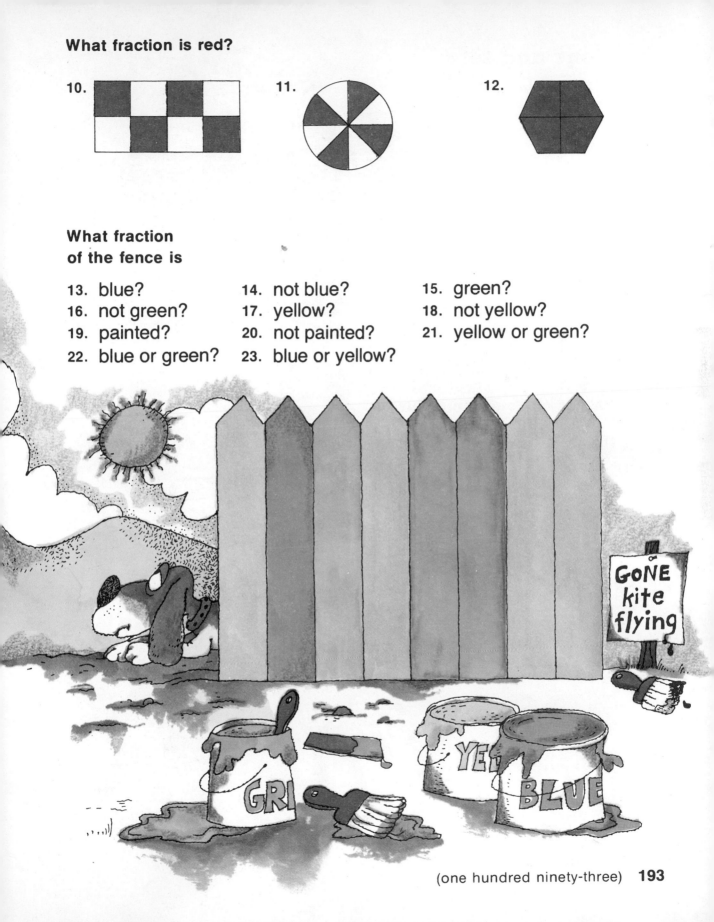

11.

12.

What fraction of the fence is

13. blue?
14. not blue?
15. green?
16. not green?
17. yellow?
18. not yellow?
19. painted?
20. not painted?
21. yellow or green?
22. blue or green?
23. blue or yellow?

GONE
kite
flying

Fractions and sets

2 shoes are blue.
5 shoes in all.

$\frac{2}{5}$ of the shoes are blue.

EXERCISES
What fraction of the toys are blue?

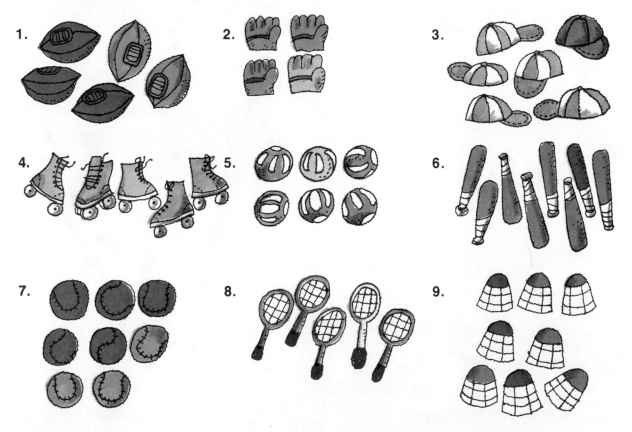

1.

2.

3.

4.

5.

6.

7.

8.

9.

What fraction of the helmets are

10. yellow?
11. green?
12. red?
13. orange?

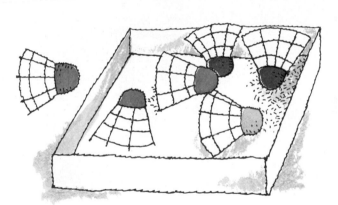

What fraction of the birdies are

14. outside the box?
15. inside the box?
16. blue?
17. green?
18. red?

What fraction of the buttons are

19. large?
20. small?
21. green?
22. blue?
23. yellow?
24. red?
25. in the box?
26. out of the box?
27. four-hole?
28. two-hole?
29. large and yellow?
30. small and green?

Problem solving

EXERCISES
What fraction of the puppies are

1. yellow?
2. black?
3. spotted?
4. being held?
5. in the box?
6. out of the box?
7. eating?
8. not eating?

196 (one hundred ninety-six)

Our Pet Graph

Look at the graph to answer the following questions.
How many

9. cats?   10. dogs?   11. fish?
12. birds?   13. pets in all?
14. How many more dogs than cats?
15. How many fewer birds than dogs?

What fraction of the pets are

16. cats?   17. dogs?
18. fish?   19. birds?
20. not dogs?   21. not cats?

Fraction of a number

To find $\frac{1}{2}$,

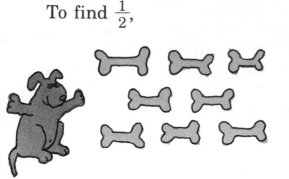

divide by 2.

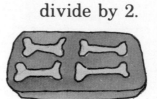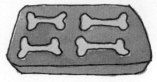

$\frac{1}{2}$ of 8 = 4

To find $\frac{1}{3}$,

divide by 3.

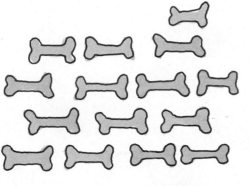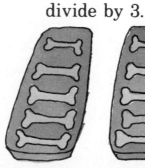

$\frac{1}{3}$ of 15 = 5

EXERCISES
Complete.

1. $\frac{1}{2}$ of 6 = ?

2. $\frac{1}{3}$ of 6 = ?

3. $\frac{1}{4}$ of 8 = ?

4. $\frac{1}{3}$ of 9 = ?

5. $\frac{1}{2}$ of 10 = ?

6. $\frac{1}{4}$ of 16 = ?

Complete.

7. $\frac{1}{2}$ of 8 = _?_

8. $\frac{1}{5}$ of 5 = _?_

9. $\frac{1}{3}$ of 18 = _?_

10. $\frac{1}{6}$ of 12 = _?_

11. $\frac{1}{4}$ of 8 = _?_

12. $\frac{1}{8}$ of 24 = _?_

13. $\frac{1}{3}$ of 21 = _?_

14. $\frac{1}{8}$ of 16 = _?_

15. $\frac{1}{2}$ of 16 = _?_

16. $\frac{1}{5}$ of 10 = _?_

17. $\frac{1}{2}$ of 14 = _?_

18. $\frac{1}{5}$ of 35 = _?_

19. $\frac{1}{8}$ of 40 = _?_

20. $\frac{1}{5}$ of 15 = _?_

21. $\frac{1}{3}$ of 24 = _?_

22. $\frac{1}{6}$ of 30 = _?_

23. $\frac{1}{2}$ of 12 = _?_

24. $\frac{1}{6}$ of 18 = _?_

25. $\frac{1}{4}$ of 24 = _?_

26. $\frac{1}{4}$ of 32 = _?_

27. $\frac{1}{3}$ of 27 = _?_

28. $\frac{1}{4}$ of 28 = _?_

29. $\frac{1}{6}$ of 24 = _?_

30. $\frac{1}{8}$ of 32 = _?_

Solve.

31. Had 24¢.
    Spent $\frac{1}{3}$ of it.
    How much was spent?

32. Had 36¢.
    Gave $\frac{1}{4}$ of it away.
    How much was given away?

33. Had 32¢.
    Spent $\frac{1}{4}$ of it.
    How much was left?

34. Had 24¢.
    Spent $\frac{1}{6}$ of it.
    How much was left?

Who am I?

★ 35. If you take $\frac{1}{2}$ of me and then add 2, you get 6.

36. If you take $\frac{1}{3}$ of me ★ and then subtract 1, you get 7.

Problem solving

EXERCISES
Complete.

Regular price	Amount off	Sale price
1. 24¢	$\frac{1}{4}$ of 24¢ = _6_¢	$\begin{array}{r}24\\-6\\\hline 18\end{array}$ _18_¢
2. 36¢	$\frac{1}{4}$ of 36¢ = _?_¢	_?_¢
3. 8¢	$\frac{1}{2}$ of 8¢ = _?_¢	_?_¢
4. 16¢	$\frac{1}{2}$ of 16¢ = _?_¢	_?_¢
5. 18¢	$\frac{1}{3}$ of 18¢ = _?_¢	_?_¢
6. 27¢	$\frac{1}{3}$ of 27¢ = _?_¢	_?_¢

Complete.

	Regular price	Amount off	Sale price
7.	32¢	$\frac{1}{4}$ of 32¢ = $\underline{?}$ ¢	$\underline{?}$ ¢
8.	35¢	$\frac{1}{5}$ of 35¢ = $\underline{?}$ ¢	$\underline{?}$ ¢
9.	24¢	$\frac{1}{8}$ of 24¢ = $\underline{?}$ ¢	$\underline{?}$ ¢
10.	24¢	$\frac{1}{6}$ of 24¢ = $\underline{?}$ ¢	$\underline{?}$ ¢
11.	21¢	$\frac{1}{3}$ of 21¢ = $\underline{?}$ ¢	$\underline{?}$ ¢
12.	32¢	$\frac{1}{8}$ of 32¢ = $\underline{?}$ ¢	$\underline{?}$ ¢
13.	14¢	$\frac{1}{2}$ of 14¢ = $\underline{?}$ ¢	$\underline{?}$ ¢
14.	48¢	$\frac{1}{6}$ of 48¢ = $\underline{?}$ ¢	$\underline{?}$ ¢
15.	45¢	$\frac{1}{5}$ of 45¢ = $\underline{?}$ ¢	$\underline{?}$ ¢

Give each sale price.

16. Regular price:
    Sale: $\frac{1}{4}$ off — 28¢

17. Regular price:
    Sale: $\frac{1}{3}$ off — 24¢

18. Regular price:
    Sale: $\frac{1}{5}$ off — 30¢

19. Regular price:
    Sale: $\frac{1}{8}$ off — 40¢

Equivalent fractions

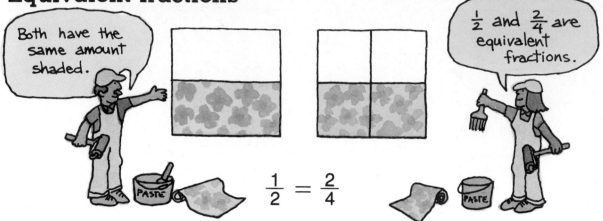

Both have the same amount shaded.

$\frac{1}{2}$ and $\frac{2}{4}$ are equivalent fractions.

$$\frac{1}{2} = \frac{2}{4}$$

EXERCISES

Complete.

1.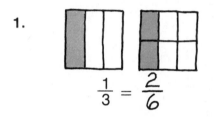

$$\frac{1}{3} = \frac{2}{6}$$

2.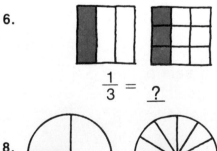

$$\frac{1}{2} = \underline{?}$$

3.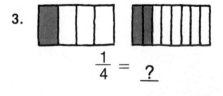

$$\frac{1}{4} = \underline{?}$$

4.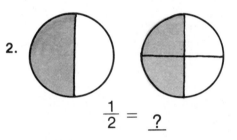

$$\frac{1}{5} = \underline{?}$$

5.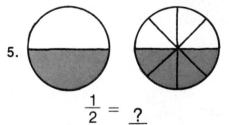

$$\frac{1}{2} = \underline{?}$$

6.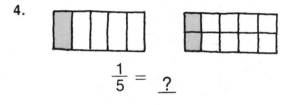

$$\frac{1}{3} = \underline{?}$$

7.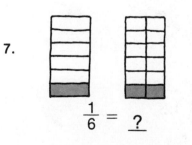

$$\frac{1}{6} = \underline{?}$$

8.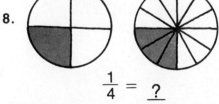

$$\frac{1}{4} = \underline{?}$$

Give two equivalent fractions.

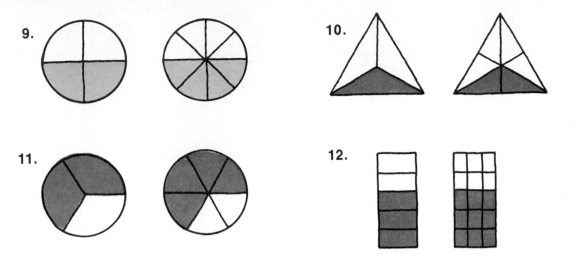

9.

10.

11.

12.

Complete. If you need to, draw pictures.

13. $\frac{1}{2} = \frac{?}{4}$ 14. $\frac{1}{2} = \frac{?}{6}$ 15. $\frac{1}{2} = \frac{?}{8}$ 16. $\frac{1}{2} = \frac{?}{10}$

17. $\frac{1}{3} = \frac{?}{6}$ 18. $\frac{1}{3} = \frac{?}{9}$ 19. $\frac{1}{3} = \frac{?}{12}$ 20. $\frac{1}{3} = \frac{?}{15}$

21. $\frac{1}{4} = \frac{?}{8}$ 22. $\frac{1}{4} = \frac{?}{12}$ 23. $\frac{1}{4} = \frac{?}{16}$ 24. $\frac{1}{4} = \frac{?}{20}$

25. $\frac{2}{3} = \frac{?}{6}$ 26. $\frac{2}{3} = \frac{?}{9}$ 27. $\frac{2}{3} = \frac{?}{12}$ 28. $\frac{2}{3} = \frac{?}{15}$

Keeping Skills Sharp

1.	593 − 258	2.	745 − 329	3.	852 − 171	4.	819 − 420	5.	635 − 254
6.	621 − 435	7.	830 − 666	8.	523 − 155	9.	742 − 374	10.	945 − 259
11.	302 − 154	12.	506 − 378	13.	708 − 249	14.	300 − 126	15.	900 − 358

Comparing fractions

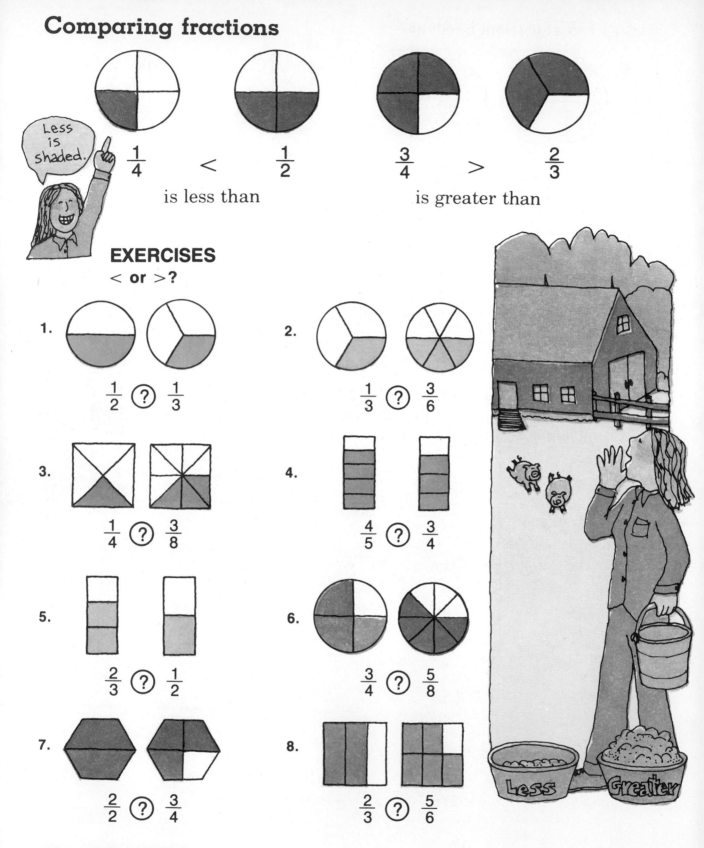

Less is shaded.

$\frac{1}{4}$ < $\frac{1}{2}$

is less than

$\frac{3}{4}$ > $\frac{2}{3}$

is greater than

EXERCISES

< or >?

1. $\frac{1}{2}$ (?) $\frac{1}{3}$

2. $\frac{1}{3}$ (?) $\frac{3}{6}$

3. $\frac{1}{4}$ (?) $\frac{3}{8}$

4. $\frac{4}{5}$ (?) $\frac{3}{4}$

5. $\frac{2}{3}$ (?) $\frac{1}{2}$

6. $\frac{3}{4}$ (?) $\frac{5}{8}$

7. $\frac{2}{2}$ (?) $\frac{3}{4}$

8. $\frac{2}{3}$ (?) $\frac{5}{6}$

Less   Greater

< or >? (Hint: Use the picture.)

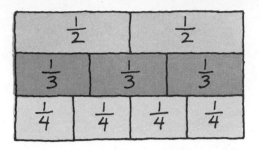

9. $\frac{1}{2}$ (?) $\frac{1}{3}$ 10. $\frac{1}{2}$ (?) $\frac{1}{4}$

11. $\frac{1}{3}$ (?) $\frac{1}{2}$ 12. $\frac{1}{3}$ (?) $\frac{1}{4}$

13. $\frac{1}{4}$ (?) $\frac{1}{2}$ 14. $\frac{1}{4}$ (?) $\frac{1}{3}$

15. $\frac{1}{3}$ (?) $\frac{1}{6}$ 16. $\frac{1}{3}$ (?) $\frac{1}{8}$

17. $\frac{1}{6}$ (?) $\frac{1}{3}$ 18. $\frac{1}{6}$ (?) $\frac{1}{8}$

19. $\frac{1}{8}$ (?) $\frac{1}{3}$ 20. $\frac{1}{8}$ (?) $\frac{1}{6}$

21. $\frac{1}{3}$ (?) $\frac{3}{8}$ 22. $\frac{1}{6}$ (?) $\frac{2}{8}$

23. $\frac{2}{3}$ (?) $\frac{5}{8}$ 24. $\frac{7}{8}$ (?) $\frac{5}{6}$

Solve.

25. Jon and Jennifer each had 24¢. Jon spent $\frac{1}{2}$ of his money. Jennifer spent $\frac{1}{3}$ of hers. Who spent more money?

26. Jill and Alan won a pie. Jill ate $\frac{1}{3}$ of the pie. Alan ate $\frac{1}{4}$ of it. Who ate less pie?

27. Maria knocked down $\frac{1}{2}$ of the pins. George knocked down $\frac{1}{6}$ of the pins. Who knocked down more pins?

Problem solving

A baker makes cakes, pies, bread, cookies, and doughnuts. Cookies and doughnuts are often priced by the dozen.

1 dozen = 12

EXERCISES

1. How many doughnuts in $\frac{1}{2}$ dozen?

   $\frac{1}{2}$ of $12 = ?$

2. How many doughnuts in $\frac{1}{3}$ dozen?

3. How many cookies in $\frac{1}{4}$ dozen?

4. Which would cost less, $\frac{1}{3}$ dozen cookies or $\frac{1}{2}$ dozen cookies?

5. Which would you rather have, $\frac{1}{2}$ dozen cupcakes or $\frac{1}{4}$ dozen cupcakes?

Give the total price.

6.

7.

8.

9.

How much money will be left?

10. You have $1.00.

    You buy

11. You have $3.00.

    You buy

12. You have $1.60.

    You buy

13. You have $1.32.

    You buy

What fraction is shaded? [pages 191–193]

1.

2.

3.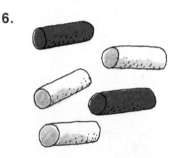

What fraction of the objects are red? [pages 194–197]

4.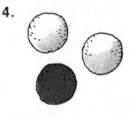

5.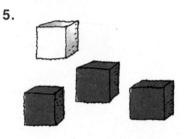

6.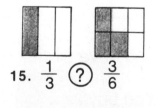

Complete. [pages 198–199]

7. $\frac{1}{2}$ of 6 = __?__

8. $\frac{1}{4}$ of 12 = __?__

9. $\frac{1}{3}$ of 18 = __?__

10. $\frac{1}{6}$ of 30 = __?__

11. $\frac{1}{8}$ of 24 = __?__

12. $\frac{1}{5}$ of 25 = __?__

<, =, or >? [pages 202–205]

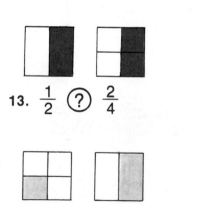

13. $\frac{1}{2}$ ⓪ $\frac{2}{4}$

14. $\frac{1}{3}$ ⓪ $\frac{1}{4}$

15. $\frac{1}{3}$ ⓪ $\frac{3}{6}$

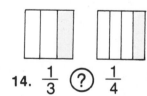

16. $\frac{1}{4}$ ⓪ $\frac{1}{2}$

17. $\frac{1}{3}$ ⓪ $\frac{1}{5}$

18. $\frac{1}{8}$ ⓪ $\frac{1}{6}$

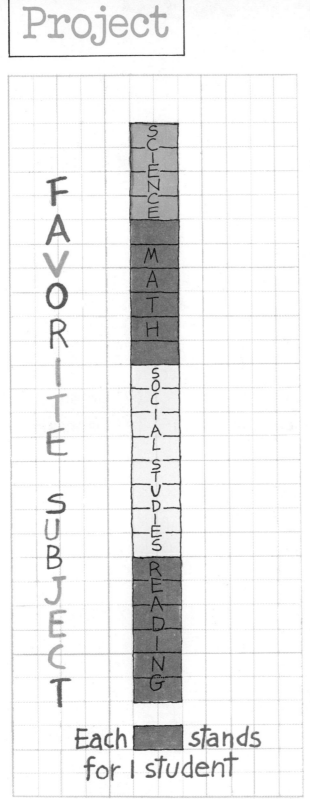

Project

FAVORITE SUBJECT

SCIENCE

MATH

SOCIAL STUDIES

READING

Each ▨ stands for I student

Use the graph to answer the questions.

1. How many students in the class?

2. How many students' favorite subject is
   a. reading?
   b. science?
   c. social studies?
   d. math?

3. a. What fraction of the students like science best?
   b. What fraction like reading best?
   c. What fraction like social studies best?

4. a. Make a "favorite subject" graph for your class.
   b. What fraction of your class has math as favorite subject?
   c. What fraction of your class likes reading best?
   d. Tell some other things that your graph shows.

CHAPTER REVIEW

What fraction is blue?

1.
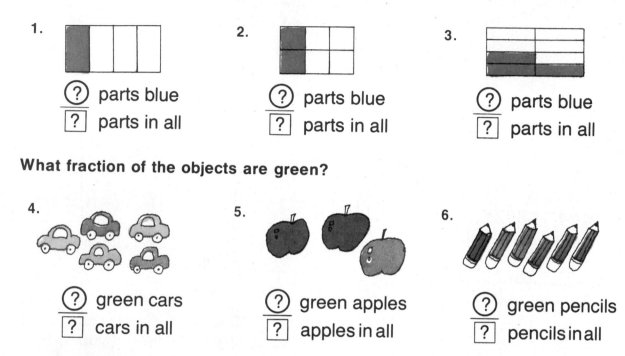

$\dfrac{?}{?}$ parts blue

parts in all

2.

$\dfrac{?}{?}$ parts blue

parts in all

3.

$\dfrac{?}{?}$ parts blue

parts in all

What fraction of the objects are green?

4.

$\dfrac{?}{?}$ green cars

cars in all

5.

$\dfrac{?}{?}$ green apples

apples in all

6.

$\dfrac{?}{?}$ green pencils

pencils in all

Complete.

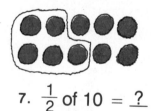

7. $\dfrac{1}{2}$ of 10 = $\underline{?}$

8. $\dfrac{1}{4}$ of 8 = $\underline{?}$

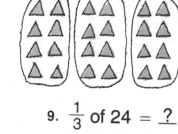

9. $\dfrac{1}{3}$ of 24 = $\underline{?}$

<, =, or >?

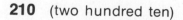

10. $\dfrac{1}{2}$ ⃝ $\dfrac{1}{3}$

11. $\dfrac{2}{4}$ ⃝ $\dfrac{1}{2}$

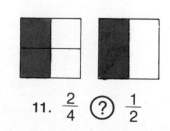

12. $\dfrac{1}{4}$ ⃝ $\dfrac{4}{8}$

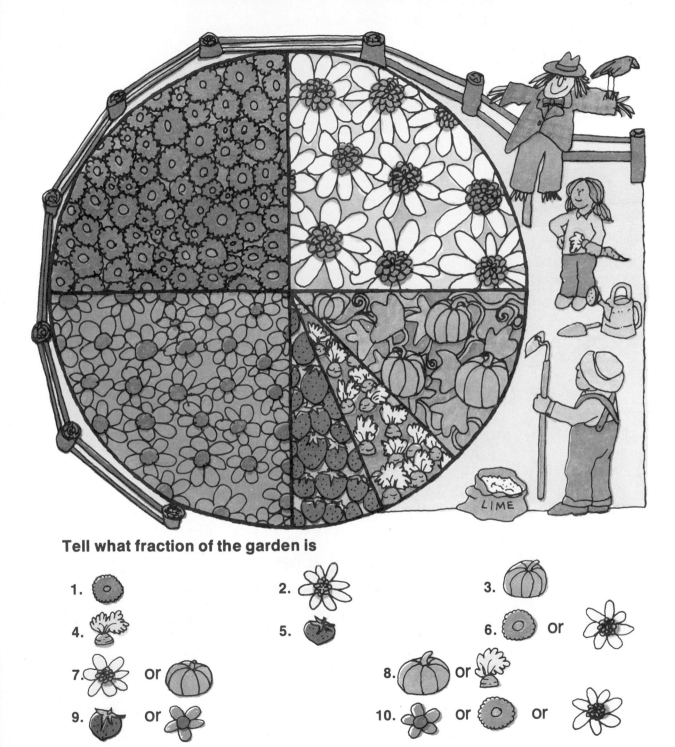

Tell what fraction of the garden is

1.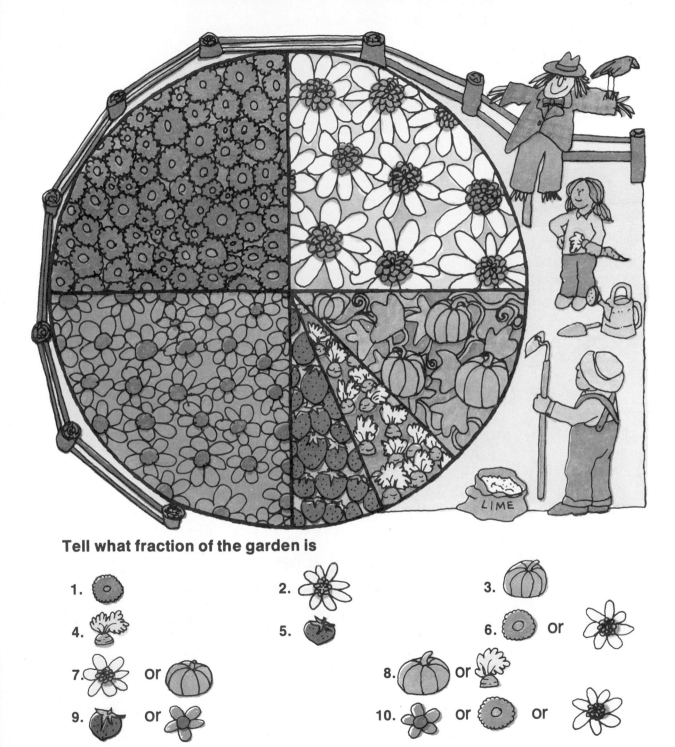

2.

3.

4.

5.

6. or

7. or

8. or

9. or

10. or or

MAJOR CHECKUP
Standardized Format

Give the correct letter.

1. Add.

7
2
+8

    a. 16
    b. 17
    c. 18
    d. none of these

2. Which letter is the fifth letter?

ARITHMETIC

    a. T
    b. M
    c. E
    d. H

3. Which number is the greatest?

    a. 756
    b. 576
    c. 765
    d. 675

4. Three thousand forty-four is

    a. 3044
    b. 3404
    c. 3440
    d. none of these

5. Add.

75
29
+68

    a. 152
    b. 172
    c. 162
    d. none of these

6. Subtract.

624
−358

    a. 334
    b. 376
    c. 366
    d. 266

7. What time is shown?

    a. 4:30
    b. 3:30
    c. 6:20
    d. none of these

8. How much money?

2 quarters
1 dime
2 nickels
1 penny

    a. 71¢
    b. 67¢
    c. 91¢
    d. 80¢

9. How much money?

1 dollar
1 half-dollar
1 quarter
1 nickel
3 pennies

    a. $2.03
    b. $1.58
    c. $2.08
    d. $1.83

10. Multiply.

4
×7

    a. 24
    b. 28
    c. 32
    d. none of these

11. Divide.

$3 \overline{)24}$

    a. 6
    b. 9
    c. 7
    d. none of these

12. Divide.

$4 \overline{)27}$

    a. 3 R6
    b. 8 R3
    c. 6 R3
    d. none of these

9 Measurement

Centimeter

The **centimeter** is a unit for measuring length
in the metric system.
Here is a centimeter ruler.

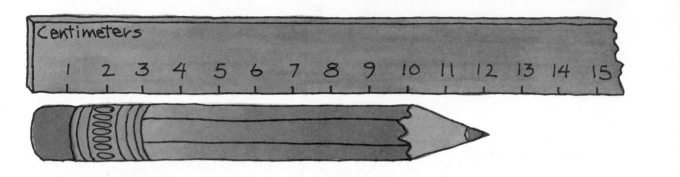

The pencil is between 12 and 13 centimeters (cm) long.
It is nearer 12 cm.
It is about 12 cm long.

EXERCISES

About how long is each pencil?
Measure with a centimeter ruler.

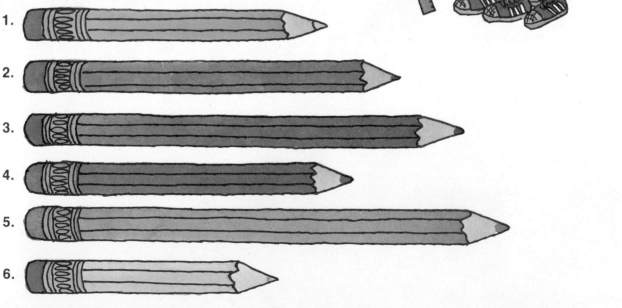

1.

2.

3.

4.

5.

6.

Measure each segment with a centimeter ruler.

7. _____   8. _____

9. _____   10. _____

Draw segments with these lengths.

11. 3 cm   12. 8 cm   13. 11 cm   14. 16 cm

15. 10 cm   16. 13 cm   17. 18 cm   18. 21 cm

Measure with a centimeter ruler

19. the width of your math book.

20. the length of your shoe.

21. the thickness of your desk top.

22. the height of your desk.

23. your height.

Centimeters and meters

The **meter** is used to measure longer lengths. The picture shows some children measuring a basketball court.

1 meter (m) = 100 centimeters (cm)

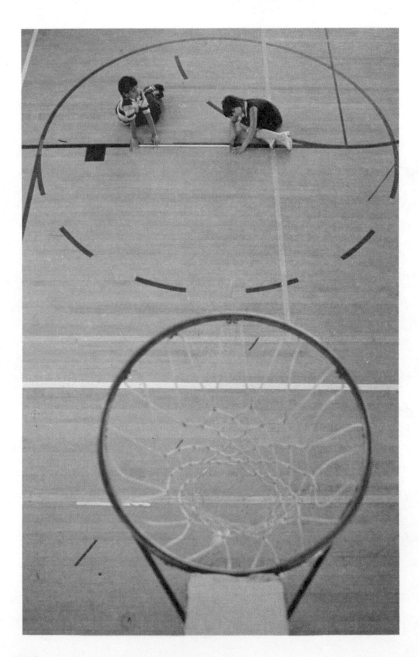

Complete. If you need to, look at a meter stick.

1. 1 m = _?_ cm

2. 2 m = _?_ cm

3. 3 m = _?_ cm

4. 6 m = _?_ cm

5. 8 m = _?_ cm

6. 9 m = _?_ cm

7. 7 m = _?_ cm

8. 100 cm = _?_ m

9. 400 cm = _?_ m

10. 700 cm = _?_ m

11. 800 cm = _?_ m

12. 500 cm = _?_ m

13. 200 cm = _?_ m

14. 600 cm = _?_ m

★15. 1000 cm = _?_ m

Measure with a meter stick

16. the width of the door.

17. the length of the chalkboard.

18. the height of the chalkboard.

19. the length of the room.

20. the width of the room.

21. the height of the ceiling.

Keeping Skills Sharp

Write the number.

1. eleven
2. seventy
3. forty-six
4. sixty-nine
5. two hundred five
6. five hundred twenty-three
7. three thousand ninety
8. one thousand seven
9. eight thousand two hundred fifty
10. nine thousand four hundred sixty-one

Perimeter

The distance around a figure is called the **perimeter** of the figure.

The perimeter of this rectangle is 18 cm. To find a perimeter, you can add the lengths of the sides.

EXERCISES
Give the perimeter.

1.

2.

3.

4.

5.

6.

7.

Centimeters

1 2 3 4 5 6

The length of each side is given. Find the perimeter.

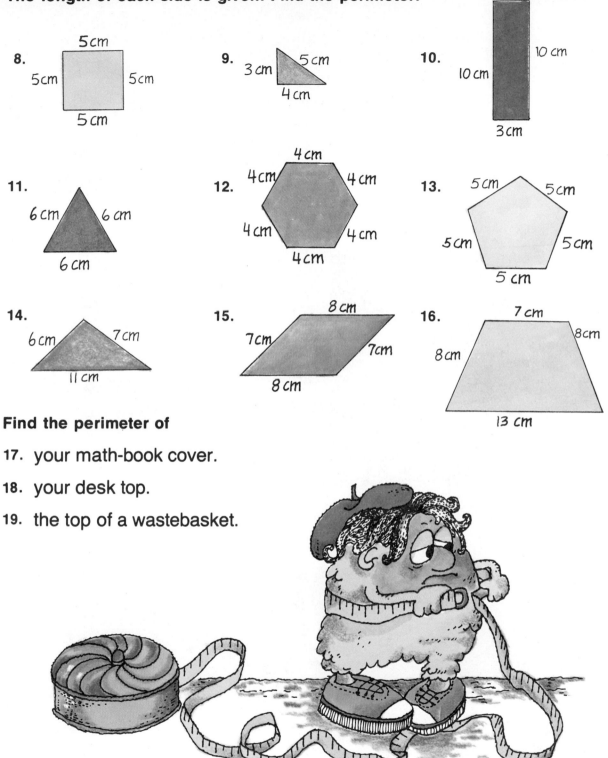

8. 5cm / 5cm / 5cm / 5cm

9. 3cm / 5cm / 4cm

10. 3cm / 10cm / 10cm / 3cm

11. 6cm / 6cm / 6cm

12. 4cm / 4cm / 4cm / 4cm / 4cm / 4cm

13. 5cm / 5cm / 5cm / 5cm / 5cm

14. 6cm / 7cm / 11cm

15. 8cm / 7cm / 7cm / 8cm

16. 7cm / 8cm / 8cm / 13cm

Find the perimeter of

17. your math-book cover.

18. your desk top.

19. the top of a wastebasket.

Area

To find the **area** of the blue region, we can count the **square centimeter** tiles that it takes to cover the region.

square centimeter

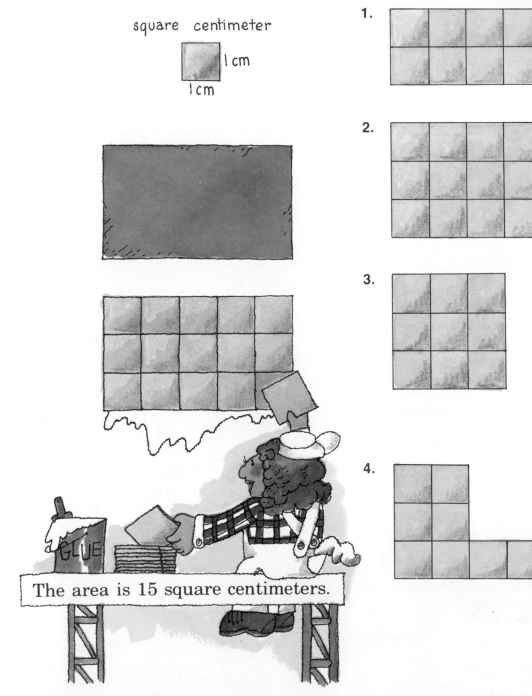

1 cm
1 cm

The area is 15 square centimeters.

EXERCISES
Give each area.

1.

2.

3.

4.

These pieces were cut from graph paper. Each square is one square centimeter. Give each area.

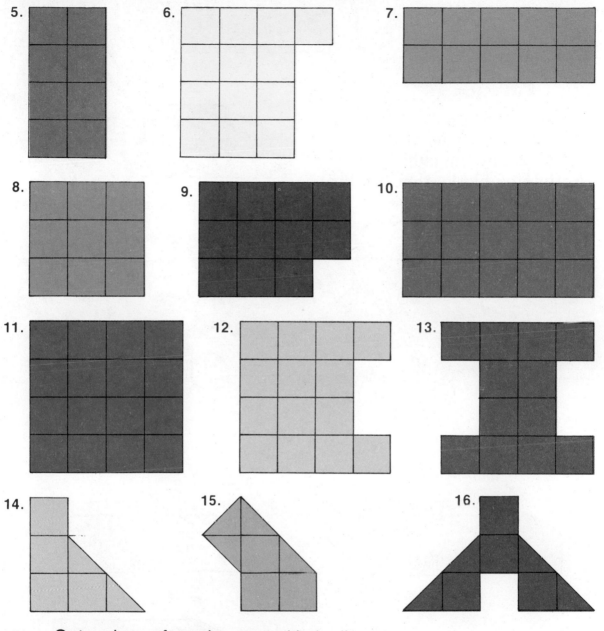

5.

6.

7.

8.

9.

10.

11.

12.

13.

14.

15.

16.

17. a. Get a piece of graph paper with the lines one centimeter apart.
 b. Trace around your hand.
 c. Find the area of your hand print.

18. Find the area of your footprint.

Volume

cubic centimeter

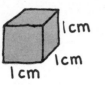

1 cm
1 cm
1 cm

To find the **volume** of this box, we can count the **cubic centimeter** blocks that it takes to fill the box.

The volume is 8 cubic centimeters.

EXERCISES
Give the volume of each box.

1.

2.

3.

4.

Liquid measure

The **liter** is a unit used for measuring liquids.

1 liter = 1000 cubic centimeters

← 10 cm →

1. a. Get some containers and a liter container.
   b. Guess whether each container holds less than a liter, more than a liter, or just a liter.
   c. Check your guesses.
   d. Order your containers from smallest to largest.

2. a. Get a paper cup. Keep a record of how many paper cups of water you drink in a day.
   b. Do you drink more or less than a liter of water in a day?

Measuring weight

The **kilogram** (kg) is used for measuring weight. A liter of water weighs about 1 kg.

EXERCISES
Give each weight.

1.

2.

3.

4.

5.

6.

Get a kilogram scale.

7. Weigh some objects.

8. Find an object that weighs about 1 kg.

9. Weigh yourself on a kilogram scale.

Measuring temperature

The **degree Celsius** (°C) is a unit for measuring **temperature**.

This thermometer shows a temperature reading of 24°C.

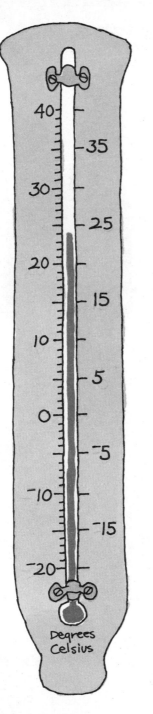

Give each temperature.

1.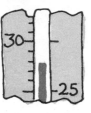

2.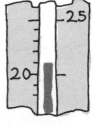

3.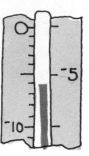

Get a Celsius thermometer. What is the temperature

4. inside your classroom?
5. outdoors?

Inch

In the customary system, the **inch** is used to measure length.

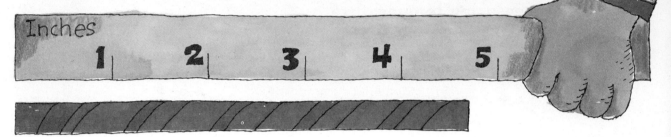

The straw is between 4 and 5 inches (in.) long.
It is nearer 5 in.
It is about 5 in. long.

EXERCISES

About how long is each straw?
Measure with an inch ruler.

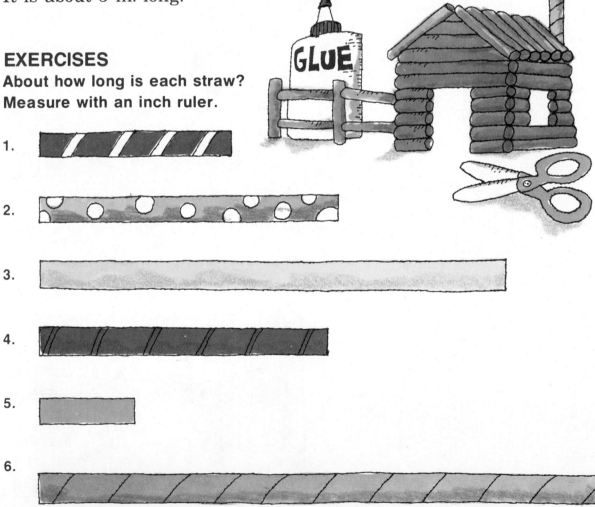

1.

2.

3.

4.

5.

6.

Measure each segment in inches.

7.

8.

9.

10.

Draw segments of

11. 2 in.
12. 3 in.
13. 6 in.
14. 1 in.
15. 5 in.
16. 7 in.
17. 4 in.
18. 8 in.

Measure with an inch ruler.

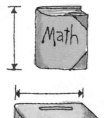

19. the height of your math book

20. the width of your desk top

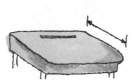

21. the length of your desk top

22. the height of your desk top

23. your height

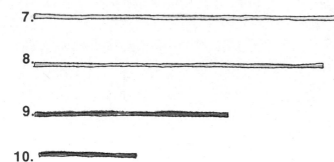

Half-inch

This ruler is marked in half-inches.

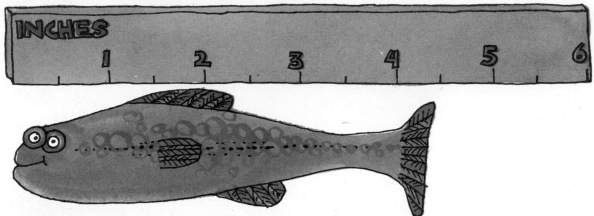

The fish is between 4 and 5 inches long.

It is nearer $4\frac{1}{2}$ (4 and $\frac{1}{2}$) inches long.

The fish is about $4\frac{1}{2}$ in. long.

EXERCISES

About how long is each object?
Measure with a half-inch ruler.

1.

2.

3.

4.

5.

6.

7.

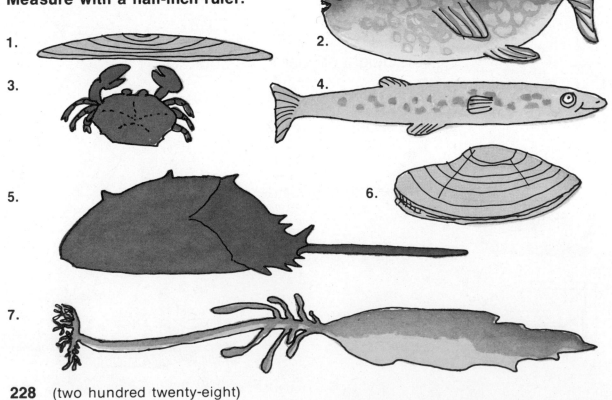

Measure each segment.

8. _____ 9. _____

10. _____ 11. _____

Draw segments with these lengths.

12. 3 in. 13. $3\frac{1}{2}$ in. 14. 4 in. 15. $4\frac{1}{2}$ in.

16. $7\frac{1}{2}$ in. 17. 5 in. 18. 6 in. 19. $5\frac{1}{2}$ in.

Measure with a half-inch ruler.

20. the length of your little finger
21. the width of your hand
22. the length of your arm span
23. your height

Inches, feet, and yards

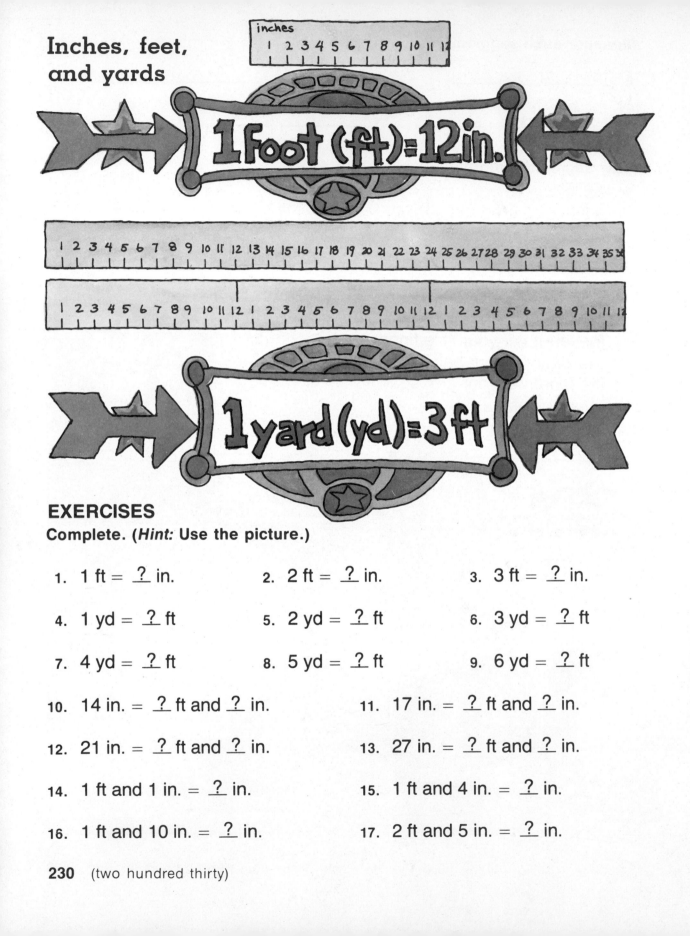

inches
1 2 3 4 5 6 7 8 9 10 11 12

1 foot (ft) = 12 in.

1 2 3 4 5 6 7 8 9 10 11 12 13 14 15 16 17 18 19 20 21 22 23 24 25 26 27 28 29 30 31 32 33 34 35 36

1 2 3 4 5 6 7 8 9 10 11 12 1 2 3 4 5 6 7 8 9 10 11 12 1 2 3 4 5 6 7 8 9 10 11 12

1 yard (yd) = 3 ft

EXERCISES

Complete. (*Hint:* Use the picture.)

1. 1 ft = _?_ in.

2. 2 ft = _?_ in.

3. 3 ft = _?_ in.

4. 1 yd = _?_ ft

5. 2 yd = _?_ ft

6. 3 yd = _?_ ft

7. 4 yd = _?_ ft

8. 5 yd = _?_ ft

9. 6 yd = _?_ ft

10. 14 in. = _?_ ft and _?_ in.

11. 17 in. = _?_ ft and _?_ in.

12. 21 in. = _?_ ft and _?_ in.

13. 27 in. = _?_ ft and _?_ in.

14. 1 ft and 1 in. = _?_ in.

15. 1 ft and 4 in. = _?_ in.

16. 1 ft and 10 in. = _?_ in.

17. 2 ft and 5 in. = _?_ in.

Measure in feet.

18. the width of the door

19. the height of the door

Measure in yards.

20. the length of the room

21. the width of the room

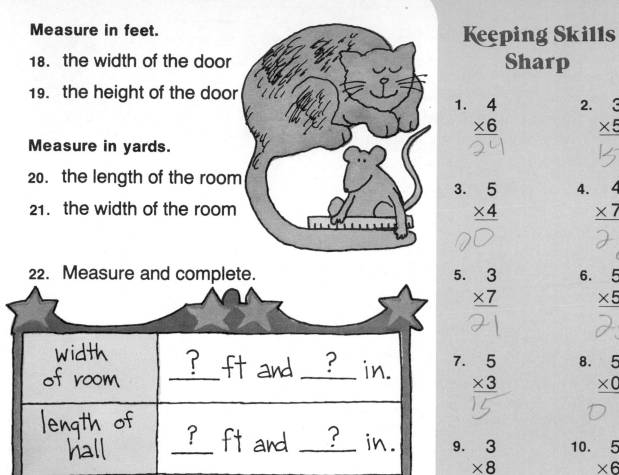

22. Measure and complete.

width of room	___ ft and ___ in.
length of hall	___ ft and ___ in.
length of chalkboard	___ ft and ___ in.
length of bulletin board	___ ft and ___ in.
length of sidewalk	___ yd and ___ ft
length of playground	___ yd and ___ ft

23. You may want to measure some other things.

Keeping Skills Sharp

1. $\begin{array}{r} 4 \\ \times 6 \\ \hline \end{array}$ 24

2. $\begin{array}{r} 3 \\ \times 5 \\ \hline \end{array}$ 15

3. $\begin{array}{r} 5 \\ \times 4 \\ \hline \end{array}$ 20

4. $\begin{array}{r} 4 \\ \times 7 \\ \hline \end{array}$ 28

5. $\begin{array}{r} 3 \\ \times 7 \\ \hline \end{array}$ 21

6. $\begin{array}{r} 5 \\ \times 5 \\ \hline \end{array}$ 25

7. $\begin{array}{r} 5 \\ \times 3 \\ \hline \end{array}$ 15

8. $\begin{array}{r} 5 \\ \times 0 \\ \hline \end{array}$ 0

9. $\begin{array}{r} 3 \\ \times 8 \\ \hline \end{array}$ 24

10. $\begin{array}{r} 5 \\ \times 6 \\ \hline \end{array}$ 30

11. $\begin{array}{r} 4 \\ \times 8 \\ \hline \end{array}$ 32

12. $\begin{array}{r} 4 \\ \times 5 \\ \hline \end{array}$ 20

13. $\begin{array}{r} 3 \\ \times 9 \\ \hline \end{array}$ 27

14. $\begin{array}{r} 3 \\ \times 4 \\ \hline \end{array}$ 12

15. $\begin{array}{r} 5 \\ \times 9 \\ \hline \end{array}$ 45

16. $\begin{array}{r} 3 \\ \times 6 \\ \hline \end{array}$ 18

17. $\begin{array}{r} 4 \\ \times 4 \\ \hline \end{array}$ 16

18. $\begin{array}{r} 5 \\ \times 8 \\ \hline \end{array}$ 40

Perimeter and area

The perimeter and area of the figure are given. The perimeter was measured in inches. The area was measured in **square inches**.

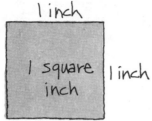

1 inch

1 square inch

1 inch

Inches

The perimeter is 8 inches.

The area is 4 square inches

EXERCISES
Give the perimeter and area of each figure.

1.

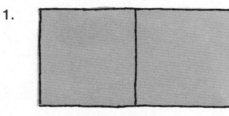

2.

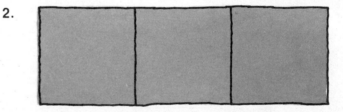

3.

4.

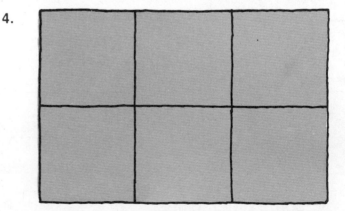

These rectangles were cut from graph paper. Each square is one square inch. Give the perimeter and area of each rectangle.

5.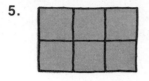

6.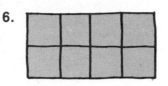

7.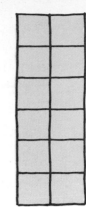

8.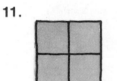

9.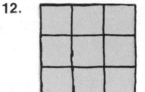

10.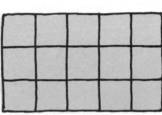

11.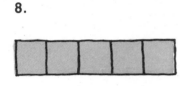

12.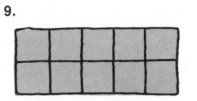

13.

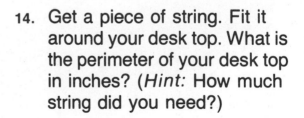

14. Get a piece of string. Fit it around your desk top. What is the perimeter of your desk top in inches? (*Hint:* How much string did you need?)

★ 15. See if you can find the area of your desk top in square inches.

Volume

The **cubic inch** is a unit for measuring volume.

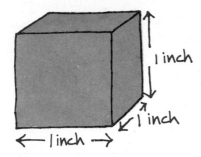

1 inch
1 inch
1 inch

We can find the volume of the box by counting the number of cubic-inch blocks it holds.

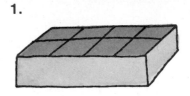

The volume is 9 cubic inches.

These boxes have been filled with cubic-inch blocks. Give each volume.

1.

2.

3.

4.

Liquid measure

Complete.

1. 2 pints = <u>?</u> quart
2. 2 c = <u>?</u> pt
3. 4 qt = <u>?</u> gal

4. 1 qt = <u>?</u> pt
5. 8 qt = <u>?</u> gal
6. 3 qt = <u>?</u> pt

7. 2 qt = <u>?</u> pt
8. 3 pt = <u>?</u> c
9. 2 gal = <u>?</u> qt

Which is more?

10. 3 pt or 1 qt
11. 3 qt or 1 gal
12. 3 c or 1 pt

13. 3 pt or 2 qt
14. 5 c or 2 pt
15. 5 qt or 1 gal

Complete.

16. 8 c = <u>?</u> qt
17. 8 pt = <u>?</u> gal
18. $\frac{1}{2}$ gal = <u>?</u> pt

19. $\frac{1}{2}$ gal = <u>?</u> qt
20. 12 pt = 1 gal and <u>?</u> qt

Measuring weight

In our customary system, the **pound** (lb) is a unit for measuring weight.

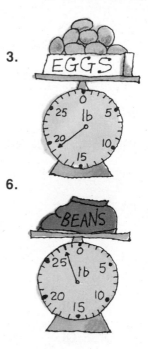

EXERCISES
Give each weight.

1.

2.

3.

4.

5.

6.

Get a pound scale.

7. Weigh some objects.

8. Guess the weights of some objects. Then check your guesses by weighing.

9. Weigh yourself on a pound scale.

Measuring temperature

The degree **Fahrenheit** (°F) is a unit for measuring temperature. This thermometer shows a reading of 62°F.

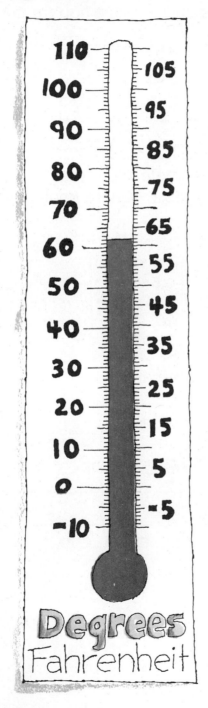

Degrees Fahrenheit

Give each temperature.

1.

2.

3.

Get a Fahrenheit thermometer. What is the temperature

4. inside your classroom?

5. outdoors?

Complete. [pages 213–229, 232–234, 236–237]

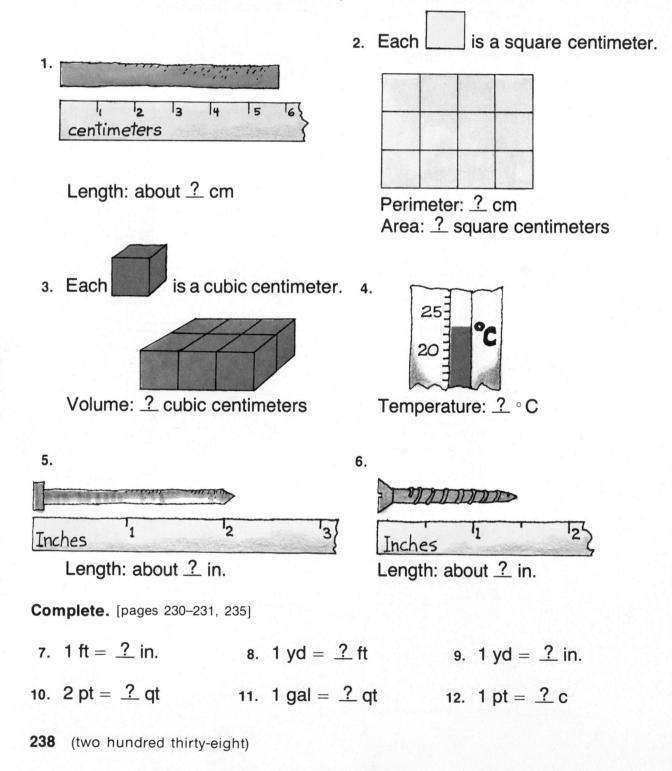

1. Length: about _?_ cm

2. Each ☐ is a square centimeter.

   Perimeter: _?_ cm
   Area: _?_ square centimeters

3. Each ☐ is a cubic centimeter.

   Volume: _?_ cubic centimeters

4. Temperature: _?_ °C

5. Inches

   Length: about _?_ in.

6. Inches

   Length: about _?_ in.

Complete. [pages 230–231, 235]

7. 1 ft = _?_ in.

8. 1 yd = _?_ ft

9. 1 yd = _?_ in.

10. 2 pt = _?_ qt

11. 1 gal = _?_ qt

12. 1 pt = _?_ c

Project

P:10
A:6

P:10
A:5

P:14
A:8

P:8
A:4

P:16
A:10

1. Get a piece of graph paper.
2. Color some regions.
3. Give the perimeter and area of each region.

CHAPTER REVIEW

Complete.

1.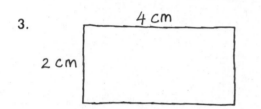

Length: about _?_ cm

2.

Length: about _?_ cm

3.

4 cm

2 cm

Perimeter: _?_ cm

4.

5 cm

3 cm

Perimeter: _?_ cm

5.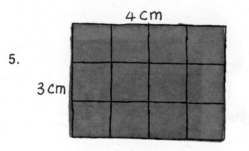

4 cm

3 cm

Area: _?_ square centimeters

6.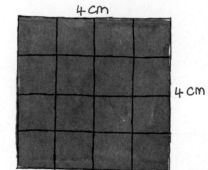

4 cm

4 cm

Area: _?_ square centimeters

7.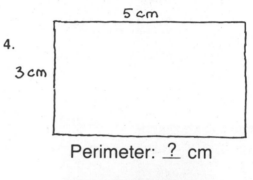

3 cm

2 cm

1 cm

Volume: _?_ cubic centimeters

8.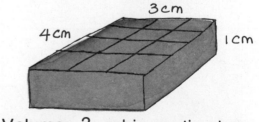

3 cm

4 cm

1 cm

Volume: _?_ cubic centimeters

CHAPTER CHALLENGE

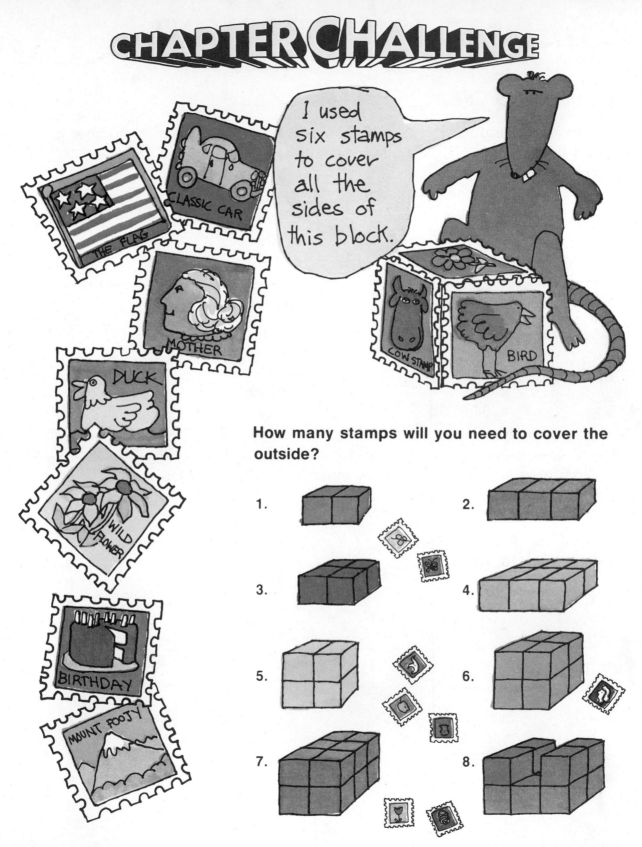

I used six stamps to cover all the sides of this block.

How many stamps will you need to cover the outside?

1.

2.

3.

4.

5.

6.

7.

8.

Form

14 a b c d   34 a b c d   14 a b c d   4 a b c d   30 a b c d
15 a b c d   c d   31   a b c d
                                    a b c d   a b c

MAJOR CHECKUP
Standardized Format

Give the correct letter.

1. Which numeral has a 4 in the tens place?

    a. 7934
    b. 9473
    c. 3749
    d. 4793

2. Six hundred twenty-eight is

    a. 682
    b. 608
    c. 628
    d. none of these

3. Which number is the smallest?

    a. 5605
    b. 3829
    c. 3759
    d. 3795

4. Add.

$$\begin{array}{r} 59 \\ 38 \\ +17 \\ \hline \end{array}$$

    a. 114
    b. 104
    c. 94
    d. none of these

5. Add.

$$\begin{array}{r} 759 \\ +386 \\ \hline \end{array}$$

    a. 1035
    b. 1045
    c. 1145
    d. none of these

6. Subtract.

$$\begin{array}{r} 535 \\ -276 \\ \hline \end{array}$$

    a. 261
    b. 259
    c. 347
    d. 359

7. What time is shown?

    a. 12:00
    b. 12:30
    c. 6:00
    d. none of these

8. How much money?

1 dollar
1 half-dollar
1 quarter
1 dime
1 nickel

    a. $1.65
    b. $1.76
    c. $1.81
    d. $1.90

9. Multiply.

$$\begin{array}{r} 4 \\ \times 7 \\ \hline \end{array}$$

    a. 24
    b. 21
    c. 29
    d. 28

10. Divide.

$4\overline{)18}$

    a. 3 R2
    b. 4 R2
    c. 5 R2
    d. 2 R4

11. Complete.

$\frac{1}{3}$ of $12 = \underline{\ ?\ }$

    a. 9
    b. 4
    c. 6
    d. 3

12. Complete.

$\frac{1}{2} = \underline{\ ?\ }$

    a. $\frac{1}{3}$
    b. $\frac{2}{3}$
    c. $\frac{1}{4}$
    d. $\frac{2}{4}$

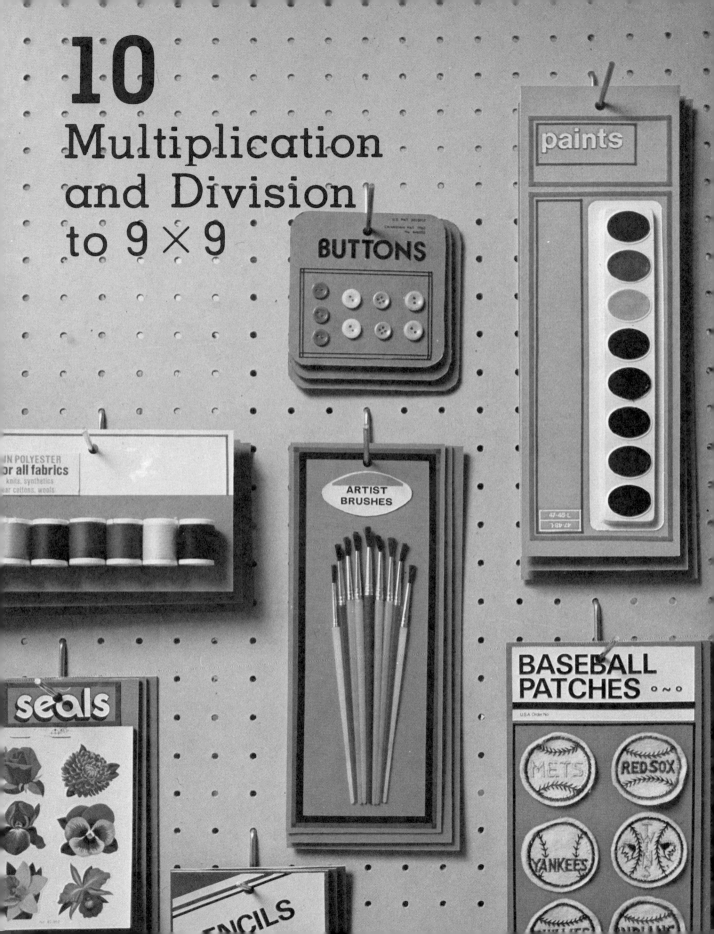

10
Multiplication and Division to 9 × 9

Multiplication review

1. $1 \times 0 = \underline{?}$

2. $2 \times 0 = \underline{?}$

3. $3 \times 0 = \underline{?}$

4. $4 \times 0 = \underline{?}$

5. $5 \times 0 = \underline{?}$

6. $6 \times 0 = \underline{?}$

7. $7 \times 0 = \underline{?}$

8. $8 \times 0 = \underline{?}$

9. $9 \times 0 = \underline{?}$

10. $1 \times 1 = \underline{?}$

11. $2 \times 1 = \underline{?}$

12. $3 \times 1 = \underline{?}$

13. $4 \times 1 = \underline{?}$

14. $5 \times 1 = \underline{?}$

15. $6 \times 1 = \underline{?}$

16. $7 \times 1 = \underline{?}$

17. $8 \times 1 = \underline{?}$

18. $9 \times 1 = \underline{?}$

19. $1 \times 2 = \underline{?}$

20. $2 \times 2 = \underline{?}$

21. $3 \times 2 = \underline{?}$

22. $4 \times 2 = \underline{?}$

23. $5 \times 2 = \underline{?}$

24. $6 \times 2 = \underline{?}$

25. $7 \times 2 = \underline{?}$

26. $8 \times 2 = \underline{?}$

27. $9 \times 2 = \underline{?}$

28. $1 \times 3 = \underline{?}$

29. $2 \times 3 = \underline{?}$

30. $3 \times 3 = \underline{?}$

31. $4 \times 3 = \underline{?}$

32. $5 \times 3 = \underline{?}$

33. $6 \times 3 = \underline{?}$

34. $7 \times 3 = \underline{?}$

35. $8 \times 3 = \underline{?}$

36. $9 \times 3 = \underline{?}$

37. $1 \times 4 = \underline{?}$

38. $2 \times 4 = \underline{?}$

39. $3 \times 4 = \underline{?}$

40. $4 \times 4 = \underline{?}$

41. $5 \times 4 = \underline{?}$

42. $6 \times 4 = \underline{?}$

43. $7 \times 4 = \underline{?}$

44. $8 \times 4 = \underline{?}$

45. $9 \times 4 = \underline{?}$

46. $1 \times 5 = \underline{?}$

47. $2 \times 5 = \underline{?}$

48. $3 \times 5 = \underline{?}$

49. $4 \times 5 = \underline{?}$

50. $5 \times 5 = \underline{?}$

51. $6 \times 5 = \underline{?}$

52. $7 \times 5 = \underline{?}$

53. $8 \times 5 = \underline{?}$

54. $9 \times 5 = \underline{?}$

Division review

Division is finding a missing factor.

55. $1 \div 1 = \underline{?}$

56. $2 \div 1 = \underline{?}$

57. $3 \div 1 = \underline{?}$

58. $4 \div 1 = \underline{?}$

59. $5 \div 1 = \underline{?}$

60. $6 \div 1 = \underline{?}$

61. $7 \div 1 = \underline{?}$

62. $8 \div 1 = \underline{?}$

63. $9 \div 1 = \underline{?}$

64. $2 \div 2 = \underline{?}$

65. $4 \div 2 = \underline{?}$

66. $6 \div 2 = \underline{?}$

67. $8 \div 2 = \underline{?}$

68. $10 \div 2 = \underline{?}$

69. $12 \div 2 = \underline{?}$

70. $14 \div 2 = \underline{?}$

71. $16 \div 2 = \underline{?}$

72. $18 \div 2 = \underline{?}$

73. $3 \div 3 = \underline{?}$

74. $6 \div 3 = \underline{?}$

75. $9 \div 3 = \underline{?}$

76. $12 \div 3 = \underline{?}$

77. $15 \div 3 = \underline{?}$

78. $18 \div 3 = \underline{?}$

79. $21 \div 3 = \underline{?}$

80. $24 \div 3 = \underline{?}$

81. $27 \div 3 = \underline{?}$

82. $4 \div 4 = \underline{?}$

83. $8 \div 4 = \underline{?}$

84. $12 \div 4 = \underline{?}$

85. $16 \div 4 = \underline{?}$

86. $20 \div 4 = \underline{?}$

87. $24 \div 4 = \underline{?}$

88. $28 \div 4 = \underline{?}$

89. $32 \div 4 = \underline{?}$

90. $36 \div 4 = \underline{?}$

91. $5 \div 5 = \underline{?}$

92. $10 \div 5 = \underline{?}$

93. $15 \div 5 = \underline{?}$

94. $20 \div 5 = \underline{?}$

95. $25 \div 5 = \underline{?}$

96. $30 \div 5 = \underline{?}$

97. $35 \div 5 = \underline{?}$

98. $40 \div 5 = \underline{?}$

99. $45 \div 5 = \underline{?}$

6 as a factor

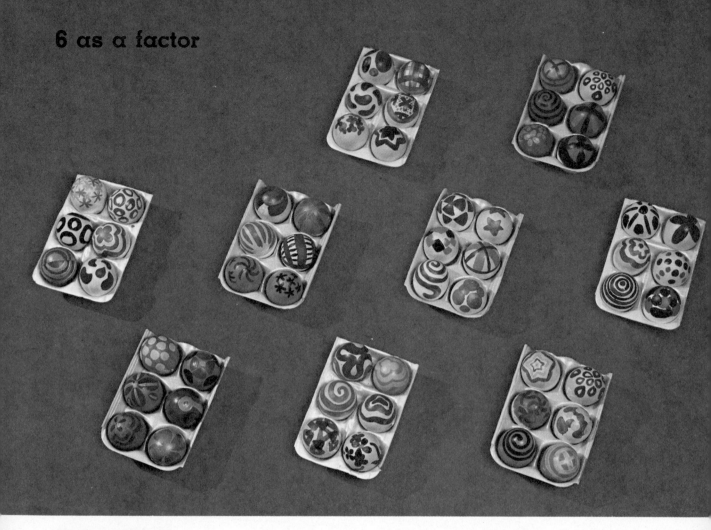

EXERCISES
Give each product.

1. $1 \times 6 = \underline{?}$

2. $2 \times 6 = \underline{?}$

3. $3 \times 6 = \underline{?}$

4. $4 \times 6 = \underline{?}$

5. $5 \times 6 = \underline{?}$

6. $6 \times 6 = \underline{?}$

7. $7 \times 6 = \underline{?}$

8. $8 \times 6 = \underline{?}$

9. $9 \times 6 = \underline{?}$

10. $2 \times 6 = \underline{?}$

11. $4 \times 6 = \underline{?}$

12. $1 \times 6 = \underline{?}$

13. $6 \times 6 = \underline{?}$

14. $3 \times 6 = \underline{?}$

15. $8 \times 6 = \underline{?}$

16. $5 \times 6 = \underline{?}$

17. $9 \times 6 = \underline{?}$

18. $7 \times 6 = \underline{?}$

Multiply.

19. $\begin{array}{r} 3 \\ \times 5 \\ \hline \end{array}$	20. $\begin{array}{r} 2 \\ \times 7 \\ \hline \end{array}$	21. $\begin{array}{r} 4 \\ \times 5 \\ \hline \end{array}$	22. $\begin{array}{r} 6 \\ \times 5 \\ \hline \end{array}$	23. $\begin{array}{r} 5 \\ \times 3 \\ \hline \end{array}$	24. $\begin{array}{r} 2 \\ \times 6 \\ \hline \end{array}$
25. $\begin{array}{r} 4 \\ \times 6 \\ \hline \end{array}$	26. $\begin{array}{r} 6 \\ \times 4 \\ \hline \end{array}$	27. $\begin{array}{r} 5 \\ \times 4 \\ \hline \end{array}$	28. $\begin{array}{r} 3 \\ \times 9 \\ \hline \end{array}$	29. $\begin{array}{r} 5 \\ \times 7 \\ \hline \end{array}$	30. $\begin{array}{r} 6 \\ \times 2 \\ \hline \end{array}$
31. $\begin{array}{r} 6 \\ \times 9 \\ \hline \end{array}$	32. $\begin{array}{r} 4 \\ \times 7 \\ \hline \end{array}$	33. $\begin{array}{r} 5 \\ \times 8 \\ \hline \end{array}$	34. $\begin{array}{r} 6 \\ \times 1 \\ \hline \end{array}$	35. $\begin{array}{r} 2 \\ \times 9 \\ \hline \end{array}$	36. $\begin{array}{r} 3 \\ \times 7 \\ \hline \end{array}$
37. $\begin{array}{r} 5 \\ \times 5 \\ \hline \end{array}$	38. $\begin{array}{r} 6 \\ \times 8 \\ \hline \end{array}$	39. $\begin{array}{r} 2 \\ \times 8 \\ \hline \end{array}$	40. $\begin{array}{r} 4 \\ \times 9 \\ \hline \end{array}$	41. $\begin{array}{r} 6 \\ \times 7 \\ \hline \end{array}$	42. $\begin{array}{r} 5 \\ \times 6 \\ \hline \end{array}$
43. $\begin{array}{r} 3 \\ \times 8 \\ \hline \end{array}$	44. $\begin{array}{r} 4 \\ \times 8 \\ \hline \end{array}$	45. $\begin{array}{r} 6 \\ \times 3 \\ \hline \end{array}$	46. $\begin{array}{r} 5 \\ \times 9 \\ \hline \end{array}$	47. $\begin{array}{r} 3 \\ \times 6 \\ \hline \end{array}$	48. $\begin{array}{r} 6 \\ \times 6 \\ \hline \end{array}$

Solve.

49. How many

in 7 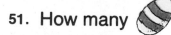 ?

50. How many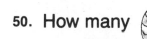

in 6 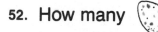 ?

51. How many

in 9 ?

52. How many

in 8  ?

Dividing by 6

Remember that division is finding a missing factor.

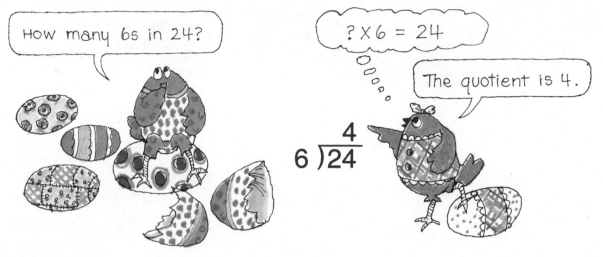

How many 6s in 24?

$? \times 6 = 24$

$$6 \overline{)24} \quad \overset{4}{}$$

The quotient is 4.

To divide by 6, think of the multiplication facts for 6.

EXERCISES
Divide.

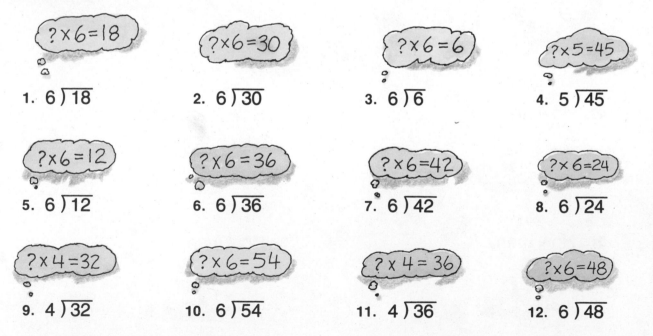

$? \times 6 = 18$

1. $6 \overline{)18}$

$? \times 6 = 30$

2. $6 \overline{)30}$

$? \times 6 = 6$

3. $6 \overline{)6}$

$? \times 5 = 45$

4. $5 \overline{)45}$

$? \times 6 = 12$

5. $6 \overline{)12}$

$? \times 6 = 36$

6. $6 \overline{)36}$

$? \times 6 = 42$

7. $6 \overline{)42}$

$? \times 6 = 24$

8. $6 \overline{)24}$

$? \times 4 = 32$

9. $4 \overline{)32}$

$? \times 6 = 54$

10. $6 \overline{)54}$

$? \times 4 = 36$

11. $4 \overline{)36}$

$? \times 6 = 48$

12. $6 \overline{)48}$

Give each quotient.

13. $6\overline{)18}$ 14. $6\overline{)12}$ 15. $6\overline{)24}$ 16. $6\overline{)6}$ 17. $6\overline{)30}$

18. $6\overline{)42}$ 19. $6\overline{)36}$ 20. $6\overline{)54}$ 21. $6\overline{)48}$ 22. $3\overline{)18}$

23. $4\overline{)36}$ 24. $3\overline{)24}$ 25. $4\overline{)12}$ 26. $3\overline{)21}$ 27. $6\overline{)12}$

28. $6\overline{)36}$ 29. $6\overline{)54}$ 30. $4\overline{)32}$ 31. $4\overline{)16}$ 32. $6\overline{)18}$

33. $4\overline{)20}$ 34. $6\overline{)24}$ 35. $3\overline{)15}$ 36. $6\overline{)48}$ 37. $4\overline{)28}$

38. $3\overline{)27}$ 39. $6\overline{)42}$ 40. $4\overline{)24}$ 41. $6\overline{)6}$ 42. $6\overline{)30}$

Solve.

43.

6 buttons on a card.
5 cards.
How many buttons?

44.

54 buttons in all.
6 buttons on a card.
How many cards?

Use the numbers in two multiplication equations and two division equations.

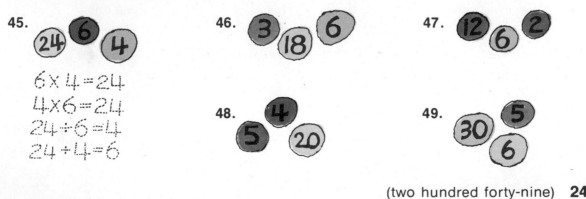

45. (24) (6) (4)

6 × 4 = 24
4 × 6 = 24
24 ÷ 6 = 4
24 ÷ 4 = 6

46. (3) (18) (6)

47. (12) (6) (2)

48. (4) (5) (20)

49. (30) (5) (6)

7 as a factor

EXERCISES
Give each product.

1. $1 \times 7 = \underline{?}$

2. $2 \times 7 = \underline{?}$

3. $3 \times 7 = \underline{?}$

4. $4 \times 7 = \underline{?}$

5. $5 \times 7 = \underline{?}$

6. $6 \times 7 = \underline{?}$

7. $7 \times 7 = \underline{?}$

8. $8 \times 7 = \underline{?}$

9. $9 \times 7 = \underline{?}$

10. $3 \times 7 = \underline{?}$

11. $5 \times 7 = \underline{?}$

12. $2 \times 7 = \underline{?}$

13. $4 \times 7 = \underline{?}$

14. $1 \times 7 = \underline{?}$

15. $8 \times 7 = \underline{?}$

16. $7 \times 7 = \underline{?}$

17. $9 \times 7 = \underline{?}$

18. $6 \times 7 = \underline{?}$

Multiply.

19. $\begin{array}{r} 7 \\ \times 1 \\ \hline \end{array}$ 20. $\begin{array}{r} 6 \\ \times 5 \\ \hline \end{array}$ 21. $\begin{array}{r} 7 \\ \times 5 \\ \hline \end{array}$ 22. $\begin{array}{r} 6 \\ \times 1 \\ \hline \end{array}$

23. $\begin{array}{r} 7 \\ \times 2 \\ \hline \end{array}$ 24. $\begin{array}{r} 7 \\ \times 3 \\ \hline \end{array}$ 25. $\begin{array}{r} 4 \\ \times 8 \\ \hline \end{array}$ 26. $\begin{array}{r} 7 \\ \times 4 \\ \hline \end{array}$

27. $\begin{array}{r} 3 \\ \times 9 \\ \hline \end{array}$ 28. $\begin{array}{r} 7 \\ \times 8 \\ \hline \end{array}$ 29. $\begin{array}{r} 3 \\ \times 7 \\ \hline \end{array}$ 30. $\begin{array}{r} 6 \\ \times 2 \\ \hline \end{array}$

31. $\begin{array}{r} 7 \\ \times 9 \\ \hline \end{array}$ 32. $\begin{array}{r} 6 \\ \times 4 \\ \hline \end{array}$ 33. $\begin{array}{r} 7 \\ \times 7 \\ \hline \end{array}$ 34. $\begin{array}{r} 7 \\ \times 8 \\ \hline \end{array}$

35. $\begin{array}{r} 6 \\ \times 3 \\ \hline \end{array}$ 36. $\begin{array}{r} 7 \\ \times 9 \\ \hline \end{array}$ 37. $\begin{array}{r} 6 \\ \times 5 \\ \hline \end{array}$ 38. $\begin{array}{r} 7 \\ \times 4 \\ \hline \end{array}$

39. $\begin{array}{r} 4 \\ \times 9 \\ \hline \end{array}$ 40. $\begin{array}{r} 7 \\ \times 7 \\ \hline \end{array}$ 41. $\begin{array}{r} 6 \\ \times 9 \\ \hline \end{array}$ 42. $\begin{array}{r} 7 \\ \times 6 \\ \hline \end{array}$

43. $\begin{array}{r} 8 \\ \times 4 \\ \hline \end{array}$ 44. $\begin{array}{r} 6 \\ \times 6 \\ \hline \end{array}$ 45. $\begin{array}{r} 7 \\ \times 5 \\ \hline \end{array}$ 46. $\begin{array}{r} 6 \\ \times 8 \\ \hline \end{array}$

47. $\begin{array}{r} 8 \\ \times 7 \\ \hline \end{array}$ 48. $\begin{array}{r} 6 \\ \times 7 \\ \hline \end{array}$ 49. $\begin{array}{r} 3 \\ \times 6 \\ \hline \end{array}$ 50. $\begin{array}{r} 9 \\ \times 6 \\ \hline \end{array}$

51. $\begin{array}{r} 4 \\ \times 5 \\ \hline \end{array}$ 52. $\begin{array}{r} 5 \\ \times 7 \\ \hline \end{array}$ 53. $\begin{array}{r} 8 \\ \times 6 \\ \hline \end{array}$ 54. $\begin{array}{r} 9 \\ \times 5 \\ \hline \end{array}$

Multiply the corner numbers to fill in the circles. Complete.

55.

56.

57.

★ 58.

Dividing by 7

$1 \times 7 = 7$ $2 \times 7 = 14$ $3 \times 7 = 21$ $4 \times 7 = 28$ $5 \times 7 = 35$ $6 \times 7 = 42$ $7 \times 7 = 49$ $8 \times 7 = 56$ $9 \times 7 = 63$

42 divided by 7.

$7 \overline{)42}$ quotient 6

The quotient is 6.

EXERCISES
Divide.

1. $? \times 7 = 14$ $7 \overline{)14}$
2. $? \times 7 = 7$ $7 \overline{)7}$
3. $? \times 6 = 48$ $6 \overline{)48}$
4. $? \times 6 = 42$ $6 \overline{)42}$

5. $? \times 6 = 54$ $6 \overline{)54}$
6. $? \times 7 = 35$ $7 \overline{)35}$
7. $? \times 7 = 21$ $7 \overline{)21}$
8. $? \times 7 = 63$ $7 \overline{)63}$

9. $7 \overline{)56}$
10. $7 \overline{)42}$
11. $7 \overline{)49}$
12. $7 \overline{)28}$

13. $2 \overline{)16}$
14. $3 \overline{)27}$
15. $4 \overline{)24}$
16. $5 \overline{)35}$

17. $5 \overline{)40}$
18. $4 \overline{)36}$
19. $3 \overline{)18}$
20. $5 \overline{)45}$

Give each quotient.

21. $7\overline{)35}$ 22. $4\overline{)36}$ 23. $7\overline{)21}$

24. $4\overline{)28}$ 25. $7\overline{)49}$ 26. $7\overline{)42}$

27. $6\overline{)42}$ 28. $5\overline{)30}$ 29. $6\overline{)24}$

30. $6\overline{)48}$ 31. $6\overline{)18}$ 32. $7\overline{)56}$

33. $6\overline{)36}$ 34. $6\overline{)54}$ 35. $7\overline{)63}$

There are seven days in a week.

36. How many days in 2 weeks?

37. How many days in 4 weeks?

38. How many weeks in 21 days?

39. How many weeks in 35 days?

Who am I?

40. If you divide me by 7, you get 8.

41. If you multiply me by 6, you get 42.

★ 42. If you multiply me by 5 and add 7, you get 37.

1. $\begin{array}{r} 53 \\ +21 \\ \hline \end{array}$ 2. $\begin{array}{r} 58 \\ +34 \\ \hline \end{array}$

3. $\begin{array}{r} 29 \\ +83 \\ \hline \end{array}$ 4. $\begin{array}{r} 75 \\ +75 \\ \hline \end{array}$

5. $\begin{array}{r} 98 \\ +56 \\ \hline \end{array}$ 6. $\begin{array}{r} 352 \\ +741 \\ \hline \end{array}$

7. $\begin{array}{r} 529 \\ +138 \\ \hline \end{array}$ 8. $\begin{array}{r} 652 \\ +278 \\ \hline \end{array}$

9. $\begin{array}{r} 946 \\ +387 \\ \hline \end{array}$ 10. $\begin{array}{r} 274 \\ +888 \\ \hline \end{array}$

11. $\begin{array}{r} 56 \\ 34 \\ +75 \\ \hline \end{array}$ 12. $\begin{array}{r} 58 \\ 39 \\ +\ 3 \\ \hline \end{array}$

13. $\begin{array}{r} 76 \\ 5 \\ +48 \\ \hline \end{array}$ 14. $\begin{array}{r} 64 \\ 27 \\ +89 \\ \hline \end{array}$

Problem solving

Carpenters build and repair the homes we live in. They work with many tools.

EXERCISES

Give the total cost.

1.

$.95 $2.58

2.

$5.95 $2.65

3.

$9.39 $8.45

4.

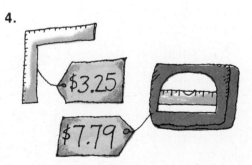

$3.25 $7.79

**Which costs more?
How much more?**

5.  $7.65 $10.29

6.  $3.39 $5.00

7.  $4.25 $1.19

8.  $8.69 $9.50

Solve.

9. How many screws will be needed for 8 ?

10. How many screws will be needed for 7  ?

11. One panel needs 6 nails.

48 NAILS

How many panels can be put up with these nails?

12. One shelf needs 7 nails.

60 NAILS

How many shelves can be put up with these nails? How many nails will be left over?

8 as a factor

EXERCISES
Give each product.

1. $1 \times 8 = \underline{?}$

2. $2 \times 8 = \underline{?}$

3. $3 \times 8 = \underline{?}$

4. $4 \times 8 = \underline{?}$

5. $5 \times 8 = \underline{?}$

6. $6 \times 8 = \underline{?}$

7. $7 \times 8 = \underline{?}$

8. $8 \times 8 = \underline{?}$

9. $9 \times 8 = \underline{?}$

10. $4 \times 8 = \underline{?}$

11. $1 \times 8 = \underline{?}$

12. $3 \times 8 = \underline{?}$

13. $2 \times 8 = \underline{?}$

14. $5 \times 8 = \underline{?}$

15. $7 \times 8 = \underline{?}$

16. $9 \times 8 = \underline{?}$

17. $6 \times 8 = \underline{?}$

18. $8 \times 8 = \underline{?}$

Multiply.

19. 8
    ×2

20. 6
    ×4

21. 7
    ×2

22. 8
    ×3

23. 6
    ×3

24. 7
    ×6

25. 8
    ×8

26. 7
    ×5

27. 8
    ×6

28. 6
    ×5

29. 8
    ×4

30. 7
    ×7

31. 6
    ×9

32. 8
    ×1

33. 6
    ×7

34. 7
    ×8

35. 6
    ×8

36. 8
    ×9

37. 7
    ×4

38. 6
    ×6

39. 8
    ×7

40. 7
    ×3

41. 8
    ×5

42. 7
    ×9

Complete.

43. 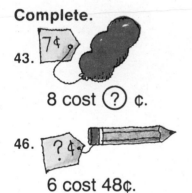 8 cost (?) ¢.

44. 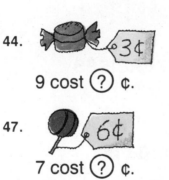 9 cost (?) ¢.

45. 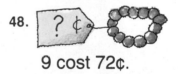 5 cost 35¢.

46.  6 cost 48¢.

47. 7 cost (?) ¢.

48. 9 cost 72¢.

Give the missing digits.

49.
    ×7
    ──
    56

50. 6
    ×
    ──
    54

51.
    ×7
    ──
    49

52. 8
    ×
    ──
    48

Dividing by 8

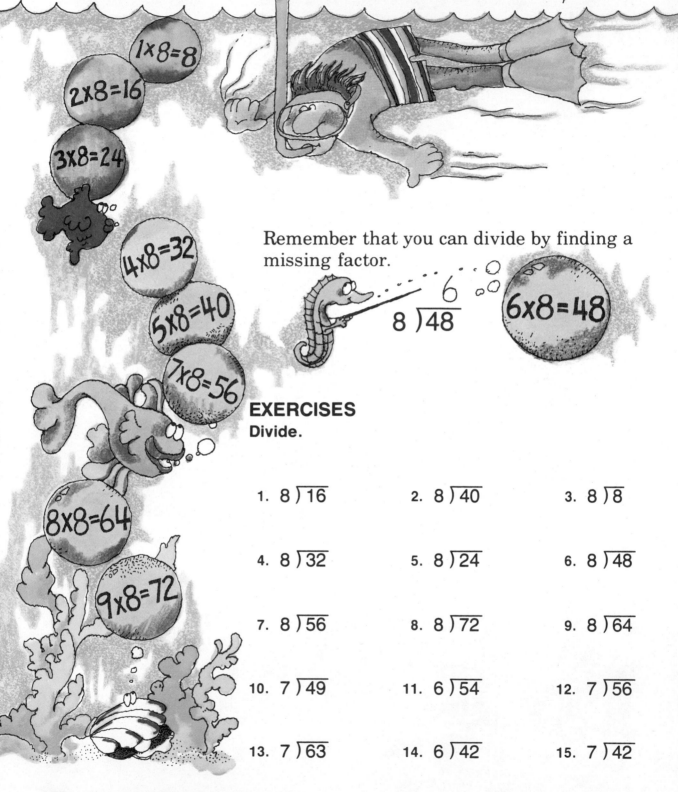

$1 \times 8 = 8$

$2 \times 8 = 16$

$3 \times 8 = 24$

$4 \times 8 = 32$

$5 \times 8 = 40$

$7 \times 8 = 56$

$8 \times 8 = 64$

$9 \times 8 = 72$

$6 \times 8 = 48$

Remember that you can divide by finding a missing factor.

$8 \overline{)48}$ with quotient 6

EXERCISES
Divide.

1. $8 \overline{)16}$ 2. $8 \overline{)40}$ 3. $8 \overline{)8}$

4. $8 \overline{)32}$ 5. $8 \overline{)24}$ 6. $8 \overline{)48}$

7. $8 \overline{)56}$ 8. $8 \overline{)72}$ 9. $8 \overline{)64}$

10. $7 \overline{)49}$ 11. $6 \overline{)54}$ 12. $7 \overline{)56}$

13. $7 \overline{)63}$ 14. $6 \overline{)42}$ 15. $7 \overline{)42}$

Divide.

16. $8\overline{)16}$ 17. $6\overline{)18}$ 18. $7\overline{)28}$ 19. $6\overline{)12}$ 20. $8\overline{)56}$

21. $7\overline{)35}$ 22. $6\overline{)24}$ 23. $8\overline{)8}$ 24. $7\overline{)14}$ 25. $8\overline{)72}$

26. $8\overline{)48}$ 27. $7\overline{)21}$ 28. $6\overline{)30}$ 29. $8\overline{)24}$ 30. $7\overline{)49}$

31. $6\overline{)36}$ 32. $8\overline{)32}$ 33. $6\overline{)42}$ 34. $7\overline{)42}$ 35. $8\overline{)64}$

36. $7\overline{)56}$ 37. $6\overline{)48}$ 38. $7\overline{)63}$ 39. $6\overline{)54}$ 40. $8\overline{)40}$

Solve.

41. 6 pencils in a box.
7 boxes.
How many pencils?

42. 48 pencils in all.
6 pencils in a box.
How many boxes?

43. 48 balls.
8 balls in a package.
How many packages?

44. 9 marbles in a package.
8 packages.
How many marbles?

45. 4 screws in a package.
9 packages.
How many screws?

46. 42 bolts.
7 bolts in a package.
How many packages?

9 as a factor

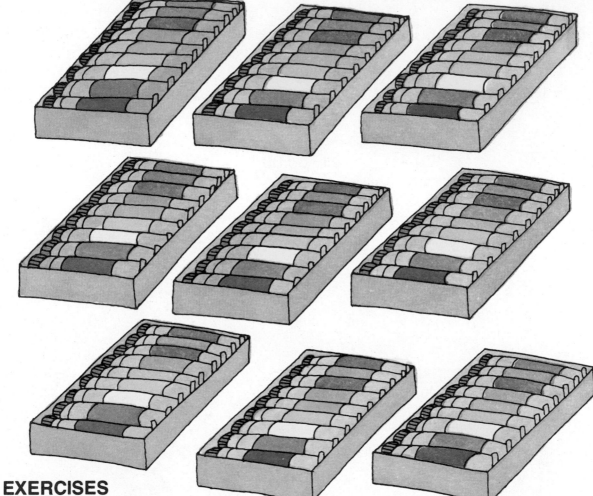

EXERCISES
Give each product.

1. $1 \times 9 = \underline{?}$

2. $2 \times 9 = \underline{?}$

3. $3 \times 9 = \underline{?}$

4. $4 \times 9 = \underline{?}$

5. $5 \times 9 = \underline{?}$

6. $6 \times 9 = \underline{?}$

7. $7 \times 9 = \underline{?}$

8. $8 \times 9 = \underline{?}$

9. $9 \times 9 = \underline{?}$

10. $3 \times 9 = \underline{?}$

11. $1 \times 9 = \underline{?}$

12. $4 \times 9 = \underline{?}$

13. $2 \times 9 = \underline{?}$

14. $5 \times 9 = \underline{?}$

15. $7 \times 9 = \underline{?}$

16. $9 \times 9 = \underline{?}$

17. $6 \times 9 = \underline{?}$

18. $8 \times 9 = \underline{?}$

Multiply.

19. 9
    ×1

20. 9
    ×3

21. 7
    ×8

22. 9
    ×2

23. 8
    ×5

24. 9
    ×8

25. 7
    ×9

26. 7
    ×5

27. 8
    ×3

28. 7
    ×6

29. 8
    ×9

30. 9
    ×7

31. 7
    ×4

32. 9
    ×5

33. 8
    ×8

34. 9
    ×4

35. 8
    ×6

36. 8
    ×2

37. 8
    ×4

38. 7
    ×7

39. 9
    ×9

40. 8
    ×7

41. 8
    ×1

42. 9
    ×6

Solve.

43.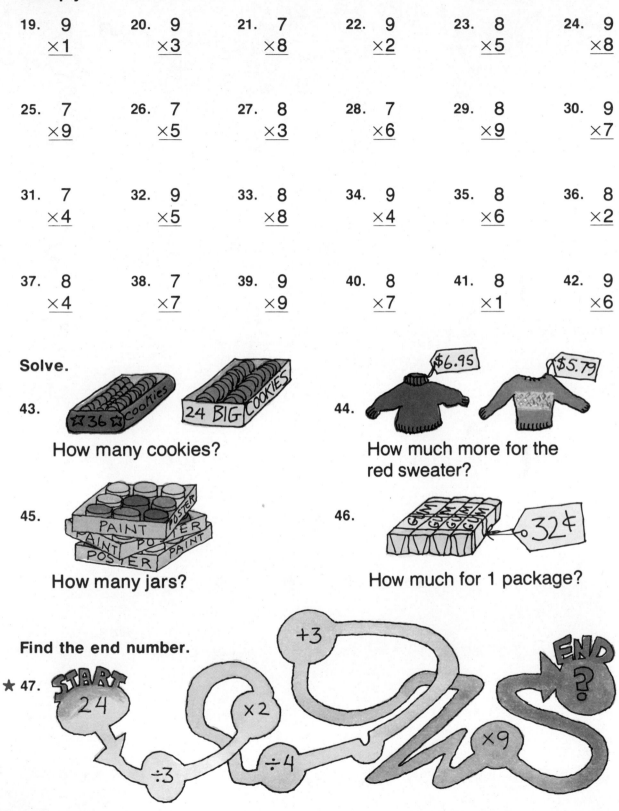

How many cookies?

44.

How much more for the red sweater?

45.

How many jars?

46.

How much for 1 package?

Find the end number.

★ 47.

Dividing by 9

EXERCISES

Divide.

1. $9\overline{)27}$ 2. $9\overline{)36}$ 3. $9\overline{)9}$ 4. $9\overline{)45}$ 5. $9\overline{)18}$

6. $9\overline{)63}$ 7. $9\overline{)54}$ 8. $9\overline{)81}$ 9. $9\overline{)72}$ 10. $7\overline{)28}$

11. $8\overline{)40}$ 12. $7\overline{)49}$ 13. $8\overline{)64}$ 14. $7\overline{)63}$ 15. $8\overline{)48}$

16. $8\overline{)32}$ 17. $8\overline{)56}$ 18. $7\overline{)42}$ 19. $7\overline{)35}$ 20. $8\overline{)72}$

21. $6\overline{)48}$ 22. $9\overline{)9}$ 23. $6\overline{)36}$ 24. $6\overline{)54}$ 25. $9\overline{)27}$

26. $8\overline{)24}$ 27. $9\overline{)18}$ 28. $9\overline{)81}$ 29. $6\overline{)30}$ 30. $6\overline{)24}$

31. $7\overline{)21}$ 32. $6\overline{)42}$ 33. $8\overline{)16}$ 34. $9\overline{)63}$ 35. $9\overline{)72}$

36. $9\overline{)45}$ 37. $7\overline{)56}$ 38. $9\overline{)36}$ 39. $6\overline{)18}$ 40. $9\overline{)54}$

Solve.

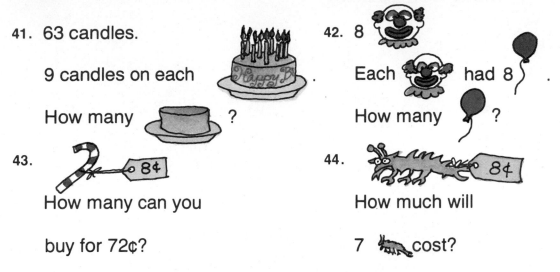

41. 63 candles.

9 candles on each .

How many ?

42. 8

Each had 8 .

How many ?

43.

How many can you

buy for 72¢?

44.

How much will

7 cost?

Complete.

45.

2	3	?
4	1	?
?	?	?

★ 46.

3	?	3
3	?	6
?	?	?

★ 47.

?	?	?
?	?	6
4	9	?

Keeping Skills Sharp

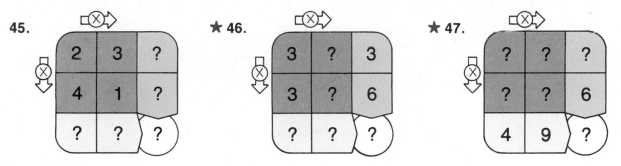

1. 523
   − 109

2. 462
   − 446

3. 842
   − 538

4. 629
   − 448

5. 728
   − 658

6. 743
   − 259

7. 516
   − 348

8. 832
   − 176

9. 924
   − 455

10. 635
    − 199

11. 506
    − 278

12. 307
    − 159

13. 402
    − 148

14. 600
    − 267

15. 500
    − 345

Division with remainder

Kim had 43¢.

She spent it for  8¢

How many 8¢ did she buy?

$$\begin{array}{r} 5\,R\,3 \\ 8\overline{)43} \\ -40 \\ \hline 3 \end{array}$$

She got 5 8¢ and had 3¢ left over.

EXERCISES
Divide.

1. $6\overline{)13}$ 2. $6\overline{)14}$ 3. $8\overline{)25}$ 4. $6\overline{)29}$ 5. $8\overline{)11}$

6. $8\overline{)29}$ 7. $8\overline{)23}$ 8. $9\overline{)85}$ 9. $6\overline{)50}$ 10. $6\overline{)38}$

11. $6\overline{)19}$ 12. $9\overline{)43}$ 13. $7\overline{)46}$ 14. $9\overline{)36}$ 15. $8\overline{)47}$

16. $8\overline{)19}$ 17. $9\overline{)58}$ 18. $6\overline{)55}$ 19. $7\overline{)29}$ 20. $7\overline{)38}$

21. $7\overline{)45}$ 22. $8\overline{)53}$ 23. $6\overline{)49}$ 24. $9\overline{)50}$ 25. $8\overline{)50}$

Solve.

26. How many 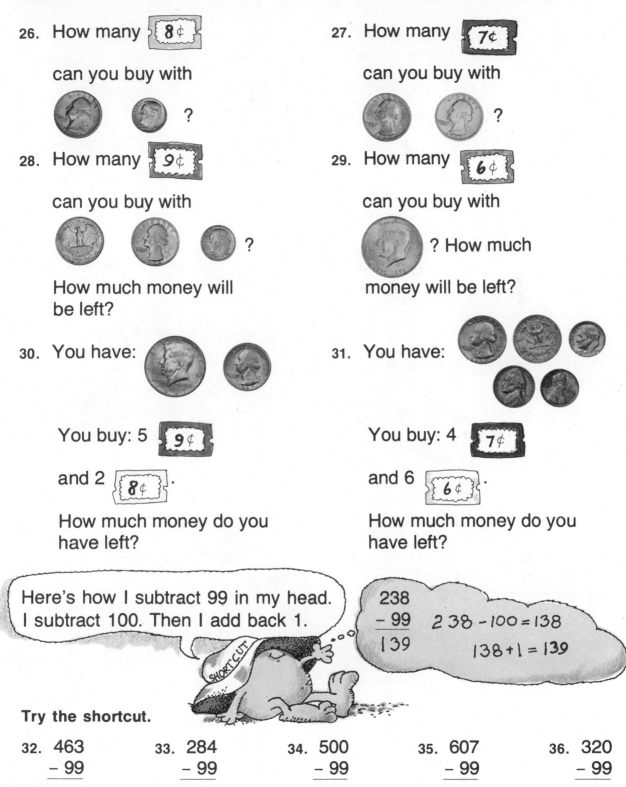 **8¢**

    can you buy with

    (quarter) (dime) ?

27. How many **7¢**

    can you buy with

    (quarter) (quarter) ?

28. How many **9¢**

    can you buy with

    (quarter) (quarter) (dime) ?

    How much money will
    be left?

29. How many **6¢**

    can you buy with

    (half dollar) ? How much

    money will be left?

30. You have:

    (half dollar) (quarter)

    You buy: 5 **9¢**

    and 2 **8¢**.

    How much money do you
    have left?

31. You have:

    (quarter) (nickel) (dime)
    (nickel) (penny)

    You buy: 4 **7¢**

    and 6 **6¢**.

    How much money do you
    have left?

Here's how I subtract 99 in my head.
I subtract 100. Then I add back 1.

$$\begin{array}{r} 238 \\ -\ 99 \\ \hline 139 \end{array}$$ 238 − 100 = 138

138 + 1 = 139

Try the shortcut.

32. $\begin{array}{r} 463 \\ -\ 99 \\ \hline \end{array}$
33. $\begin{array}{r} 284 \\ -\ 99 \\ \hline \end{array}$
34. $\begin{array}{r} 500 \\ -\ 99 \\ \hline \end{array}$
35. $\begin{array}{r} 607 \\ -\ 99 \\ \hline \end{array}$
36. $\begin{array}{r} 320 \\ -\ 99 \\ \hline \end{array}$

Grouping symbols

The grouping symbols tell us what to do first.

Add first.

$3 + 2 = 5$

Multiply first.

$2 \times 4 = 8$

$$(3 + 2) \times 4 = 20$$

$$3 + (2 \times 4) = 11$$

Subtract first.

$8 - 6 = 2$

Divide first.

$$(8 - 6) \div 2 = 1$$

$6 \div 2 = 3$

$$8 - (6 \div 2) = 5$$

EXERCISES

Complete.

12

1. $(8 + 4) \div 2 = \underline{?}$

2

2. $8 + (4 \div 2) = \underline{?}$

3

3. $(6 - 3) \div 3 = \underline{?}$

1

4. $6 - (3 \div 3) = \underline{?}$

6

5. $(4 + 2) + 3 = \underline{?}$

5

6. $4 + (2 + 3) = \underline{?}$

7. $(3 \times 2) \times 2 = \underline{?}$

8. $4 \times (2 \times 2) = \underline{?}$

9. $(8 - 3) - 1 = \underline{?}$

10. $8 - (3 - 1) = \underline{?}$

11. $(8 \div 4) \div 2 = \underline{?}$

12. $8 \div (4 \div 2) = \underline{?}$

13. $8 \times (4 \div 2) = \underline{?}$

Complete.

14. $(5 - 2) \times 4 = \underline{?}$

15. $(8 \div 2) - 4 = \underline{?}$

16. $3 \times (0 \div 5) = \underline{?}$

17. $(3 + 6) \times 5 = \underline{?}$

18. $17 - (4 \times 2) = \underline{?}$

19. $18 \div (2 + 4) = \underline{?}$

20. $24 \div (1 + 7) = \underline{?}$

21. $(18 \div 3) - 2 = \underline{?}$

22. $(6 \times 4) \div 8 = \underline{?}$

23. $(4 + 8) \div 3 = \underline{?}$

24. $9 + (36 \div 4) = \underline{?}$

25. $7 \times (9 - 3) = \underline{?}$

Solve.

26. Bought 3 pencils for 8¢ each and 1 eraser for 6¢. What was the total cost?

27. Had 53¢. Bought 6 pieces of gum for 4¢ each. How much money was left?

Give the missing signs.

★ 28. $(8 \,⬭\, 2) \,⬭\, 5 = 2$

★ 29. $(8 \,⬭\, 2) \,⬭\, 5 = 9$

★ 30. $8 \,⬭\, (2 \,⬭\, 5) = 15$

★ 31. $8 \,⬭\, (2 \,⬭\, 5) = 1$

★ 32. $(8 \,⬭\, 2) \,⬭\, 5 = 30$

Another meaning of division

Division tells how
many in each set.

4 IN EACH SET

3)12 IN ALL

SETS

EXERCISES
**How many doughnuts would be
on each plate?**

1.

2.

3.

4.

5.

6.

Write 2 divisions for each picture.

7.

$$2\overline{)8} = 4$$

$$4\overline{)8} = 2$$

8.

9.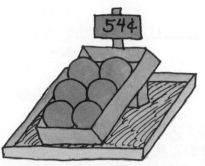

10.

11.

Solve.

12.

How many apples are in the bag?

13.

How much does 1 orange cost?

14. Each box weighs the same.

How much does 1 box weigh?

15. Each bag weighs 6 kg.

How many bags are there?

16. Mr. Alan had 28 dimes. He divided them among his 4 children. How many dimes did each child get?

17. Miss Stevens can save $9.00 a week. How long will it take her to save $72.00?

Problem solving

Sometimes you can solve a story problem without knowing all the words.

Julie had 8 apples.
Jim had 2 apples.
How many apples did they have in all?

Julie had 8 🐾.
Jim had 2 🐾.
How many 🐾 did they have in all?

$$8 + 2 = 10$$

Answer: 10 apples in all.

Answer: 10 🐾 in all.

Multiplication Problem

George put 8 ● in each 🍃.
He has 2 🍃.
How many ● in all?

$$2 \times 8 = 16$$

Answer: 16 ● in all.

Division Problem

Sarah had 8 ●.
She put 2 ● in each 🍃.
How many 🍃 ?

$$8 \div 2 = 4$$

Answer: 4 🍃.

EXERCISES
Solve.

1. Bill bought 8 ● and 4 ●. How many ● and ● did he buy in all?

2. Jill bought 8 ● and 4 ●. How many more ● did she buy?

3. There were 6 ⬤ with
   3 ▬ in each ⬤ . How
   many ▬ in all?

4. Mary bought 8 ⬤ .
   There were 4 ⬤ in each ⬤ .
   How many ⬤ did she buy?

5. Harry bought 8 ▬ .
   He put 4 of them in
   each ▬ . How many
   ▬ did he use?

6. ⬤ bought 10 ▬ .
   ⬤ bought 4 ▬ .
   How many more
   did ⬤ buy?

7. ▪ had 10 ⬤ .
   ▫ had 4 ⬤ .
   How many ⬤ did
   they have together?

8. ▲ had 10 ⬤ .
   ▲ gave 4 ⬤ to ⬤ .
   How many ⬤ did
   ▲ have left?

Multiply. [pages 243–247, 250–251, 256–257, 260–261]

1. 8 ×4	2. 8 ×6	3. 7 ×5	4. 6 ×6	5. 8 ×7	6. 7 ×4
7. 8 ×8	8. 8 ×9	9. 9 ×6	10. 7 ×7	11. 7 ×6	12. 9 ×7
13. 7 ×8	14. 9 ×5	15. 8 ×5	16. 9 ×9	17. 6 ×8	18. 8 ×9

Divide. [pages 248–249, 252–253, 258–259, 262]

19. 8)32 20. 6)42 21. 9)36 22. 6)30 23. 9)45

24. 8)40 25. 6)48 26. 9)27 27. 6)54 28. 7)49

29. 7)35 30. 7)63 31. 8)24 32. 7)28 33. 8)72

34. 7)56 35. 7)21 36. 9)81 37. 6)36 38. 8)64

Solve. [pages 254–255, 263, 265, 272–273]

39.

How much will 7 cost?

40. 9¢

How many 9¢ can you buy with 63¢?

41. 48 students went on a field trip. There were 6 students in each car. How many cars were there?

42. 54 students went to the zoo in 9 cars. The same number of students were in each car. How many students were in each car?

1. Copy and complete this multiplication table.

X	0	1	2	3	4	5	6	7	8	9
0	0	0	0	0	0	0	0	0	0	0
1	0	1	2	3	4	5	6	7	8	9
2	0	2	4	6						
3	0	3								
4										
5										
6										
7										
8										
9										

2. Look at your completed table.

3. What patterns can you find?
   Hint: Look at the rows.
   Look at the columns.
   Look at the diagonals.

ERASER

Multiply or divide.

1. 6
    ×2

2. 6
    ×7

3. 6
    ×4

4. 6
    ×9

5. 6)18

6. 6)36

7. 6)48

8. 6)30

9. 7
    ×7

10. 7
     ×2

11. 7
     ×9

12. 7
     ×5

13. 7)21

14. 7)42

15. 7)28

16. 7)56

17. 8
     ×3

18. 8
     ×8

19. 8
     ×4

20. 8
     ×6

21. 8)16

22. 8)40

23. 8)72

24. 8)56

25. 9
     ×5

26. 9
     ×2

27. 9
     ×9

28. 9
     ×6

29. 9)27

30. 9)63

31. 9)36

32. 9)72

CHAPTER CHALLENGE

When you multiply, the product of each row is 24.

CEMENT

Fill in the blocks.
Do not use any 1s.
(There is more than one way to fill in the blocks.)

1. 12 / 6 × 2 / ? × ? × ?

2. 45 / ? × ? / ? × ? × ?

3. 36 / ? × ? / ? × ? × ? / ? × ? × ? × ?

4. 54 / ? × ? / ? × ? × ? / ? × ? × ? × ?

5. 48 / ? × ? / ? × ? × ? / ? × ? × ? × ? / ? × ? × ? × ? × ?

6. 72 / ? × ? / ? × ? × ? / ? × ? × ? × ? / ? × ? × ? × ? × ?

MAJOR CHECKUP
Standardized Format

Give the correct letter.

1. Which letter is seventh?

QUOTIENT

- **a.** I
- **b.** N
- **c.** E
- **d.** T

2. Round 74 to the nearest ten.

- **a.** 70
- **b.** 50
- **c.** 80
- **d.** none of these

3. Which number is smallest?

- **a.** 5738
- **b.** 5381
- **c.** 5138
- **d.** 5173

---

4. Add.

$$538 \atop +296$$

- **a.** 724
- **b.** 834
- **c.** 824
- **d.** none of these

5. Subtract.

$$526 \atop -384$$

- **a.** 262
- **b.** 142
- **c.** 242
- **d.** none of these

6. Subtract.

$$600 \atop -238$$

- **a.** 462
- **b.** 372
- **c.** 472
- **d.** 362

---

7. What time is shown?

- **a.** 2:35
- **b.** 7:13
- **c.** 3:35
- **d.** none of these

8. Multiply.

$$3 \atop \times 8$$

- **a.** 18
- **b.** 16
- **c.** 21
- **d.** none of these

9. Divide.

$24 \div 4$

- **a.** 4
- **b.** 6
- **c.** 8
- **d.** 9

---

10. Divide.

$5\overline{)28}$

- **a.** 5 R3
- **b.** 3 R5
- **c.** 4 R3
- **d.** 6 R3

11. What fraction is yellow?

- **a.** $\frac{3}{8}$
- **b.** $\frac{3}{5}$
- **c.** $\frac{5}{8}$
- **d.** $\frac{5}{3}$

12. How long?

inches 1

- **a.** about 1 in.
- **b.** about 3 in.
- **c.** about 1½ in.
- **d.** none of these

11
Geometry

Solids

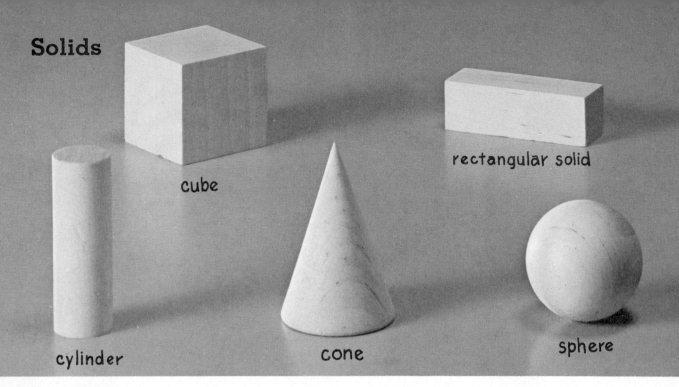

cube

rectangular solid

cylinder

cone

sphere

EXERCISES
Name each shape.

1.

2.

3.

4.

5.

6.

7.

8.

9.

Name each shape.

10.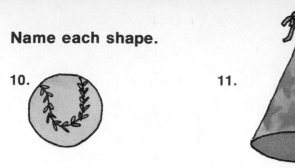

11.

12.

13.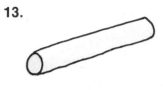

14.

15.

**Look for these shapes in your classroom.
List what you found.**

16. cube

17. rectangular solid

18. sphere

19. cylinder

20. cone

More about solids

A sphere has one curved surface.

A cube has six flat surfaces.

EXERCISES
How many?

1.

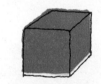

  a. flat surfaces
  b. curved surfaces

2.

  a. flat surfaces
  b. curved surfaces

3.

a. flat surfaces
b. curved surfaces

4.

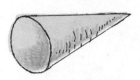

  a. flat surfaces
  b. curved surfaces

5.

  a. flat surfaces
  b. curved surfaces

Copy and complete the table.

Solid	6.	7.	8.	9.	10.
Number of flat surfaces					
Number of curved surfaces					
Number of corners					
Number of edges					

Plane figures

Place a cube on a piece of paper. Trace around it and you get a **square**.

Place a rectangular solid on a piece of paper. Trace around it and you get a **rectangle**.

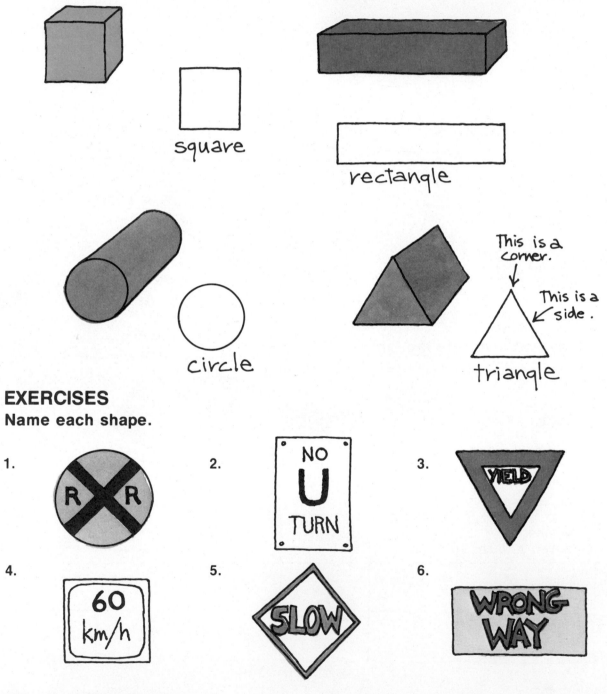

square

rectangle

circle

This is a corner.

This is a side.

triangle

EXERCISES
Name each shape.

1.

2.   NO U TURN

3.   YIELD

4.   60 km/h

5.   SLOW

6.   WRONG WAY

**Look for these shapes in your classroom.
List what you find.**

7. square

8. rectangle

9. triangle

10. circle

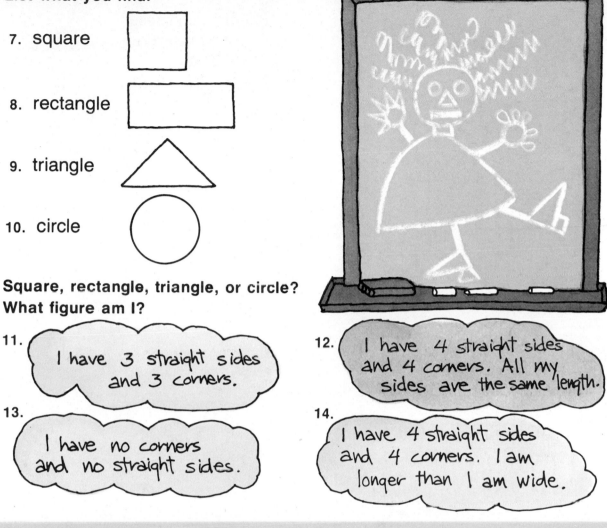

**Square, rectangle, triangle, or circle?
What figure am I?**

11. I have 3 straight sides and 3 corners.

12. I have 4 straight sides and 4 corners. All my sides are the same length.

13. I have no corners and no straight sides.

14. I have 4 straight sides and 4 corners. I am longer than I am wide.

Keeping Skills Sharp

1. 400 +168	2. 526 +381	3. 824 +200	4. 462 +258	5. 258 +462
6. 659 +352	7. 483 +275	8. 817 +359	9. 523 +214	10. 506 +384
11. 384 +267	12. 267 +384	13. 752 +258	14. 946 +359	15. 833 +108

More about plane figures

The sides of these figures are **segments**.

The edges of these figures are **segments**.

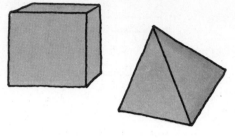

Segments

Point A and point B are the **endpoints** of the red segment.

We call it segment AB or segment BA.

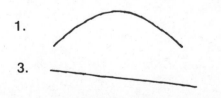

EXERCISES
Which are segments?

1.

2.

3.

4.

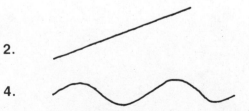

Which segment is the

5. longest?
6. shortest?

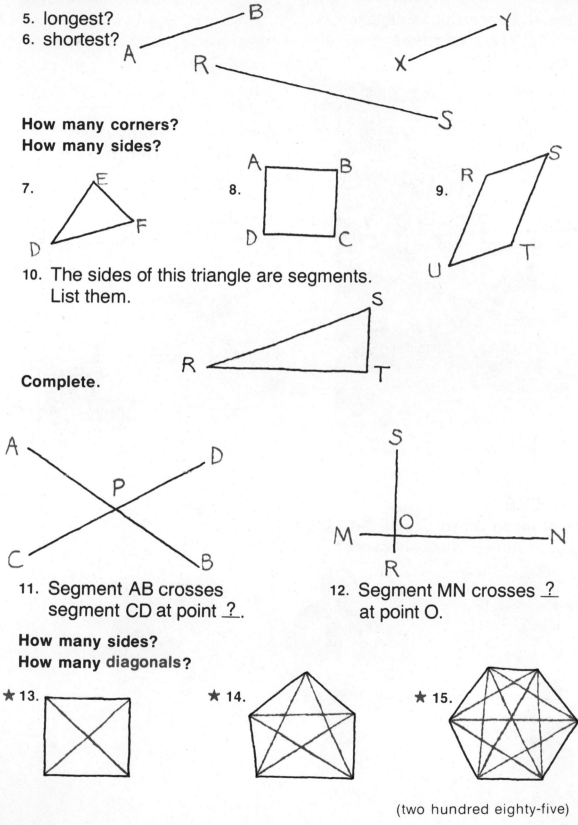

How many corners?
How many sides?

7.

8.

9.

10. The sides of this triangle are segments. List them.

Complete.

11. Segment AB crosses segment CD at point _?_.

12. Segment MN crosses _?_ at point O.

How many sides?
How many diagonals?

★ 13.

★ 14.

★ 15.

Congruent figures

Figures that are the same size and shape are **congruent figures**.

Andrew cut out some cookies with a cookie cutter. Here is one of his cookies.

EXERCISES
Which of these cookies could have been made with Andrew's cookie cutter?

1.

2.

3.

4.

5.

6.

Which two figures are congruent?

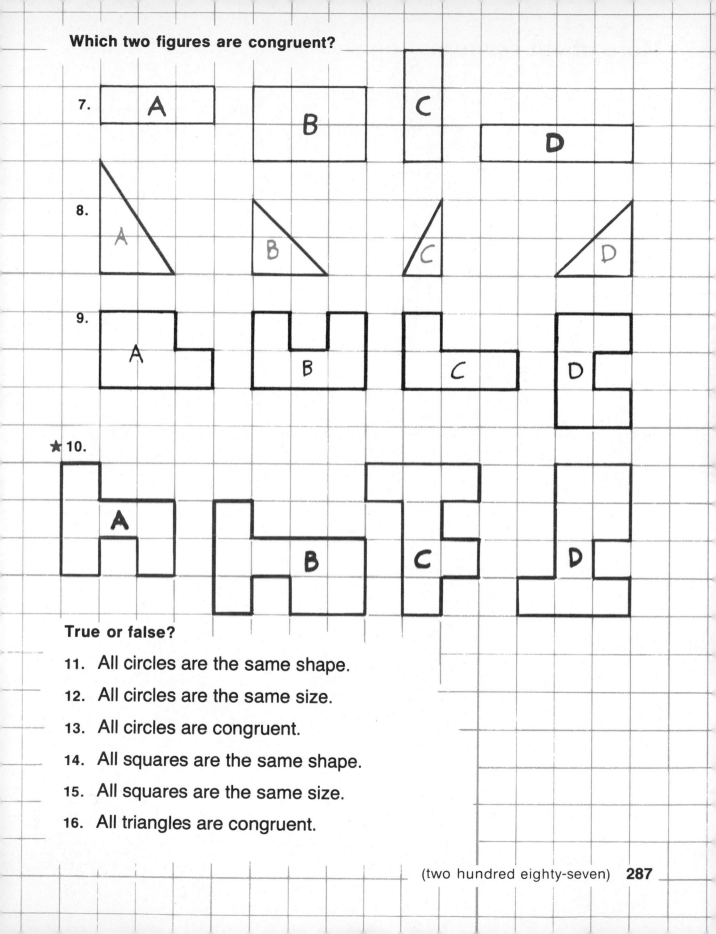

7. A B C D

8. A B C D

9. A B C D

★ 10. A B C D

True or false?

11. All circles are the same shape.

12. All circles are the same size.

13. All circles are congruent.

14. All squares are the same shape.

15. All squares are the same size.

16. All triangles are congruent.

More about congruent figures

We can use a tracing to find congruent figures.

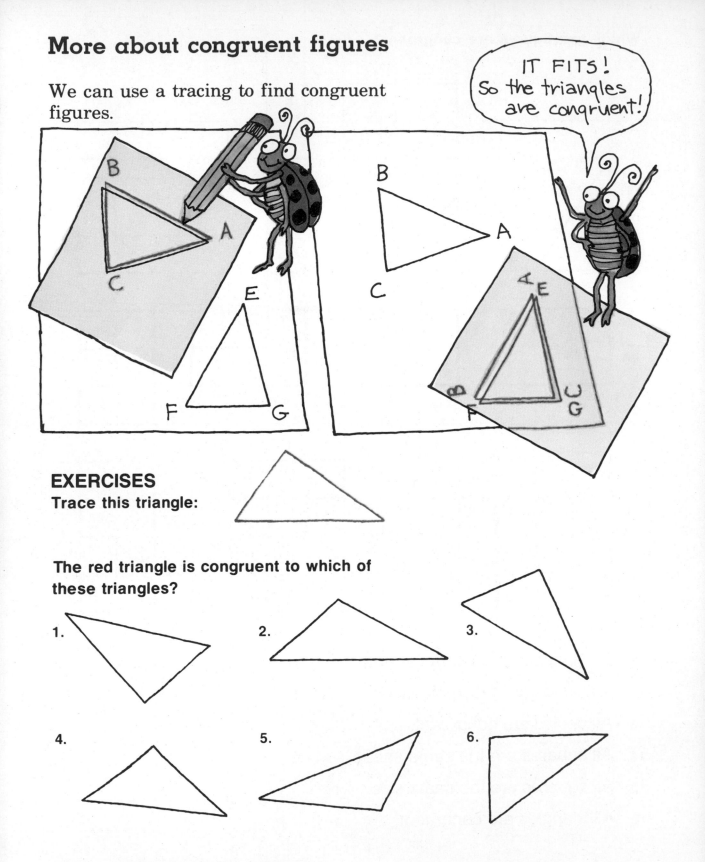

IT FITS! So the triangles are congruent!

EXERCISES
Trace this triangle:

The red triangle is congruent to which of these triangles?

1.

2.

3.

4.

5.

6.

Which figure is congruent to the red figure?

7.

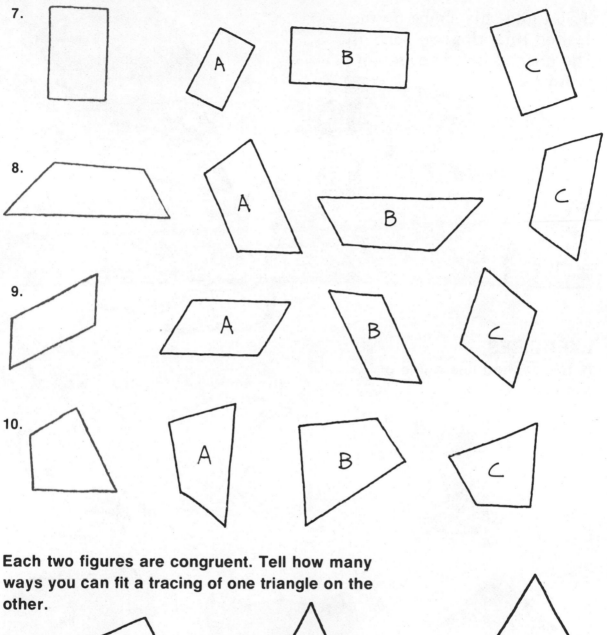

8.

9.

10.

Each two figures are congruent. Tell how many ways you can fit a tracing of one triangle on the other.

11.   ★12.   ★13.

Lines of symmetry

If you fold this shape on the dashed line, the two parts fit. The dashed line is a **line of symmetry**.

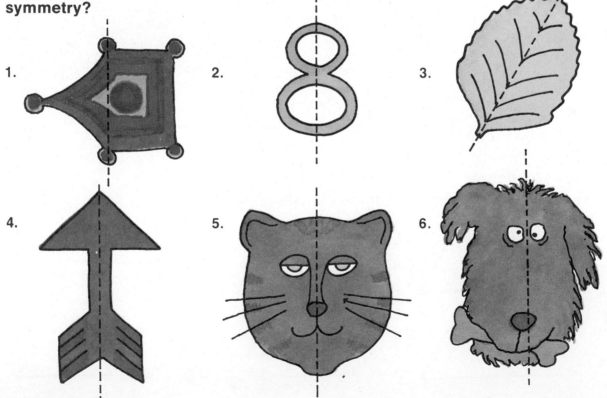

1.

2.

3.

4.

5.

6.

Project

1. Fold a piece of paper in half.

2. Cut out a shape from the folded edge.

3. Unfold your cutout. Does your cutout have a line of symmetry?

4. Cut out another shape that has a line of symmetry.

Keeping Skills Sharp

1.	746 − 214	2.	829 − 153	3.	742 − 378	4.	706 − 355	5.	436 − 395
6.	624 − 583	7.	801 − 459	8.	318 − 106	9.	900 − 253	10.	943 − 300
11.	749 − 582	12.	800 − 465	13.	607 − 558	14.	866 − 794	15.	742 − 231

More about lines of symmetry

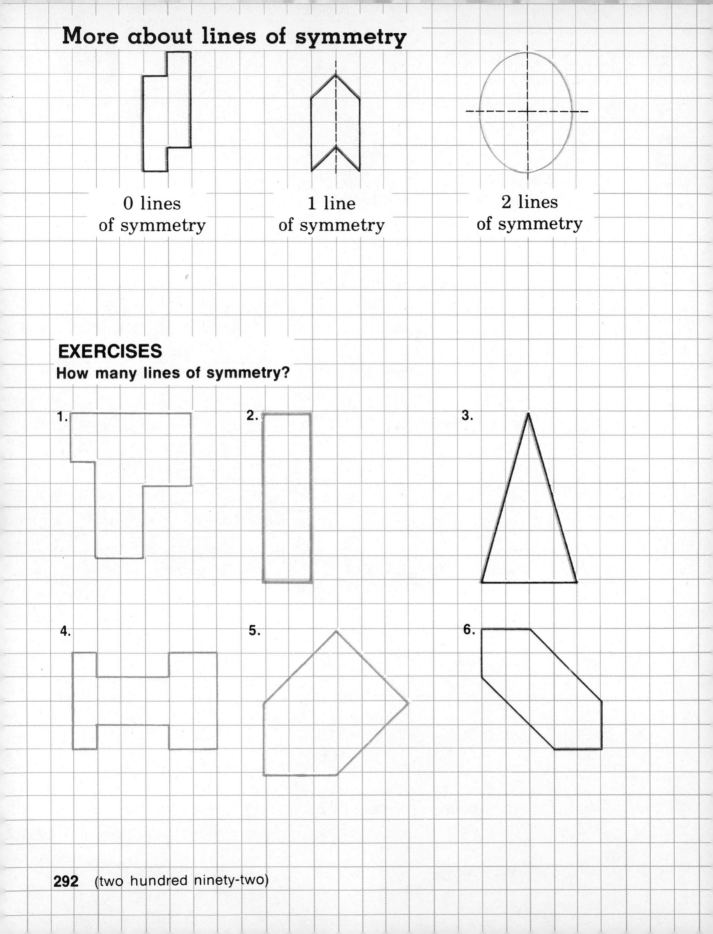

0 lines
of symmetry

1 line
of symmetry

2 lines
of symmetry

EXERCISES
How many lines of symmetry?

1.

2.

3.

4.

5.

6.

How many lines of symmetry?

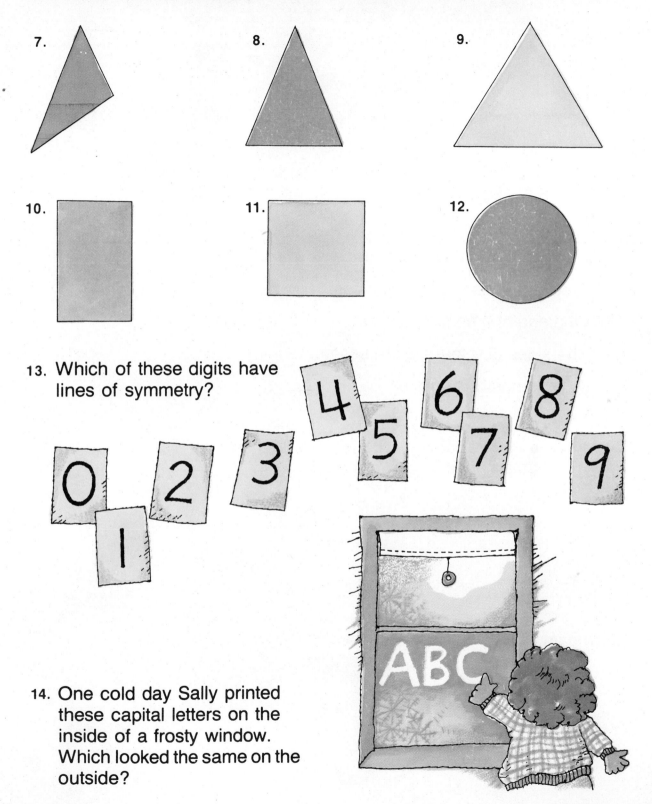

7.

8.

9.

10.

11.

12.

13. Which of these digits have lines of symmetry?

0 1 2 3 4 5 6 7 8 9

14. One cold day Sally printed these capital letters on the inside of a frosty window. Which looked the same on the outside?

ABC

Match. [pages 278–281]

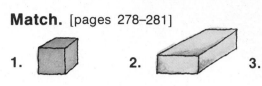

1. 2. 3. 4. 5.

a. sphere   b. cylinder   c. cube   d. cone   e. rectangular
                                                solid

True or false? [pages 284–287]

6. A cube has one curved surface.

7. A cylinder has two flat surfaces.

8. One end of a cone is a circle.

9. The sides of a triangle are segments.

10. A circle has no corners.

Are the two figures congruent? [pages 288–291]
(*Hint:* You may need to use a tracing.)

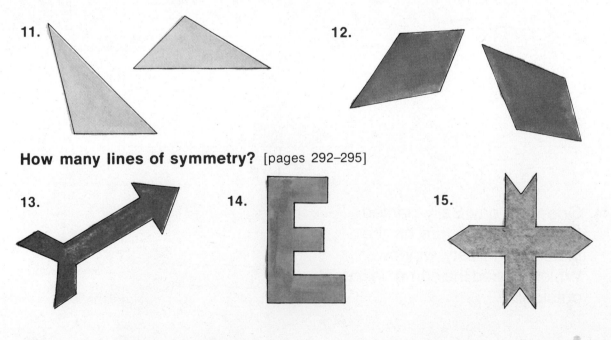

11. 12.

How many lines of symmetry? [pages 292–295]

13. 14. 15.

Project

1. a. Cut out some pictures that have only one line of symmetry.
   b. Draw the line of symmetry.
2. a. Cut out some pictures that have two lines of symmetry.
   b. Draw the lines of symmetry.
3. Paste your pictures in a symmetry scrapbook.

Match.

1. 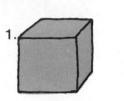 2. 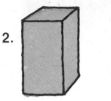 3. 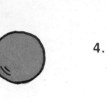 4. 5.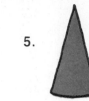

a. rectangular   b. cylinder   c. cube   d. cone   e. sphere
  solid

Match.

6.   7.   8.   9.

a. rectangle   b. circle   c. triangle   d. square

10. Are the two triangles congruent?

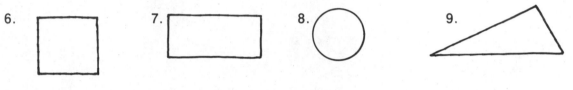

Is the dashed line a line of symmetry?

11.

12.

A number pair is used to locate points on a grid. The number pair (4,3) gives you the location of . It tells you to go right 4 spaces and then up 3 spaces.

What do you find at these locations?

1. **(3, 1)** 2. **(6, 5)** 3. **(5, 2)** 4. **(4, 3)** 5. **(7, 7)** 6. **(1, 7)**

Give each location.

7. 8. 9. 10.

11. 12. 13. 14.

a b c d · a b c d · a b c d · a b c d · a b c d
14 · 34 · 14 · 4 · 30
a b c d · a b c d · a b c d · a b c d · a b c d
15 · · · · 31
a b c · a b c · a b c · a b c · a b c d

MAJOR CHECKUP
Standardized Format

Give the correct letter.

1. What is 275 rounded to the nearest hundred?

    a. 270
    b. 300
    c. 280
    d. 200

2. Which numeral has a 6 in the hundreds place?

    a. 6483
    b. 4836
    c. 4368
    d. 8634

3. Add.

$$78$$
$$29$$
$$+65$$

    a. 152
    b. 172
    c. 162
    d. none of these

4. Subtract.

$$503$$
$$-257$$

    a. 256
    b. 254
    c. 244
    d. 246

5. What time is shown?

    a. 12:05
    b. 1:00
    c. 12:01
    d. none of these

6. How much money?

1 dollar
1 half-dollar
1 quarter
1 dime
1 nickel
2 pennies

    a. $.92
    b. $1.83
    c. $1.92
    d. $1.97

7. Multiply.

$$5$$
$$\times 7$$

    a. 25
    b. 30
    c. 45
    d. none of these

8. Divide.

$$4\overline{)36}$$

    a. 7
    b. 9
    c. 8
    d. none of these

9. Divide.

$$3\overline{)29}$$

    a. 9 R1
    b. 8 R1
    c. 7 R2
    d. 9 R2

10. What fraction of the marbles are red?

    a. $\frac{2}{5}$
    b. $\frac{3}{5}$
    c. $\frac{3}{2}$
    d. $\frac{2}{3}$

11. What is the perimeter?

3 cm
3 cm

    a. 3 cm
    b. 6 cm
    c. 9 cm
    d. 12 cm

12. Complete.

$$8 \div (4 - 2) = \underline{?}$$

    a. 10
    b. 0
    c. 4
    d. none of these

12
Multiplication and Division

READY OR NOT !

1. 6
    ×7

2. 5
    ×5

3. 9
    ×5

4. 6
    ×5

5. 3
    ×7

6. 4
    ×4

7. 3
    ×8

8. 8
    ×9

9. 6
    ×4

10. 4
     ×7

11. 6
     ×8

12. 3
     ×9

13. 3$\overline{)27}$

14. 5$\overline{)35}$

15. 5$\overline{)40}$

16. 4$\overline{)32}$

17. 4$\overline{)36}$

18. 6$\overline{)36}$

19. 8$\overline{)64}$

20. 6$\overline{)54}$

21. 6$\overline{)24}$

22. 7$\overline{)63}$

23. 7$\overline{)56}$

24. 6$\overline{)48}$

25. 9$\overline{)81}$

26. 7$\overline{)42}$

27. 9$\overline{)72}$

Multiplying a 2- or 3-digit number

3 sets of 12

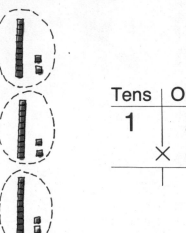

Tens	Ones
1	2
×	3

Multiply the ones.

Tens	Ones
	2
×	3
	6

Multiply the tens.

Tens	Ones
1	2
×	3
3	6

300 (three hundred)

EXERCISES
Multiply.

1.

Tens	Ones
2	3
$\times$	2

2.

Hundreds	Tens	Ones
1	2	3
	$\times$	3

3.

Tens	Ones
2	1
$\times$	3

4. 32
   $\times 3$

5. 22
   $\times 3$

6. 10
   $\times 6$

7. 20
   $\times 3$

8. 22
   $\times 2$

9. 21
   $\times 4$

10. 11
    $\times 4$

11. 12
    $\times 2$

12. 42
    $\times 2$

13. 22
    $\times 4$

14. 14
    $\times 2$

15. 13
    $\times 3$

16. 23
    $\times 3$

17. 21
    $\times 3$

18. 11
    $\times 7$

19. 41
    $\times 2$

20. 12
    $\times 3$

21. 11
    $\times 9$

22. 181
    $\times 0$

23. 234
    $\times 2$

24. 112
    $\times 4$

25. 100
    $\times 8$

26. 432
    $\times 1$

27. 403
    $\times 2$

To find this product, I multiply 2 and 4 and then write a zero.

$2 \times 40 = 80$

Use the shortcut to find these products.

28. $2 \times 20 = \underline{?}$

29. $5 \times 10 = \underline{?}$

30. $3 \times 30 = \underline{?}$

31. $3 \times 20 = \underline{?}$

32. $2 \times 30 = \underline{?}$

33. $4 \times 20 = \underline{?}$

(three hundred one) **301**

Multiplying with regrouping

Sometimes you will need to regroup when you multiply.

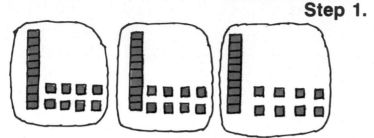

Step 1. Multiply in the ones column.

$$\begin{array}{r} 18 \\ \times\ 3 \\ \hline \end{array}$$

Step 2. Regroup 24 ones as 2 tens and 4 ones.

$$\begin{array}{r} {\scriptstyle 2} \\ 18 \\ \times\ 3 \\ \hline 4 \end{array}$$

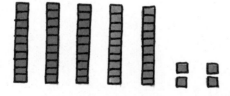

Step 3. Multiply the tens. Then add the two tens that were regrouped.

$$\begin{array}{r} {\scriptstyle 2} \\ 18 \\ \times\ 3 \\ \hline 54 \end{array}$$

EXERCISES

Complete.

1. $\overset{1}{24}$ $\times4$ ⎯⎯ 6

2. $\overset{2}{19}$ $\times3$ ⎯⎯ 7

3. $\overset{1}{25}$ $\times2$ ⎯⎯ 0

4. $\overset{3}{19}$ $\times4$ ⎯⎯ 6

5. $\overset{1}{37}$ $\times2$ ⎯⎯ 4

6. $\overset{1}{26}$ $\times3$ ⎯⎯ 8

Multiply.

7. 14 $\times4$

8. 35 $\times2$

9. 27 $\times3$

10. 18 $\times4$

11. 25 $\times3$

12. 14 $\times7$

13. 36 $\times2$

14. 39 $\times2$

15. 17 $\times3$

16. 16 $\times3$

17. 17 $\times5$

18. 16 $\times6$

19. 16 $\times4$

20. 12 $\times7$

21. 24 $\times3$

22. 28 $\times3$

23. 38 $\times2$

24. 18 $\times5$

25. 13 $\times6$

26. 27 $\times2$

27. 48 $\times2$

28. 19 $\times5$

29. 17 $\times4$

30. 29 $\times3$

Complete.

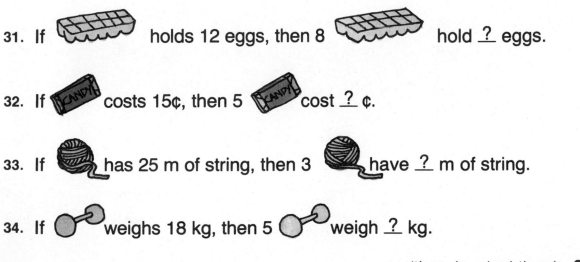

31. If [illustration] holds 12 eggs, then 8 [illustration] hold _?_ eggs.

32. If [illustration] costs 15¢, then 5 [illustration] cost _?_ ¢.

33. If [illustration] has 25 m of string, then 3 [illustration] have _?_ m of string.

34. If [illustration] weighs 18 kg, then 5 [illustration] weigh _?_ kg.

Multiplication with two regroupings

Sometimes we get hundreds when we
multiply the tens.

Step 1. Multiply ones.

$$\begin{array}{r} 42 \\ \times\ 3 \\ \hline 6 \end{array}$$

Step 2. Multiply tens.

$$\begin{array}{r} 42 \\ \times\ 3 \\ \hline 126 \end{array}$$

12 Tens =
1 hundred +
2 tens

Here is another example.

Step 1.

$$\begin{array}{r} \overset{1}{5}4 \\ \times\ 4 \\ \hline 6 \end{array}$$

Step 2.

$$\begin{array}{r} \overset{1}{5}4 \\ \times\ 4 \\ \hline 216 \end{array}$$

EXERCISES
Multiply.

1. $\begin{array}{r} 20 \\ \times 8 \\ \hline \end{array}$
   2. $\begin{array}{r} 30 \\ \times 4 \\ \hline \end{array}$
   3. $\begin{array}{r} 40 \\ \times 5 \\ \hline \end{array}$
   4. $\begin{array}{r} 32 \\ \times 4 \\ \hline \end{array}$
   5. $\begin{array}{r} 51 \\ \times 6 \\ \hline \end{array}$
   6. $\begin{array}{r} 43 \\ \times 3 \\ \hline \end{array}$

7. $\begin{array}{r} 84 \\ \times 2 \\ \hline \end{array}$
   8. $\begin{array}{r} 70 \\ \times 7 \\ \hline \end{array}$
   9. $\begin{array}{r} 74 \\ \times 2 \\ \hline \end{array}$
   10. $\begin{array}{r} 40 \\ \times 9 \\ \hline \end{array}$
   11. $\begin{array}{r} 83 \\ \times 3 \\ \hline \end{array}$
   12. $\begin{array}{r} 31 \\ \times 8 \\ \hline \end{array}$

13. $\begin{array}{r} 40 \\ \times 5 \\ \hline \end{array}$
   14. $\begin{array}{r} 67 \\ \times 6 \\ \hline \end{array}$
   15. $\begin{array}{r} 74 \\ \times 7 \\ \hline \end{array}$
   16. $\begin{array}{r} 66 \\ \times 5 \\ \hline \end{array}$
   17. $\begin{array}{r} 78 \\ \times 5 \\ \hline \end{array}$
   18. $\begin{array}{r} 36 \\ \times 3 \\ \hline \end{array}$

Multiply.

19. 73 ×8	20. 89 ×6	21. 45 ×3	22. 85 ×4	23. 37 ×5	24. 55 ×4
25. 79 ×6	26. 54 ×6	27. 88 ×6	28. 70 ×3	29. 87 ×7	30. 76 ×9
31. 68 ×7	32. 37 ×4	33. 93 ×5	34. 53 ×8	35. 46 ×3	36. 86 ×7
37. 90 ×7	38. 75 ×8	39. 69 ×8	40. 46 ×5	41. 77 ×8	42. 72 ×9

Give each end number.

43. START 72 ÷8 +43 ×8 −149 END ?

44. START 63 ÷7 +76 ×8 −271 END ?

Keeping Skills Sharp

1. $8\overline{)48}$ 2. $4\overline{)32}$ 3. $9\overline{)54}$ 4. $9\overline{)36}$ 5. $5\overline{)45}$

6. $6\overline{)36}$ 7. $8\overline{)56}$ 8. $9\overline{)45}$ 9. $8\overline{)64}$ 10. $9\overline{)63}$

11. $7\overline{)49}$ 12. $6\overline{)48}$ 13. $9\overline{)72}$ 14. $6\overline{)42}$ 15. $6\overline{)54}$

Problem solving

Find each total.

1. GRAPEFRUIT JUICE $.73, ORANGE JELLY $1.58

2. Pitted DATES $1.79, CRACKERS $1.25

3. HONEY $1.28, POPCORN $1.46

4. Shampoo $1.87, MIXED NUTS $1.35

5. OATMEAL CEREAL $.73, MAPLE SYRUP $.69, MARGARINE $.37

6. MUSTARD $.59, MILK $.48, VEGETABLE OIL $1.29

Multiply to find each total.

7.

SCRUBS $.18
SCRUBS $.18
SCRUBS $.18

8.

OLIVES $.79
OLIVES $.79
OLIVES $.79
OLIVES $.79
OLIVES $.79

9.

$.87
$.87
$.87
$.87
PEANUT BUTTER
PEANUT BUTTER

10.

$.96 SARDINES
$.96 SARDINES
$.96 SARDINES

11.

$.65
$.65
$.65
$.65
MIXED FRUIT

12.

$1.13
$1.13
$1.13
LIQUID SOAP

Division

The example shows how to divide larger numbers.

$$4 \overline{)48}$$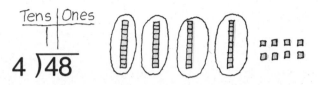

Step 1. Divide the tens. Put 1 ten in each set.

Tens | Ones

$$4 \overline{)48}$$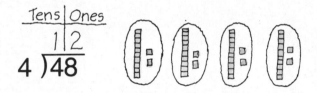

Step 2. Divide the ones. Put 2 ones in each set.

Tens | Ones

$$4 \overline{)48}$$

EXERCISES
Divide.

Tens | Ones

1. $2 \overline{)24}$

Tens | Ones

2. $2 \overline{)42}$

Tens | Ones

3. $3 \overline{)36}$

Tens | Ones

4. $3 \overline{)60}$

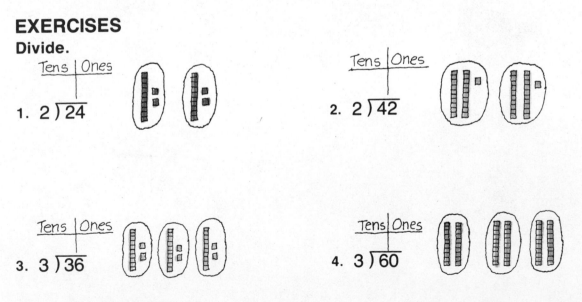

Divide.

5. $2\overline{)62}$ 6. $2\overline{)44}$ 7. $4\overline{)88}$ 8. $4\overline{)84}$ 9. $2\overline{)42}$

10. $2\overline{)46}$ 11. $3\overline{)39}$ 12. $3\overline{)63}$ 13. $2\overline{)22}$ 14. $3\overline{)90}$

15. $3\overline{)93}$ 16. $2\overline{)24}$ 17. $4\overline{)80}$ 18. $3\overline{)33}$ 19. $3\overline{)36}$

20. $2\overline{)26}$ 21. $3\overline{)60}$ 22. $3\overline{)66}$ 23. $4\overline{)40}$ 24. $2\overline{)48}$

25. $3\overline{)30}$ 26. $2\overline{)40}$ 27. $4\overline{)44}$ 28. $2\overline{)20}$ 29. $2\overline{)28}$

30. $6\overline{)66}$ 31. $8\overline{)80}$ 32. $5\overline{)55}$ 33. $7\overline{)77}$ 34. $5\overline{)50}$

Solve.

35. 48¢.
4 children.
How much money for
each child?

36. 24 raisins.
2 children.
How many raisins for
each child?

37. 36¢ for 3 balloons.
How much for 1 balloon?

38. 36¢ for 1 balloon.
How much for 3 balloons?

39. 69 marbles.
3 marbles in each bag.
How many bags?

40. 69 marbles in two bags.
3 marbles in one of the bags.
How many marbles in the
other bag?

Give the end number.

41.

18 Start → +19 → −13 → ÷2 → ×7 → ÷4 → End ?

More about division

Divide.

$$3\overline{)51}$$

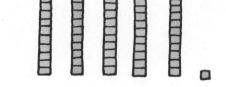

Step 1. Divide the tens. Subtract.

1 ten in each set ⇨

Used 3 tens ⇨

2 tens left ⇨

Tens	Ones
1	

$$3\overline{)51}$$
$$-3$$
$$\overline{2}$$

Step 2. Regroup the remaining tens.

Think 2! ones ⇨

Tens	Ones
1	

$$3\overline{)51}$$
$$-3$$
$$\overline{21}$$

Step 3. Divide the ones. Subtract.

Tens	Ones
1	7

$$3\overline{)51}$$
$$-3$$
$$\overline{21}$$

Used 21 ones ⇨

0 ones left ⇨

$$-21$$
$$\overline{0}$$

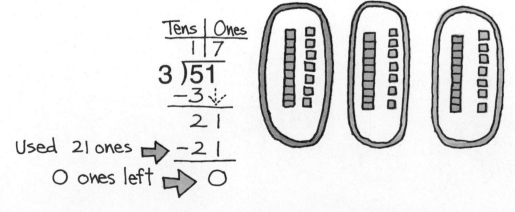
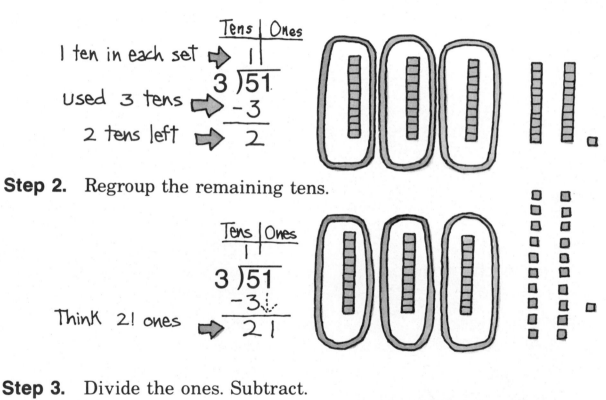

EXERCISES

Copy and complete each division.

1.
$$
\begin{array}{r}
15 \\
3\overline{)45} \\
-3 \\
\hline
15 \\
-\square\square \\
\hline
\square
\end{array}
$$

2.
$$
\begin{array}{r}
14 \\
4\overline{)56} \\
4 \\
\hline
16 \\
-\square\square \\
\hline
\square
\end{array}
$$

3.
$$
\begin{array}{r}
1\square \\
5\overline{)85} \\
-5 \\
\hline
35 \\
-\square\square \\
\hline
\square
\end{array}
$$

4.
$$
\begin{array}{r}
2\square \\
3\overline{)81} \\
-6 \\
\hline
21 \\
-\square\square \\
\hline
\square
\end{array}
$$

5.
$$
\begin{array}{r}
1\square \\
4\overline{)72} \\
4 \\
\hline
32 \\
-\square\square \\
\hline
\square
\end{array}
$$

6.
$$
\begin{array}{r}
1 \\
6\overline{)84} \\
-6 \\
\hline
2
\end{array}
$$

7.
$$
\begin{array}{r}
4 \\
2\overline{)94} \\
-8 \\
\hline
1
\end{array}
$$

8.
$$
\begin{array}{r}
2 \\
3\overline{)87} \\
-6 \\
\hline
2
\end{array}
$$

9.
$$
\begin{array}{r}
1 \\
6\overline{)78} \\
-6
\end{array}
$$

10.
$$
\begin{array}{r}
1 \\
4\overline{)68} \\
-4
\end{array}
$$

Divide.

11. $3\overline{)45}$ 12. $5\overline{)65}$ 13. $2\overline{)58}$ 14. $5\overline{)70}$ 15. $4\overline{)52}$

16. $6\overline{)96}$ 17. $3\overline{)84}$ 18. $4\overline{)76}$ 19. $3\overline{)57}$ 20. $6\overline{)72}$

21. $2\overline{)38}$ 22. $5\overline{)95}$ 23. $2\overline{)74}$ 24. $5\overline{)60}$ 25. $6\overline{)90}$

26. $3\overline{)78}$ 27. $4\overline{)96}$ 28. $3\overline{)75}$ 29. $4\overline{)92}$ 30. $2\overline{)56}$

Solve.

31. 72 eggs in all.
6 eggs in each carton.
How many cartons?

32. 56 sweet rolls in all.
4 sweet rolls per package.
How many packages?

Who am I?

33. If you divide me by 6, you get 13.

34. If you multiply me by 4, you get 92.

Problem solving

1. The Andrews family took a trip. They started at 7:30 A.M. They drove for 3 hours before stopping. What time was their first stop?

2. During the first 2 hours they traveled 92 miles. How many miles did they drive each hour?

4. The whole trip was to be 425 miles. At their first stop they had driven 141 miles. How many miles did they have left to travel?

5. They started driving again at 10:45 A.M. They drove for 2 hours and 30 minutes before their next stop. What time was it then?

6. At the service station they spent $7.45 for gasoline, $.85 for oil, and $1.80 for snacks. How much did they spend in all?

7. They bought 6 hamburgers for $.89 each. What was the total cost?

8. They also bought 4 malts for $.95 each. How much did the malts cost?

9. They drove from 2:15 P.M. until 4:30 P.M. How much time was that?

3. At their first stop they spent $10.85 for gasoline and $.95 for oil. What was the total spent?

10. Their dinner cost $16.75. The tip was $2.25. How much change did they get from a $20 bill?

Practice

C	H	R	I	A	V	E	U	M	S	N
27	85	177	273	324	469	576	1135	1206	1240	1371

What is the message?

302 − 217	36 × 9	173 + 296	72 × 8
85			
H			

54 × 6

495 + 876	700 − 427	3)‾81‾	277 + 299

547 + 693	389 + 746	599 + 607	783 + 423	801 − 225	926 − 749

Which product is greater?

1. 2 6
   × 7

   6 2
   × 7

2. 6 4
   × 3

   6 3
   × 4

3. 9 8
   × 5

   8 9
   × 5

4. 0 6
   × 4

   4 6
   × 0

Play this game.

1. Draw a table like the ones shown above.

2. As your teacher picks a card, write the digit in any place in your table.

3. After three digits have been picked, multiply.

4. The player with the greatest product wins!

CHAPTER CHECKUP

Multiply [pages 300–305]

1. 24 ×2	2. 13 ×3	3. 21 ×4	4. 11 ×6	5. 43 ×2
6. 27 ×3	7. 48 ×2	8. 19 ×5	9. 37 ×2	10. 18 ×4
11. 65 ×5	12. 58 ×4	13. 76 ×8	14. 94 ×9	15. 87 ×7

Divide. [pages 308–311]

16. 2)42	17. 4)48	18. 3)93	19. 5)55	20. 3)69
21. 2)72	22. 2)54	23. 3)72	24. 5)85	25. 3)48
26. 4)52	27. 5)65	28. 3)51	29. 2)94	30. 4)68

Solve. [pages 303, 309, 311]

31.

How much will 9 stamps cost?

32.

How much will 4 boxes weigh?

33.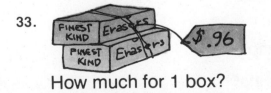

How much for 1 box?

34.

How many belts in 1 box?

Project

1. a. How many minutes of the school day do you spend eating lunch?
   b. How many minutes do you spend eating lunch in a school week?

2. a. How many minutes do you spend on the playground during a school day?
   b. How many minutes do you spend on the playground during a school week?

3. How many minutes do you spend eating in a day? In a week?

4. How many minutes do you spend sleeping in a week? In 4 weeks?

CHAPTER REVIEW

MULTIPLY WITH CARE

Multiply.

1. 32
   ×3

2. 42
   ×2

3. 22
   ×4

REGROUP ONCE

1
48
×2
96

4. 37
   ×2

5. 28
   ×3

6. 19
   ×4

REGROUP TWICE

2
76
×4
304

7. 85
   ×5

8. 74
   ×7

9. 96
   ×6

DIVIDE WITH CARE

32
$3\overline{)96}$

Divide.

10. $4\overline{)48}$

11. $2\overline{)86}$

12. $3\overline{)63}$

REGROUP ONCE

19
$3\overline{)57}$
-3
27
-27
0

13. $4\overline{)96}$

14. $3\overline{)84}$

15. $5\overline{)95}$

CHAPTER CHALLENGE

1. Give the missing numbers.

25	+	15	=	40
–		–		–
10	+	5	=	?
=		=		=
15	+	?	=	?

2. Give the missing signs.

6	?	6	=	36
?		?		?
2	?	3	=	6
=		=		=
3	?	2	=	6

3. Complete.

?	×	4	=	32
×		?		?
?	×	?	=	8
=		=		=
16	+	8	=	?

4. Make up one of your own.

MAJOR CHECKUP
Standardized Format

Give the correct letter.

1. Which number is greatest?

    a. 3826
    b. 3854
    c. 3796
    d. 2978

2. Add.

    579
   +846

    a. 1415
    b. 1325
    c. 1425
    d. 1315

3. Subtract.

    624
   −278

    a. 356
    b. 456
    c. 454
    d. 346

4. What time is shown?

    a. 3:35
    b. 7:18
    c. 4:35
    d. none of these

5. How much money?

1 quarter
1 dime
2 nickels
1 penny

    a. $.37
    b. $.46
    c. $.42
    d. $.47

6. Multiply.

    4
  ×9

    a. 32
    b. 28
    c. 24
    d. none of these

7. Divide.

$5 \overline{)38}$

    a. 3 R7
    b. 6 R3
    c. 8 R3
    d. 7 R3

8. Complete.

$\frac{1}{4}$ of 12 = ?

    a. 6
    b. 8
    c. 3
    d. 2

9. What is the length?

    a. about 2 cm
    b. about 4 cm
    c. about 3 cm
    d. none of these

10. What is the area?

    a. 5 cm
    b. 5 square cm
    c. 6 square cm
    d. none of these

11. Which figure is congruent to ◺ ?

    a.
    b.
    c.
    d.

12. Which figure has no line of symmetry?

    a.
    b.
    c.
    d.

SKILL TEST

1 Basic addition facts, sums to 10

5	3	8	2	3
+4	+7	+2	+6	+4

2 Basic subtraction facts, sums to 10

10	8	7	10	9
−9	−3	−4	−7	−5

3 Basic addition facts, sums to 18

9	6	9	6	8
+5	+7	+8	+6	+7

4 Basic subtraction facts, sums to 18

16	11	14	13	15
−7	−9	−8	−5	−6

5 Addition, no regrouping

48	165	3841	2607
+21	+324	+2044	+5322

6 Addition, regrouping ones to tens

57	38	268	4825
+24	+52	+127	+1138

7 Addition, one regrouping

23	52	276	3457
+95	+38	+183	+3812

8 Addition, several regroupings

27	35	243	1521
+96	+68	+689	+5899

9 Subtraction, no regrouping

57	246	385	5834
−23	−25	−163	−2813

10	Subtraction, regrouping tens to ones	83 − 57	46 − 19	324 − 106	4832 − 1729

11	Subtraction, one regrouping	227 − 183	542 − 81	324 − 106	4932 − 1929

12	Subtraction, several regroupings	163 − 87	243 − 168	3442 − 1651	8324 − 685

13 Multiplication, basic facts to 5 × 9

$$4 \times 3 \qquad 4 \times 8 \qquad 5 \times 6 \qquad 5 \times 9 \qquad 3 \times 7$$

14 Division, basic facts to 45 ÷ 9

$$3\overline{)21} \qquad 5\overline{)30} \qquad 4\overline{)16}$$
$$4\overline{)36} \qquad 2\overline{)16}$$

15 Fraction of a region

What fraction is red?

16 Fraction of a set

What fraction is red?

17	Multiplication, basic facts to 9 × 9	8 ×7	9 ×9	6 ×8	7 ×7	9 ×6

18	Division, basic facts to 81 ÷ 9	9)63		6)36		8)64
			7)42		9)72	

19	Division with remainder	2)13		5)24		3)19
			4)26		6)52	

20	Multiplication, no regrouping	20 ×4	31 ×3	203 ×3	423 ×2

21	Multiplication, regrouping ones to tens	25 ×2	13 ×7	15 ×5	36 ×2

22	Multiplication, regrouping tens to hundreds	31 ×4	82 ×3	142 ×4	151 ×4

23	Multiplication, two regroupings	37 ×3	44 ×5	26 ×5	157 ×4

24	Division, no regrouping	3)63	5)50	2)48	4)84

25	Division, one regrouping	2)52	6)72	4)76	5)85

EXTRA PRACTICE

Set 1

1. 4
   +3

2. 2
   +4

3. 4
   +1

4. 1
   +5

5. 5
   +5

6. 3
   +5

7. 5
   +2

8. 7
   +2

9. 0
   +8

10. 6
    +4

11. 2
    +8

12. 6
    +3

13. 5
    +4

14. 7
    +0

15. 0
    +1

16. 1
    +6

17. 6
    +2

18. 3
    +7

19. 4
    +4

20. 2
    +3

21. 1
    +9

Set 2

1. 7
   +8

2. 9
   +7

3. 9
   +3

4. 6
   +7

5. 9
   +9

6. 8
   +8

7. 4
   +8

8. 9
   +6

9. 7
   +5

10. 6
    +5

11. 8
    +4

12. 8
    +3

13. 5
    +8

14. 9
    +4

15. 9
    +8

16. 6
    +6

17. 5
    +9

18. 7
    +4

19. 9
    +2

20. 8
    +6

21. 7
    +7

Set 3

1. $6 + 8 = \underline{?}$

2. $3 + 8 = \underline{?}$

3. $6 + 6 = \underline{?}$

4. $9 + 6 = \underline{?}$

5. $5 + 6 = \underline{?}$

6. $2 + 9 = \underline{?}$

7. $7 + 9 = \underline{?}$

8. $5 + 9 = \underline{?}$

9. $8 + 8 = \underline{?}$

10. $9 + 4 = \underline{?}$

11. $5 + 8 = \underline{?}$

12. $9 + 8 = \underline{?}$

13. $9 + 3 = \underline{?}$

14. $9 + 9 = \underline{?}$

15. $7 + 7 = \underline{?}$

16. $7 + 8 = \underline{?}$

Set 4

1. $7 + \underline{?} = 16$

2. $4 + \underline{?} = 6$

3. $5 + \underline{?} = 8$

4. $5 + \underline{?} = 7$

5. $3 + \underline{?} = 12$

6. $8 + \underline{?} = 12$

7. $3 + \underline{?} = 4$

8. $6 + \underline{?} = 9$

9. $9 + \underline{?} = 13$

10. $5 + \underline{?} = 14$

11. $9 + \underline{?} = 17$

12. $8 + \underline{?} = 10$

13. $5 + \underline{?} = 13$

14. $9 + \underline{?} = 15$

15. $6 + \underline{?} = 12$

16. $5 + \underline{?} = 10$

Set 5

1. 5 4 +3	2. 3 6 +5	3. 1 4 +5	4. 3 3 +3	5. 2 4 +6	6. 6 2 +3	7. 4 4 +4
8. 7 1 +9	9. 2 3 +7	10. 6 3 +4	11. 2 5 +8	12. 3 6 +7	13. 2 5 +9	14. 1 2 +6

Set 6

1. 8 −3	2. 8 −5	3. 10 −2	4. 8 −8	5. 6 −3	6. 9 −4	7. 10 −3
8. 8 −6	9. 7 −5	10. 4 −2	11. 10 −5	12. 9 −6	13. 8 −2	14. 10 −7

Set 7

1. a. $4 + 3 = \underline{?}$
    b. $7 - 3 = \underline{?}$
    c. $3 + 4 = \underline{?}$
    d. $7 - 4 = \underline{?}$

2. a. $5 + 1 = \underline{?}$
    b. $6 - 1 = \underline{?}$
    c. $1 + 5 = \underline{?}$
    d. $6 - 5 = \underline{?}$

3. a. $5 + 3 = \underline{?}$
    b. $8 - 3 = \underline{?}$
    c. $3 + 5 = \underline{?}$
    d. $8 - 5 = \underline{?}$

4. a. $5 + 4 = \underline{?}$
    b. $9 - 4 = \underline{?}$
    c. $4 + 5 = \underline{?}$
    d. $9 - 5 = \underline{?}$

5. a. $6 + 2 = \underline{?}$
    b. $8 - 2 = \underline{?}$
    c. $2 + 6 = \underline{?}$
    d. $8 - 6 = \underline{?}$

6. a. $9 + 1 = \underline{?}$
    b. $10 - 1 = \underline{?}$
    c. $1 + 9 = \underline{?}$
    d. $10 - 9 = \underline{?}$

Set 8

1. 13 −8	2. 12 −7	3. 14 −6	4. 14 −7	5. 14 −5	6. 12 −8	7. 13 −7
8. 17 −8	9. 12 −6	10. 18 −9	11. 12 −5	12. 15 −8	13. 13 −5	14. 16 −9

Set 9

1. $11 - 2 = \underline{?}$
2. $14 - 7 = \underline{?}$
3. $16 - 8 = \underline{?}$
4. $14 - 9 = \underline{?}$
5. $13 - 6 = \underline{?}$
6. $14 - 6 = \underline{?}$
7. $12 - 8 = \underline{?}$
8. $18 - 9 = \underline{?}$
9. $16 - 9 = \underline{?}$
10. $17 - 8 = \underline{?}$
11. $11 - 8 = \underline{?}$
12. $14 - 5 = \underline{?}$
13. $13 - 4 = \underline{?}$
14. $16 - 7 = \underline{?}$
15. $17 - 9 = \underline{?}$

Set 10 MATHEMATICS Which letter is

1. first?
2. fifth?
3. fourth?
4. tenth?
5. second?
6. seventh?
7. ninth?
8. third?

Set 11 How many?

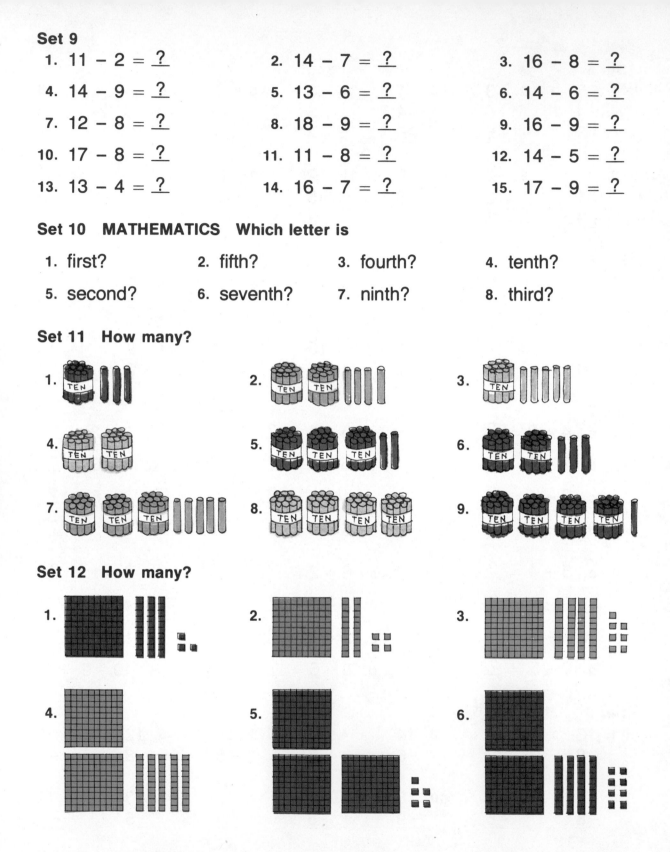

Set 12 How many?

Set 13 < or >?

1. 23 (?) 33   2. 18 (?) 21   3. 29 (?) 28

4. 32 (?) 29   5. 30 (?) 28   6. 29 (?) 32

7. 41 (?) 40   8. 43 (?) 45   9. 52 (?) 48

10. 45 (?) 54   11. 86 (?) 73   12. 65 (?) 56

Set 14 Round to the nearest ten.

1. 9   2. 23   3. 19   4. 36   5. 25   6. 43
7. 52   8. 46   9. 68   10. 73   11. 85   12. 94

Round to the nearest hundred.

13. 234   14. 156   15. 380   16. 259   17. 418   18. 451
19. 526   20. 638   21. 687   22. 750   23. 808   24. 923

Set 15 How many?

1.

2.

3.

4.

5.

6.

Set 16 < or >?

1. 57 (?) 58   2. 37 (?) 47   3. 851 (?) 723

4. 287 (?) 290   5. 306 (?) 320   6. 873 (?) 598

7. 4326 (?) 4321   8. 2806 (?) 2811   9. 3954 (?) 3754

10. 3000 (?) 2999   11. 4573 (?) 2188   12. 9999 (?) 6103

(three hundred twenty-seven) **327**

Set 17

1. 28
  +31

2. 51
  +35

3. 24
  +12

4. 44
  +30

5. 42
  +40

6. 21
  +54

7. 51
  +32

8. 42
  +46

9. 45
  +23

10. 33
  +15

11. 20
  +30

12. 55
  +43

Set 18

1. 65
  +29

2. 18
  +33

3. 46
  +28

4. 77
  +13

5. 74
  +16

6. 26
  +48

7. 28
  +37

8. 54
  +27

9. 36
  +36

10. 54
  +26

11. 39
  +46

12. 48
  +27

13. 35
  +25

14. 16
  +55

15. 39
  +39

16. 48
  +48

17. 27
  +53

18. 21
  +39

Set 19

1. 45
  +68

2. 57
  +74

3. 89
  +36

4. 43
  +57

5. 85
  +76

6. 87
  +45

7. 76
  +48

8. 73
  +48

9. 65
  +89

10. 55
  +85

11. 68
  +67

12. 58
  +75

13. 46
  +59

14. 78
  +49

15. 65
  +78

16. 75
  +97

17. 68
  +68

18. 85
  +29

Set 20

1. 46
  43
  +62

2. 72
  27
  +92

3. 24
  54
  +83

4. 52
  93
  +66

5. 79
  72
  +71

6. 56
  83
  +65

7. 78
  93
  +41

8. 59
  52
  +56

9. 35
  78
  +48

10. 29
  26
  +97

11. 74
  35
  +89

12. 58
  77
  +46

Set 21

1. 223
   +158

2. 312
   +179

3. 448
   +325

4. 356
   +437

5. 735
   +149

6. 533
   +227

7. 623
   + 48

8. 437
   +316

9. 545
   +225

10. 439
    +238

11. 357
    +429

12. 348
    +548

13. 486
    +405

14. 209
    +369

15. 518
    +239

Set 22

1. 356
   +282

2. 567
   +261

3. 143
   +287

4. 354
   +597

5. 443
   +288

6. 563
   +288

7. 137
   +279

8. 479
   +286

9. 351
   +399

10. 567
    +288

Set 23

1. 536
   +877

2. 395
   +866

3. 351
   +871

4. 931
   +486

5. 535
   +778

6. 694
   +844

7. 935
   +826

8. 537
   +867

9. 975
   +846

10. 477
    +888

11. 673
    +857

12. 268
    +732

13. 473
    +867

14. 543
    +295

15. 864
    +939

Set 24

1. 4647
   +1984

2. 2753
   +2654

3. 3543
   +3987

4. 4873
   +1544

5. 4357
   +3463

6. 2743
   +2541

7. 6325
   +2144

8. 7385
   +2194

9. 2358
   +4577

10. 4803
    +2877

Set 25

1. 45 −23	2. 86 −44	3. 73 −51	4. 68 −28	5. 93 −43	6. 87 −73
7. 46 −41	8. 87 −23	9. 56 −41	10. 84 −63	11. 91 −91	12. 47 −34

Set 26

1. 34 −17	2. 28 −19	3. 53 −28	4. 61 −44	5. 72 −36	6. 53 −47
7. 85 −46	8. 93 −59	9. 41 −16	10. 92 −18	11. 56 −18	12. 75 −36
13. 90 −35	14. 80 −56	15. 90 −72	16. 80 −42	17. 78 −29	18. 56 −19

Set 27

1. 543 −291	2. 628 −483	3. 383 −177	4. 423 −171	5. 570 −126
6. 381 −191	7. 653 −229	8. 674 −306	9. 403 −172	10. 503 −181

Set 28

1. 564 −298	2. 426 −197	3. 845 −396	4. 743 −645	5. 837 −238
6. 453 −177	7. 268 −199	8. 843 −586	9. 934 −655	10. 203 − 97
11. 560 −281	12. 426 −129	13. 833 −427	14. 628 −199	15. 375 −199

Set 29

1. 204 − 197	2. 603 − 248	3. 601 − 487	4. 805 − 146	5. 703 − 158
6. 402 − 146	7. 302 − 73	8. 604 − 56	9. 908 − 149	10. 603 − 116
11. 304 − 255	12. 800 − 426	13. 700 − 563	14. 800 − 443	15. 803 − 277

Set 30

1. 8357 − 2144	2. 5634 − 2783	3. 4052 − 2563	4. 4337 − 2156	5. 5831 − 2654
6. 8714 − 1999	7. 6453 − 2781	8. 6305 − 1486	9. 5000 − 4132	10. 8704 − 3526

Set 31   Give the time.

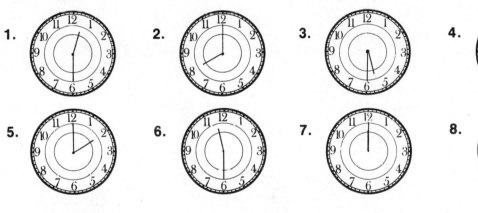

Set 32   Give the time.

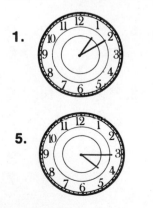
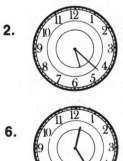
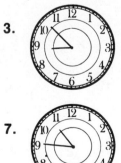

Set 33 Give the total value in dollars.

Set 34

1. 2 ×1	2. 2 ×7	3. 2 ×8	4. 2 ×9	5. 2 ×3	6. 2 ×1	7. 2 ×6
8. 2 ×5	9. 2 ×4	10. 2 ×2	11. 2 ×9	12. 2 ×8	13. 2 ×3	14. 2 ×7
15. 2 ×9	16. 2 ×5	17. 2 ×7	18. 2 ×4	19. 2 ×2	20. 2 ×6	21. 2 ×8

Set 35

1. 3 ×1	2. 2 ×1	3. 3 ×9	4. 2 ×7	5. 3 ×7	6. 3 ×3	7. 2 ×5
8. 2 ×4	9. 2 ×8	10. 3 ×2	11. 2 ×2	12. 3 ×8	13. 2 ×6	14. 3 ×5
15. 2 ×9	16. 3 ×6	17. 2 ×3	18. 3 ×8	19. 3 ×4	20. 3 ×9	21. 3 ×7

Set 36

1. $\begin{array}{r} 3 \\ \times 9 \\ \hline \end{array}$	2. $\begin{array}{r} 4 \\ \times 1 \\ \hline \end{array}$	3. $\begin{array}{r} 2 \\ \times 6 \\ \hline \end{array}$	4. $\begin{array}{r} 3 \\ \times 3 \\ \hline \end{array}$	5. $\begin{array}{r} 2 \\ \times 7 \\ \hline \end{array}$	6. $\begin{array}{r} 4 \\ \times 3 \\ \hline \end{array}$	7. $\begin{array}{r} 4 \\ \times 8 \\ \hline \end{array}$
8. $\begin{array}{r} 4 \\ \times 7 \\ \hline \end{array}$	9. $\begin{array}{r} 3 \\ \times 5 \\ \hline \end{array}$	10. $\begin{array}{r} 4 \\ \times 9 \\ \hline \end{array}$	11. $\begin{array}{r} 4 \\ \times 2 \\ \hline \end{array}$	12. $\begin{array}{r} 3 \\ \times 8 \\ \hline \end{array}$	13. $\begin{array}{r} 2 \\ \times 5 \\ \hline \end{array}$	14. $\begin{array}{r} 2 \\ \times 8 \\ \hline \end{array}$
15. $\begin{array}{r} 3 \\ \times 4 \\ \hline \end{array}$	16. $\begin{array}{r} 4 \\ \times 4 \\ \hline \end{array}$	17. $\begin{array}{r} 3 \\ \times 6 \\ \hline \end{array}$	18. $\begin{array}{r} 4 \\ \times 6 \\ \hline \end{array}$	19. $\begin{array}{r} 2 \\ \times 9 \\ \hline \end{array}$	20. $\begin{array}{r} 4 \\ \times 5 \\ \hline \end{array}$	21. $\begin{array}{r} 3 \\ \times 7 \\ \hline \end{array}$

Set 37

1. $\begin{array}{r} 5 \\ \times 3 \\ \hline \end{array}$	2. $\begin{array}{r} 5 \\ \times 9 \\ \hline \end{array}$	3. $\begin{array}{r} 5 \\ \times 1 \\ \hline \end{array}$	4. $\begin{array}{r} 4 \\ \times 5 \\ \hline \end{array}$	5. $\begin{array}{r} 3 \\ \times 9 \\ \hline \end{array}$	6. $\begin{array}{r} 5 \\ \times 4 \\ \hline \end{array}$	7. $\begin{array}{r} 3 \\ \times 8 \\ \hline \end{array}$
8. $\begin{array}{r} 5 \\ \times 2 \\ \hline \end{array}$	9. $\begin{array}{r} 4 \\ \times 4 \\ \hline \end{array}$	10. $\begin{array}{r} 4 \\ \times 8 \\ \hline \end{array}$	11. $\begin{array}{r} 5 \\ \times 6 \\ \hline \end{array}$	12. $\begin{array}{r} 4 \\ \times 6 \\ \hline \end{array}$	13. $\begin{array}{r} 3 \\ \times 7 \\ \hline \end{array}$	14. $\begin{array}{r} 5 \\ \times 8 \\ \hline \end{array}$

Set 38

1. $\begin{array}{r} 0 \\ \times 1 \\ \hline \end{array}$	2. $\begin{array}{r} 1 \\ \times 8 \\ \hline \end{array}$	3. $\begin{array}{r} 0 \\ \times 5 \\ \hline \end{array}$	4. $\begin{array}{r} 3 \\ \times 9 \\ \hline \end{array}$	5. $\begin{array}{r} 1 \\ \times 6 \\ \hline \end{array}$	6. $\begin{array}{r} 4 \\ \times 9 \\ \hline \end{array}$	7. $\begin{array}{r} 0 \\ \times 7 \\ \hline \end{array}$
8. $\begin{array}{r} 1 \\ \times 3 \\ \hline \end{array}$	9. $\begin{array}{r} 0 \\ \times 4 \\ \hline \end{array}$	10. $\begin{array}{r} 1 \\ \times 4 \\ \hline \end{array}$	11. $\begin{array}{r} 0 \\ \times 9 \\ \hline \end{array}$	12. $\begin{array}{r} 0 \\ \times 2 \\ \hline \end{array}$	13. $\begin{array}{r} 1 \\ \times 5 \\ \hline \end{array}$	14. $\begin{array}{r} 0 \\ \times 9 \\ \hline \end{array}$
15. $\begin{array}{r} 0 \\ \times 6 \\ \hline \end{array}$	16. $\begin{array}{r} 1 \\ \times 1 \\ \hline \end{array}$	17. $\begin{array}{r} 1 \\ \times 7 \\ \hline \end{array}$	18. $\begin{array}{r} 0 \\ \times 3 \\ \hline \end{array}$	19. $\begin{array}{r} 1 \\ \times 2 \\ \hline \end{array}$	20. $\begin{array}{r} 5 \\ \times 9 \\ \hline \end{array}$	21. $\begin{array}{r} 0 \\ \times 8 \\ \hline \end{array}$

Set 39

1. $\begin{array}{r} 3 \\ \times 6 \\ \hline \end{array}$	2. $\begin{array}{r} 0 \\ \times 9 \\ \hline \end{array}$	3. $\begin{array}{r} 4 \\ \times 9 \\ \hline \end{array}$	4. $\begin{array}{r} 3 \\ \times 5 \\ \hline \end{array}$	5. $\begin{array}{r} 5 \\ \times 6 \\ \hline \end{array}$	6. $\begin{array}{r} 2 \\ \times 8 \\ \hline \end{array}$	7. $\begin{array}{r} 4 \\ \times 6 \\ \hline \end{array}$
8. $\begin{array}{r} 2 \\ \times 7 \\ \hline \end{array}$	9. $\begin{array}{r} 5 \\ \times 9 \\ \hline \end{array}$	10. $\begin{array}{r} 1 \\ \times 8 \\ \hline \end{array}$	11. $\begin{array}{r} 5 \\ \times 5 \\ \hline \end{array}$	12. $\begin{array}{r} 0 \\ \times 7 \\ \hline \end{array}$	13. $\begin{array}{r} 2 \\ \times 9 \\ \hline \end{array}$	14. $\begin{array}{r} 3 \\ \times 9 \\ \hline \end{array}$

Set 40

1. $4 \div 2 = \underline{?}$ 2. $12 \div 3 = \underline{?}$ 3. $6 \div 2 = \underline{?}$ 4. $9 \div 3 = \underline{?}$

5. $15 \div 3 = \underline{?}$ 6. $2 \div 2 = \underline{?}$ 7. $6 \div 3 = \underline{?}$ 8. $18 \div 2 = \underline{?}$

9. $12 \div 2 = \underline{?}$ 10. $21 \div 3 = \underline{?}$ 11. $10 \div 2 = \underline{?}$ 12. $24 \div 3 = \underline{?}$

13. $8 \div 2 = \underline{?}$ 14. $3 \div 3 = \underline{?}$ 15. $14 \div 2 = \underline{?}$ 16. $21 \div 3 = \underline{?}$

17. $18 \div 3 = \underline{?}$ 18. $12 \div 3 = \underline{?}$ 19. $27 \div 3 = \underline{?}$ 20. $16 \div 2 = \underline{?}$

Set 41

1. $8 \div 4 = \underline{?}$ 2. $5 \div 5 = \underline{?}$ 3. $32 \div 4 = \underline{?}$ 4. $20 \div 5 = \underline{?}$

5. $30 \div 5 = \underline{?}$ 6. $24 \div 4 = \underline{?}$ 7. $35 \div 5 = \underline{?}$ 8. $20 \div 4 = \underline{?}$

9. $18 \div 3 = \underline{?}$ 10. $27 \div 3 = \underline{?}$ 11. $24 \div 3 = \underline{?}$ 12. $40 \div 5 = \underline{?}$

13. $36 \div 4 = \underline{?}$ 14. $45 \div 5 = \underline{?}$ 15. $16 \div 4 = \underline{?}$ 16. $28 \div 4 = \underline{?}$

17. $15 \div 5 = \underline{?}$ 18. $12 \div 4 = \underline{?}$ 19. $25 \div 5 = \underline{?}$ 20. $10 \div 5 = \underline{?}$

Set 42

1. $2 \overline{)12}$ 2. $3 \overline{)27}$ 3. $4 \overline{)8}$ 4. $3 \overline{)12}$ 5. $5 \overline{)5}$

6. $3 \overline{)24}$ 7. $2 \overline{)16}$ 8. $5 \overline{)45}$ 9. $4 \overline{)24}$ 10. $5 \overline{)35}$

11. $4 \overline{)16}$ 12. $5 \overline{)30}$ 13. $2 \overline{)10}$ 14. $3 \overline{)15}$ 15. $2 \overline{)6}$

Set 43

1. $3 \overline{)21}$ 2. $5 \overline{)25}$ 3. $4 \overline{)12}$ 4. $2 \overline{)8}$ 5. $3 \overline{)9}$

6. $2 \overline{)18}$ 7. $4 \overline{)32}$ 8. $5 \overline{)40}$ 9. $4 \overline{)20}$ 10. $2 \overline{)4}$

11. $5 \overline{)15}$ 12. $3 \overline{)6}$ 13. $3 \overline{)24}$ 14. $5 \overline{)35}$ 15. $2 \overline{)16}$

Set 44

1. $3\overline{)21}$ 2. $5\overline{)40}$ 3. $2\overline{)14}$ 4. $1\overline{)3}$ 5. $4\overline{)36}$

6. $2\overline{)12}$ 7. $3\overline{)27}$ 8. $4\overline{)32}$ 9. $5\overline{)45}$ 10. $3\overline{)18}$

11. $2\overline{)16}$ 12. $4\overline{)28}$ 13. $5\overline{)35}$ 14. $3\overline{)24}$ 15. $4\overline{)0}$

16. $4\overline{)24}$ 17. $1\overline{)5}$ 18. $2\overline{)18}$ 19. $2\overline{)0}$ 20. $5\overline{)30}$

Set 45

1. $3\overline{)17}$ 2. $5\overline{)21}$ 3. $4\overline{)15}$ 4. $2\overline{)15}$ 5. $4\overline{)25}$

6. $5\overline{)41}$ 7. $5\overline{)33}$ 8. $3\overline{)14}$ 9. $2\overline{)19}$ 10. $5\overline{)12}$

11. $5\overline{)27}$ 12. $3\overline{)29}$ 13. $2\overline{)7}$ 14. $5\overline{)8}$ 15. $3\overline{)7}$

16. $3\overline{)20}$ 17. $4\overline{)38}$ 18. $3\overline{)23}$ 19. $4\overline{)19}$ 20. $4\overline{)34}$

Set 46   What fraction is shaded?

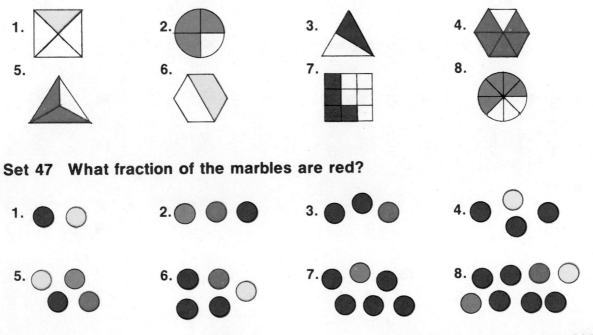

Set 47   What fraction of the marbles are red?

Set 48

1. $\frac{1}{2}$ of 6 = _?_

2. $\frac{1}{2}$ of 10 = _?_

3. $\frac{1}{3}$ of 6 = _?_

4. $\frac{1}{4}$ of 8 = _?_

5. $\frac{1}{2}$ of 12 = _?_

6. $\frac{1}{3}$ of 12 = _?_

7. $\frac{1}{4}$ of 12 = _?_

8. $\frac{1}{6}$ of 12 = _?_

9. $\frac{1}{2}$ of 4 = _?_

10. $\frac{1}{2}$ of 16 = _?_

11. $\frac{1}{3}$ of 27 = _?_

12. $\frac{1}{4}$ of 24 = _?_

13. $\frac{1}{6}$ of 24 = _?_

14. $\frac{1}{8}$ of 32 = _?_

15. $\frac{1}{5}$ of 30 = _?_

Set 49

1. $\frac{1}{2} = \frac{?}{4}$

2. $\frac{1}{3} = \frac{?}{6}$

3. $\frac{1}{3} = \frac{?}{12}$

4. $\frac{1}{5} = \frac{?}{10}$

5. $\frac{2}{3} = \frac{?}{6}$

6. $\frac{2}{3} = \frac{?}{15}$

7. $\frac{1}{2} = \frac{?}{10}$

8. $\frac{3}{4} = \frac{?}{8}$

9. $\frac{1}{3} = \frac{?}{9}$

10. $\frac{1}{4} = \frac{?}{16}$

11. $\frac{2}{3} = \frac{?}{9}$

12. $\frac{1}{4} = \frac{?}{8}$

13. $\frac{1}{2} = \frac{?}{6}$

14. $\frac{1}{2} = \frac{?}{8}$

15. $\frac{2}{5} = \frac{?}{10}$

16. $\frac{3}{4} = \frac{?}{12}$

Set 50 < or >?

1. $\frac{1}{2}$ **?** $\frac{1}{3}$

2. $\frac{1}{3}$ **?** $\frac{1}{4}$

3. $\frac{1}{3}$ **?** $\frac{1}{5}$

4. $\frac{1}{2}$ **?** $\frac{1}{5}$

5. $\frac{1}{4}$ **?** $\frac{1}{5}$

6. $\frac{1}{2}$ **?** $\frac{1}{4}$

7. $\frac{1}{4}$ **?** $\frac{1}{6}$

8. $\frac{1}{6}$ **?** $\frac{1}{2}$

9. $\frac{1}{3}$ **?** $\frac{1}{6}$

10. $\frac{1}{4}$ **?** $\frac{1}{3}$

11. $\frac{1}{6}$ **?** $\frac{1}{3}$

12. $\frac{1}{3}$ **?** $\frac{1}{2}$

13. $\frac{1}{4}$ **?** $\frac{1}{2}$

14. $\frac{1}{5}$ **?** $\frac{1}{3}$

15. $\frac{1}{5}$ **?** $\frac{1}{2}$

16. $\frac{1}{5}$ **?** $\frac{1}{4}$

Set 51

1. $\begin{array}{r} 4 \\ \times 6 \\ \hline \end{array}$

2. $\begin{array}{r} 6 \\ \times 5 \\ \hline \end{array}$

3. $\begin{array}{r} 6 \\ \times 9 \\ \hline \end{array}$

4. $\begin{array}{r} 4 \\ \times 7 \\ \hline \end{array}$

5. $\begin{array}{r} 6 \\ \times 7 \\ \hline \end{array}$

6. $\begin{array}{r} 4 \\ \times 9 \\ \hline \end{array}$

7. $\begin{array}{r} 6 \\ \times 3 \\ \hline \end{array}$

8. $\begin{array}{r} 8 \\ \times 3 \\ \hline \end{array}$

9. $\begin{array}{r} 5 \\ \times 6 \\ \hline \end{array}$

10. $\begin{array}{r} 5 \\ \times 7 \\ \hline \end{array}$

11. $\begin{array}{r} 6 \\ \times 1 \\ \hline \end{array}$

12. $\begin{array}{r} 4 \\ \times 8 \\ \hline \end{array}$

13. $\begin{array}{r} 3 \\ \times 7 \\ \hline \end{array}$

14. $\begin{array}{r} 5 \\ \times 8 \\ \hline \end{array}$

Set 52

1. $3 \overline{)24}$ 2. $6 \overline{)36}$ 3. $5 \overline{)30}$ 4. $4 \overline{)36}$ 5. $5 \overline{)35}$

6. $6 \overline{)12}$ 7. $4 \overline{)32}$ 8. $3 \overline{)27}$ 9. $6 \overline{)6}$ 10. $6 \overline{)42}$

11. $5 \overline{)40}$ 12. $6 \overline{)48}$ 13. $5 \overline{)25}$ 14. $6 \overline{)24}$ 15. $6 \overline{)0}$

Set 53

1. $\begin{array}{r} 7 \\ \times 5 \\ \hline \end{array}$ 2. $\begin{array}{r} 6 \\ \times 9 \\ \hline \end{array}$ 3. $\begin{array}{r} 7 \\ \times 7 \\ \hline \end{array}$ 4. $\begin{array}{r} 6 \\ \times 6 \\ \hline \end{array}$ 5. $\begin{array}{r} 5 \\ \times 8 \\ \hline \end{array}$ 6. $\begin{array}{r} 4 \\ \times 8 \\ \hline \end{array}$ 7. $\begin{array}{r} 7 \\ \times 4 \\ \hline \end{array}$

8. $\begin{array}{r} 6 \\ \times 3 \\ \hline \end{array}$ 9. $\begin{array}{r} 6 \\ \times 4 \\ \hline \end{array}$ 10. $\begin{array}{r} 5 \\ \times 9 \\ \hline \end{array}$ 11. $\begin{array}{r} 7 \\ \times 2 \\ \hline \end{array}$ 12. $\begin{array}{r} 7 \\ \times 8 \\ \hline \end{array}$ 13. $\begin{array}{r} 4 \\ \times 9 \\ \hline \end{array}$ 14. $\begin{array}{r} 6 \\ \times 7 \\ \hline \end{array}$

15. $\begin{array}{r} 7 \\ \times 3 \\ \hline \end{array}$ 16. $\begin{array}{r} 7 \\ \times 6 \\ \hline \end{array}$ 17. $\begin{array}{r} 6 \\ \times 5 \\ \hline \end{array}$ 18. $\begin{array}{r} 7 \\ \times 1 \\ \hline \end{array}$ 19. $\begin{array}{r} 6 \\ \times 2 \\ \hline \end{array}$ 20. $\begin{array}{r} 6 \\ \times 8 \\ \hline \end{array}$ 21. $\begin{array}{r} 7 \\ \times 9 \\ \hline \end{array}$

Set 54

1. $6 \overline{)12}$ 2. $7 \overline{)21}$ 3. $6 \overline{)30}$ 4. $7 \overline{)14}$ 5. $7 \overline{)63}$

6. $7 \overline{)0}$ 7. $6 \overline{)6}$ 8. $7 \overline{)56}$ 9. $7 \overline{)28}$ 10. $6 \overline{)36}$

11. $6 \overline{)54}$ 12. $6 \overline{)48}$ 13. $7 \overline{)7}$ 14. $6 \overline{)24}$ 15. $7 \overline{)35}$

16. $6 \overline{)42}$ 17. $7 \overline{)49}$ 18. $6 \overline{)18}$ 19. $7 \overline{)42}$ 20. $6 \overline{)0}$

Set 55

1. $\begin{array}{r} 8 \\ \times 6 \\ \hline \end{array}$ 2. $\begin{array}{r} 7 \\ \times 5 \\ \hline \end{array}$ 3. $\begin{array}{r} 7 \\ \times 7 \\ \hline \end{array}$ 4. $\begin{array}{r} 7 \\ \times 9 \\ \hline \end{array}$ 5. $\begin{array}{r} 8 \\ \times 1 \\ \hline \end{array}$ 6. $\begin{array}{r} 7 \\ \times 6 \\ \hline \end{array}$ 7. $\begin{array}{r} 8 \\ \times 8 \\ \hline \end{array}$

8. $\begin{array}{r} 6 \\ \times 7 \\ \hline \end{array}$ 9. $\begin{array}{r} 8 \\ \times 3 \\ \hline \end{array}$ 10. $\begin{array}{r} 7 \\ \times 8 \\ \hline \end{array}$ 11. $\begin{array}{r} 8 \\ \times 9 \\ \hline \end{array}$ 12. $\begin{array}{r} 5 \\ \times 8 \\ \hline \end{array}$ 13. $\begin{array}{r} 6 \\ \times 9 \\ \hline \end{array}$ 14. $\begin{array}{r} 5 \\ \times 9 \\ \hline \end{array}$

Set 56

1. 8)64   2. 7)28   3. 8)32   4. 6)42   5. 8)40

6. 8)8   7. 8)24   8. 6)36   9. 7)56   10. 7)42

11. 7)35   12. 4)36   13. 8)16   14. 6)48   15. 8)48

16. 8)56   17. 7)49   18. 6)54   19. 7)63   20. 8)72

Set 57

1. 9	2. 7	3. 9	4. 8	5. 9	6. 9	7. 9
×5	×7	×8	×8	×6	×9	×2

8. 7	9. 6	10. 8	11. 6	12. 7	13. 9	14. 7
×6	×8	×7	×9	×8	×3	×9

Set 58

1. 8)16   2. 7)42   3. 8)40   4. 8)56   5. 9)27

6. 9)18   7. 8)32   8. 9)54   9. 7)63   10. 9)0

11. 9)81   12. 9)63   13. 7)49   14. 9)36   15. 8)72

16. 9)72   17. 8)48   18. 9)45   19. 8)64   20. 9)9

Set 59

1. 8)25   2. 7)45   3. 4)37   4. 5)38   5. 7)60

6. 9)75   7. 8)37   8. 9)67   9. 9)68   10. 7)51

11. 6)38   12. 7)40   13. 8)60   14. 4)27   15. 8)49

16. 9)45   17. 6)44   18. 7)13   19. 3)19   20. 5)48

Set 60

1. $(6 - 3) - 2 = \underline{?}$ 2. $6 - (3 - 2) = \underline{?}$ 3. $(6 \div 3) - 2 = \underline{?}$

4. $8 + (2 - 2) = \underline{?}$ 5. $8 + (2 \times 2) = \underline{?}$ 6. $(8 + 2) \div 2 = \underline{?}$

7. $(8 - 4) \div 2 = \underline{?}$ 8. $(8 - 4) \times 2 = \underline{?}$ 9. $8 + (4 \div 2) = \underline{?}$

10. $(12 + 6) \div 2 = \underline{?}$ 11. $12 + (6 - 2) = \underline{?}$ 12. $(12 \div 6) \times 2 = \underline{?}$

13. $(16 \div 4) \times 3 = \underline{?}$ 14. $(16 - 8) \times 2 = \underline{?}$ 15. $18 \div (3 \times 2) = \underline{?}$

Set 61

1. $40 \\ \underline{\times 2}$ 2. $32 \\ \underline{\times 3}$ 3. $41 \\ \underline{\times 2}$ 4. $24 \\ \underline{\times 2}$ 5. $33 \\ \underline{\times 3}$ 6. $21 \\ \underline{\times 4}$

7. $11 \\ \underline{\times 6}$ 8. $12 \\ \underline{\times 4}$ 9. $10 \\ \underline{\times 7}$ 10. $10 \\ \underline{\times 8}$ 11. $10 \\ \underline{\times 9}$ 12. $12 \\ \underline{\times 3}$

Set 62

1. $19 \\ \underline{\times 4}$ 2. $36 \\ \underline{\times 2}$ 3. $27 \\ \underline{\times 3}$ 4. $24 \\ \underline{\times 3}$ 5. $12 \\ \underline{\times 7}$ 6. $13 \\ \underline{\times 5}$

7. $12 \\ \underline{\times 8}$ 8. $15 \\ \underline{\times 4}$ 9. $15 \\ \underline{\times 5}$ 10. $14 \\ \underline{\times 4}$ 11. $26 \\ \underline{\times 3}$ 12. $23 \\ \underline{\times 4}$

Set 63

1. $48 \\ \underline{\times 3}$ 2. $38 \\ \underline{\times 4}$ 3. $25 \\ \underline{\times 4}$ 4. $46 \\ \underline{\times 3}$ 5. $85 \\ \underline{\times 3}$ 6. $78 \\ \underline{\times 8}$

7. $64 \\ \underline{\times 4}$ 8. $75 \\ \underline{\times 2}$ 9. $86 \\ \underline{\times 6}$ 10. $57 \\ \underline{\times 4}$ 11. $96 \\ \underline{\times 4}$ 12. $68 \\ \underline{\times 5}$

13. $83 \\ \underline{\times 5}$ 14. $92 \\ \underline{\times 5}$ 15. $67 \\ \underline{\times 3}$ 16. $83 \\ \underline{\times 4}$ 17. $73 \\ \underline{\times 7}$ 18. $29 \\ \underline{\times 7}$

Set 64

1. $2\overline{)24}$ 2. $3\overline{)30}$ 3. $5\overline{)55}$ 4. $4\overline{)48}$ 5. $3\overline{)96}$

6. $4\overline{)44}$ 7. $2\overline{)88}$ 8. $3\overline{)33}$ 9. $3\overline{)66}$ 10. $2\overline{)40}$

11. $8\overline{)80}$ 12. $7\overline{)70}$ 13. $2\overline{)28}$ 14. $3\overline{)63}$ 15. $4\overline{)88}$

16. $3\overline{)39}$ 17. $2\overline{)86}$ 18. $4\overline{)84}$ 19. $6\overline{)66}$ 20. $2\overline{)68}$

Set 65

1. $4\overline{)64}$ 2. $3\overline{)42}$ 3. $6\overline{)96}$ 4. $2\overline{)96}$ 5. $3\overline{)45}$

6. $2\overline{)56}$ 7. $3\overline{)72}$ 8. $5\overline{)95}$ 9. $3\overline{)84}$ 10. $8\overline{)96}$

11. $5\overline{)65}$ 12. $4\overline{)72}$ 13. $2\overline{)74}$ 14. $6\overline{)72}$ 15. $2\overline{)78}$

16. $4\overline{)56}$ 17. $2\overline{)52}$ 18. $3\overline{)81}$ 19. $3\overline{)51}$ 20. $4\overline{)96}$

EXTRA PROBLEM SOLVING

Set 1

Solve.

1. There were 4

   There were 4 👩

   How many came to the party?

2. There were 7

   and 3 🎩

   How many more 🎉 were there?

3. There were 9 🔔

   3 🔔 broke.

   How many were left?

4. Bob tossed 10 🪀

   Joan tossed 7 🪀

   How many fewer did Joan toss?

5. There were 9 🕯️

   Felipe blew out 7 🕯️

   How many were not blown out?

6. Bill ate 5 🫒

   Ruth ate 4 🫒

   How many more did Bill eat?

Set 2

The graph shows the Halloween decorations made by Mr. Clark's class.

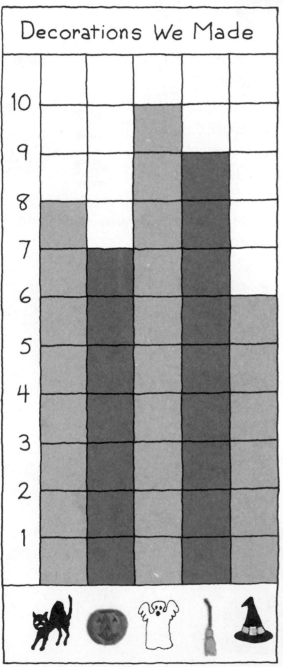

Decorations We Made

10					
9					
8					
7					
6					
5					
4					
3					
2					
1					

Solve.

1. How many did they make?

2. How many did they make?

3. Which decoration did they make the most of?

4. Which decoration did they make the fewest of?

5. How many more did

they make than ![pumpkin] ?

6. How many fewer ![hat] did

they make than ?

7. How many ![broom] and ![hat]

did they make in all?

8. How many ![cat] and ![pumpkin]

did they make in all?

9. The class had enough

paper to make 13 ![cat]

How many more could they
make?

10. There was enough paper

to make 15 ![pumpkin] . How

many more could they
make?

11. Isabel and Jon made all

the ![ghost] . Isabel made 6.

How many did Jon make?

12. Bill and Terry each made 3

![cat] . How many did they

make in all?

Set 3

$.09 each

$.06 each

$.28 each

$.65 NOTEBOOK PAPER

$.72

COLORED CRAYONS

COLORED PENCILS

$.49

PASTE

$.39 each

PASTE   PASTE

$.24 each

$.18 each

Give the total price.

1.
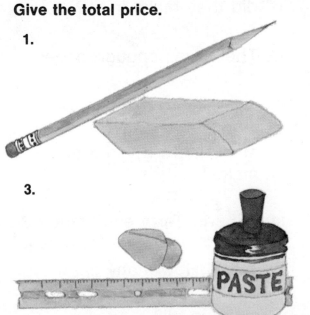

2.
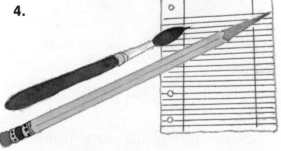

3.
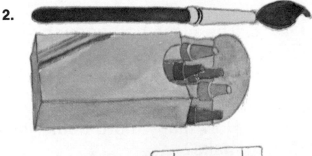

4.

5. How much more does 1  cost than 1 ?

6. How much more does 1 cost than 1 ?

7. Brad bought 2 . How much did he spend?

8. Jan bought 3 . How much did she spend?

9. Hugo had $1.12. Did he have enough money to buy and a ?

10. Beth had $.50. Did she have enough money to buy 3 ?

11. Lily bought 2 and a . How much did she spend?

12. Which cost more, 2 or a ?

Set 4

1. Getting to School

   Ride a bus: 356 students
   Do not ride a bus: 294 students

   How many students in all?

2. Math Time

   Problems worked: 12
   Problems wrong: 3

   How many problems were right?

3. Recess Time

   17 played ball
   9 on one team

   How many on the other team?

4. Reading Time

   Pages read: 6
   Pages to read: 5

   How many pages in all?

5. Lunch Time

   Chocolate milk: 279
   Plain milk: 186

   How many milks in all?

6. Lunch Time

   Hot lunches: 378
   Cold lunches: 249

   How many lunches in all?

7. Scissors

16 in one box
15 in another

How many in all?

8. Rulers

13 in all
8 in one box

How many in the other box?

9. Spelling List

First week: 24 words
Second week: 28 words

How many words in all?

10. Recess Time

15 minutes in all
6 minutes jumping rope

How many minutes left?

11. Library Time

Old books: 8,764
New books: 1,059

How many books in all?

12. Going Home

27 on one bus
29 on another

How many in all?

Set 5

Bounces Without Missing			
Name	First Try	Second Try	Third Try
Alice	37	32	27
Carmen	49	30	28
David	46	39	45
Elena	19	51	52
Frank	41	28	31
Grace	44	38	27
John	28	35	46
Lori	29	50	43
Mandy	40	43	31
Ricardo	50	42	30

1. How many bounces did Alice get on her
   a. first try?
   b. second try?
   c. third try?

2. Who had the most bounces on the
   a. first try?
   b. second try?
   c. third try?

3. What was the total number of bounces for Alice?

4. What was the total number of bounces for Carmen?

5. Who had the greater total, Alice or Carmen?

6. What was John's total?

7. What was David's total?

8. How much greater was David's total than John's total?

9. Which student had the greatest total?

10. The school record for a 3-try total was 170. By how many points did Ricardo miss the record?

Set 6

1. **Driving to Zoo**

   Before breakfast: 39 miles
   After breakfast: 27 miles

   How far was it to the zoo?

2. **Buying Tickets**

   Adult: $1.75
   Child: $.85

   How much for 2 adult's
   and 2 children's tickets?

3. **Seeing Films**

   African animals: 28 minutes
   Asian animals: 17 minutes

   How long to see both
   films?

4. **Taking a Tour**

   Tour A: 55 minutes
   Tour B: 38 minutes

   How much longer was
   Tour A?

5. **Comparing Weights**

   Mother elephant: 9000 pounds
   Baby elephant: 850 pounds

   How much heavier was the
   mother elephant?

6. **Comparing Speeds**

   Cheetah: 65 miles per hour
   Fox: 40 miles per hour

   How much faster was the
   cheetah?

7. Comparing Heights

Mother giraffe: 17 feet
Baby giraffe: 6 feet

How much taller was the mother?

8. Comparing Ages

Oldest turtle: 147 years
Youngest turtle: 9 years

What was the difference in age?

9. Eating Lunch

Milk: $.45
Hot dog: $.85

How much for 1 milk and 2 hot dogs?

10. Eating Lunch

Had: $1.50
Hot dog: $.85

How much more was needed to buy 2 hot dogs?

11. Buying Posters

Lion poster: $3.50
Elephant poster: $2.85

How much for both?

12. Buying Zoo Book

Had $4.00
Bought book for $2.25

How much money was left?

Set 7

Tea Sets $2.39

$.89 COLORING BOOKS

$1.29 YO-YO

TRUCKS $1.58

Give the total cost.

1.

2.

3.

4.

5.

6.

Solve.

7. How much more does a teddy bear cost than a boat?

8. How much more does an airplane cost than a truck?

9. What is the cost of 2 tea sets?

10. Bill bought 2 yo-yos and 1 car. What was the total cost?

11. Mary had $3.00. She bought a coloring book. How much money did she have left?

12. Lisa had $2.50. She wanted to buy a yo-yo and a truck. How much more money did she need?

1. 24 white horses
   17 brown horses

   How many horses in all?

2. 23 balloons
   15 blew away

   How many left?

3. 4 dogs in each wagon
   6 wagons

   How many dogs?

4. 3 tigers in each cage
   4 cages

   How many tigers?

5. 8 rows in the band
   4 players in each row

   How many players?

6. 13 little drums
   5 big drums

   How many more little
   drums?

7. 16 clowns in one car
19 clowns in another

How many clowns?

8. 19 clowns in a car
11 get out

How many left in car?

9. 3 monkeys in each cage
8 cages

How many monkeys?

10. 15 big elephants
9 little elephants

How many elephants in all?

11. 2307 children
1948 adults

How many people?

12. 2307 children
1948 adults

How many more children
than adults?

Set 9

1. Art Class
   Begins at 1:30
   Ends at 2:05
   How many minutes?

2. Scissors
   5 in a box
   6 boxes
   How many scissors?

3. Paste
   4 jars in a box
   7 boxes
   How many jars?

4. Paper
   36 red
   28 blue
   41 green
   How many in all?

5. Cutting Strips
   3 strips per paper
   9 papers
   How many strips?

6. Cutting Strips
   4 strips per paper
   8 papers
   How many strips?

7. Making Chains

   30 red strips
   5 strips per chain

   How many chains?

8. Making Chains

   28 blue strips
   4 strips per chain

   How many chains?

9. Comparing Chains

   John's chain: 103 strips
   Susan's chain: 67 strips

   How many more strips in John's chain?

10. Joining Chains

   John's chain: 103 strips
   Susan's chain: 67 strips

   How many strips in both?

11. Putting Away Supplies

   512 strips in all
   153 strips left

   How many strips were used?

12. Putting Away Supplies

   153 strips left
   87 were red

   How many were not red?

Set 10

1. One day Clara worked 28 minutes. The next day she worked 39 minutes. How many minutes in all?

2. Julian worked 40 minutes one day and 29 minutes the next. How many more minutes did he work the first day?

3. Julian bought a rake for $4.65 and a hoe for $3.79. What was the total cost?

4. Clara had $5.00. She bought some flower seeds for $1.69. How much did she have left?

SEEDS

5. Clara had 9 flower pots. She planted 4 seeds in each. How many seeds did she plant?

6. Julian planted 4 rows of flowers. He planted 8 flowers in each row. How many flowers did he plant?

7. Steve planted 24 flowers. He planted 6 flowers in each row. How many rows did he plant?

8. There were 18 rose bushes planted in 3 equal rows. How many bushes were in each row?

9. Sonia had 7 flower boxes. She planted 6 flowers in each box. How many flowers did she plant?

10. George had 48 flowers. He wanted to plant 8 flowers in a box. How many boxes did he need?

11. There were 129 red roses and 176 yellow roses. How many roses in all?

12. There were 156 daisies. Jane picked 48 of them. How many were left?

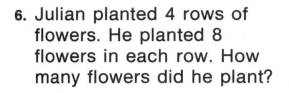

Set 11

1. Some students left Day Elementary School at 9:30. They got to the airport at 10:13. How long did the ride take?

2. There were 34 students on one bus and 29 on another. How many students in all?

3. Each tour guide led 9 students. How many students could 6 tour guides lead?

4. If each tour guide took 9 students, how many tour guides were needed for all 63 students?

5. One kind of airplane needed a crew of 7. How many crew would 8 such airplanes need?

6. One airplane had 6 seats in each row. How many seats were in 8 rows?

7. If there were 6 seats in each row, how many rows were needed to seat 54 people?

8. One airplane had 186 seats. 137 people got on. How many more people could the airplane hold?

9. There were 148 people on another airplane but only 119 meals. How many more meals were needed?

10. A pilot said that he flew 2083 miles one day and 1957 the next. How many miles did he fly in all?

11. A tour guide said that there were 5 takeoffs each minute. How many would there be in 7 minutes?

12. When the students went back to school, 27 rode on one bus. How many rode on the other? (See exercise 2.)

7¢ each

5¢ each

9¢ each

8¢ each

Set 12

1. What is the price of 6 pieces of green string?

2. How much do 5 pieces of blue string cost?

3. How many large red beads can you buy for 30¢?

4. How many large green beads can you buy for 56¢?

5. How many small blue beads can you buy with 35¢? How many cents would be left?

6. How many pieces of red string can you buy with 50¢? How many cents would be left?

7. What is the total price of 6 pieces of brown string and 5 green beads?

8. What is the total price of 7 blue beads and 8 small red beads?

9. Paul had 75¢. He bought 7 green beads. How much did he have left?

10. Rosa has 50¢. She wants to buy 8 pieces of green string. How much more money does she need?

11. Sylvia had 35¢. She bought 1 piece of each kind of string. How much did she have left?

12. Andrew had 90¢. He bought 4 large red beads and 5 blue beads. How much did he have left?

Set 13

1. Kay and Brad spent $.98 for milk and $1.27 for flour. How much did they spend in all?

2. They bought a package of red candies for $.69 and a box of raisins for $1.15. How much change did they get from $2.00?

3. Each recipe made 8 gingerbread cookies. How many cookies could be made with 6 recipes?

4. Each recipe called for 2 cups of flour. How many recipes could be made with 18 cups of flour?

5. Each cookie sheet held 6 gingerbread cookies. How many sheets would they fill with 48 cookies?

6. Each batch of cookies had to bake 12 minutes. If they put some on at 4:15, when should they have taken them out?

7. They put 3 red candies on each cookie. How many cookies could they decorate with 24 red candies?

8. They put 4 green candies on each cookie. How many cookies could they decorate with 30 candies? How many candies would be left over?

9. Kay and Brad put 5 raisins on each cookie. How many raisins did they need for 9 gingerbread men?

10. They gave 12 of the 48 cookies to their friends. How many did they have left?

11. Kay put 3 cookies in each of 5 small bags. How many cookies did she put in bags?

12. Brad sold 7 cookies for 9¢ each. What was the total price?

1. Patricia saw a red bicycle that cost $119.95 and a blue bicycle that cost $105.50. How much more did the red bicycle cost?

2. Patricia bought the blue bicycle for $105.50 and a basket for $8.59. What was the total cost?

3. There are 481 children in Patricia's school. 137 ride bicycles to school. How many do not ride bicycles to school?

4. Each day Patricia rides her bicycle 6 blocks to school and 6 blocks home. How many blocks is this a day?

5. If she rides 12 blocks each school day, how far does she ride in a school week (5 days)?

6. Patricia's friend rides her bicycle 16 blocks each day. How far does she ride in 5 days?

7. Each bicycle rack at Patricia's school holds 24 bicycles. How many bicycles can 4 racks hold?

8. During a 6-day vacation, she rode her bicycle 16 blocks each day. How many blocks did she ride in all?

9. Patricia took the bicycle safety test. She missed 23 points out of a total of 200. What was her score?

10. She got 5 points for each road sign that she got right. How many points did she get for getting 9 road signs right?

11. On Saturday, Patricia and her father rode 12 miles in 4 hours. How many miles did they average each hour?

12. Patricia had to buy 2 new tires for $2.65 each and a bell for $2.19. What was the total price?

Set 15

1. There were 467 adult tickets and 365 children's tickets sold for Fun Night. How many were sold in all?

2. If an adult ticket sold for $.65, how much did 4 cost?

3. If each bingo card cost 15¢, how much did 8 cards cost?

4. 126 people threw baseballs at bottles. Only 39 won a prize. How many did not win a prize?

5. Bob served the punch. He could fill 8 cups with 1 can of punch. How many cups could he fill with 12 cans?

6. He used 7 packages of punch cups. There were 24 cups in each package. How many cups did he use?

7. There were 32 pies. Each pie was cut into 6 pieces. How many pieces of pie was that?

8. Grace put 3 small marshmallows into each cup of hot chocolate. How many marshmallows did she need for 46 cups?

9. There were 24 peanut cookies. David put 3 cookies in each bag. How many bags did he use?

10. The students had set up 16 tables with 8 chairs at each table. How many chairs was that?

11. To decorate for Fun Night, 36 students worked 3 hours each. How many hours of work was that?

12. On Fun Night the school took in $678.54. They spent $115.25 for prizes. How much did they have left?

1. There were 138 fish. 59 of the fish were male. How many were female?

2. Colored stones for fish tanks came 12 in a box. How many stones were in 9 boxes?

3. Miguel had 2 fish tanks. He bought 48 colored stones. If he divided them evenly, how many did he put in each of his tanks?

4. Hank bought 3 plants for his fish tank. They cost 96¢. If the plants cost the same, what did 1 plant cost?

5. Vivian had $10.00. She bought a dog collar for $2.75 and a leash for $3.45. How much money did she have left?

6. Beagle puppies were on sale for $42 each. How much would 2 cost?

7. A large turtle was 41 years old. Miguel was 9 years old. How much older was the turtle?

8. A small turtle ate 4 grams of turtle food each day. How many days would 64 grams last?

9. Ann bought her kitten on sale for $22.50. A week before, it would have cost her $3.50 more. How much did it cost the week before?

10. Ann spent 7¢ a day to feed her kitten. How much did it cost to feed the kitten for the first 2 weeks?

11. Ralph spent 18¢ a day to feed his dog. How much did he spend in a week?

12. Ralph walked his dog 6 blocks each day. How many blocks would he walk his dog in a 30-day month?

Glossary

addend | A number used in an addition problem.

$$9 \leftarrow \text{addend}$$
$$\underline{+4} \leftarrow \text{addend}$$
$$13 \leftarrow \text{sum}$$

area | The number of unit squares that cover a figure. The area of this figure is 5 square centimeters.

Celsius temperature (°C) | The metric temperature scale in which 0°C is the freezing point of water and 100°C is the boiling point of water.

centimeter | A metric unit of length. One centimeter is one hundredth of a meter.

circle | A curved figure with all points a given distance from the center.

center

cone | A space figure shaped like this:

congruent figures | Figures that have the same size and shape.

cube	A rectangular solid ("box") with all edges the same length.
cylinder	A space figure shaped like this:
difference	The answer to a subtraction problem.

$$\begin{array}{r} 7 \\ -3 \\ \hline 4 \end{array} \leftarrow \text{difference}$$

digit	Any of the symbols 0, 1, 2, 3, 4, 5, 6, 7, 8, and 9.
equation	A sentence with an equals sign, such as

$$3 \times 9 = 27$$

equivalent fractions	Fractions for the same number.

$\frac{1}{2}$, $\frac{2}{4}$, and $\frac{3}{6}$ are equivalent fractions.

even number	A number that can be divided evenly by 2.

2, 4, 6, 8, 10, and 12 are even numbers.

factors	Numbers used in a multiplication problem.

$$\begin{array}{r} 8 \\ \times 6 \\ \hline 48 \end{array} \begin{array}{l} \leftarrow \text{factor} \\ \leftarrow \text{factor} \\ \leftarrow \text{product} \end{array}$$

Fahrenheit temperature (°F)	The temperature scale in which 32°F is the freezing point of water and 212°F is the boiling point of water.
fraction	A number such as $\frac{1}{2}$, $\frac{3}{4}$, and $\frac{4}{6}$.
graph	A picture used to show numerical information.
greater than	A comparison of two numbers that are not the same. The symbol is $>$. For example, $7 > 2$. (Another comparison is *less than*.)

kilogram	A unit of weight (mass) in the metric system. A kilogram is 1000 grams.
less than	A comparison of two numbers that are not the same. The symbol is <. For example, 3 < 8. (Another comparison is *greater than*.)
line of symmetry	If a figure can be folded along a line so the two parts of the figure match, the fold line is a line of symmetry.

line of symmetry

liter	A unit of volume in the metric system.
meter	A unit of length in the metric system. A meter is 100 centimeters.
metric system	An international system of measurement that uses meter, liter, gram, and Celsius temperature.
odd number	The whole numbers 1, 3, 5, 7, 9, 11, and so on, are odd numbers. An odd number cannot be divided evenly by 2.
order property of addition	The order in which two numbers are added does not change the sum. Also called the commutative property of addition.

$$7 + 9 = 9 + 7$$

order property of multiplication	The order in which two numbers are multiplied does not change the product. Also called the commutative property of multiplication.

$$7 \times 9 = 9 \times 7$$

ordinal number	The numbers *first*, *second*, *third*, *fourth*, *fifth*, and so on, are ordinal numbers. They tell the order of objects.
perimeter	The distance around a figure. The sum of the lengths of the sides.

The perimeter is 9 cm.

2 cm / 3 cm

4 cm

place value	The value given to the place, or position, of a digit in a numeral.

4 8 3 9

thousands place
hundreds place
tens place
ones place

product	The answer to a multiplication problem.

$$\begin{array}{r} 7 \\ \times 8 \\ \hline 56 \end{array} \leftarrow \text{product}$$

quotient	The answer to a division problem.

$$\overset{7}{8)\overline{56}} \leftarrow \text{quotient}$$

rectangle	A figure with four sides and four square corners.
rectangular solid	Most boxes have the shape of a rectangular solid. A rectangular solid has length, width, and height.

round	To replace a number by another one that is easier to use. You round a number to the nearest ten by choosing the nearest multiple of ten. (5 is rounded up.)

$$13 \longrightarrow 10 \quad 27 \longrightarrow 30 \quad 45 \longrightarrow 50$$

You round a number to the nearest hundred by choosing the nearest multiple of one hundred.

$$487 \longrightarrow 500 \quad 1238 \longrightarrow 1200 \quad 550 \longrightarrow 600$$ |
segment	A segment is part of a line. It has two endpoints. This is segment AB, segment BA, $\overline{AB}$, or $\overline{BA}$. A •————————————• B
sphere	The shape of a ball.
square	A rectangle with four sides that are all the same length.
sum	The answer to an addition problem.

23
+58
81 ← sum |
| **symmetry** | A figure has symmetry if it can be folded so the two parts of the figure match. |
| **triangle** | A figure with three sides. |
| **volume** | The number of unit cubes that fit inside an object.

The volume is 12 cubic centimeters.

2 cm   3 cm   2 cm |
| **whole number** | Any of the numbers 0, 1, 2, 3, 4, and so on. |

376

Index

1 2 3 4 5 6 7 8 9 0